Prentice Hall
WRITING and GRAMMAR
Communication in Action

Gold Level

Grammar Exercise
Workbook

Prentice
Hall

Upper Saddle River, New Jersey
Glenview, Illinois
Needham, Massachusetts

Student Edition

ISBN 0-13-0434744

2 3 4 5 6 7 8 9 10   04 03 02 01

Contents

Note: This workbook supports Chapters 16–29, (Part 2: Grammar, Usage, and Mechanics) of Prentice Hall *Writing and Grammar*.

19.1 Preposition or Adverb? • Practice 1

Preposition or Adverb?   Many words can be either prepositions or adverbs, depending on how they are used. Remember that prepositions always have objects. Adverbs do not.

Prepositions	Adverbs
We walked *along* the *path*.	Will Adam come *along*?
Perry sits *behind me*.	The dog followed *behind*.

▶ **Exercise 1**   **Distinguishing Between Prepositions and Adverbs.**   On each line at the right, write whether the underlined word in each sentence is a *preposition* or an *adverb*.

EXAMPLE: We planted marigolds <u>around</u> the vegetable garden. _____*preposition*_____

1. The children enjoyed playing <u>outside</u>. _____

2. A beautiful cherry tree grows <u>outside</u> my bedroom window. _____

3. An eager autograph-seeker slipped <u>past</u> the doorman. _____

4. A fire engine just sped <u>past</u>. _____

5. These belong on the shelf <u>above</u> the encyclopedia. _____

6. A seagull circled high <u>above</u>. _____

7. It was too warm to leave our jackets <u>on</u>. _____

8. Burt was wobbly <u>on</u> his new ice skates. _____

9. I must have left my notebook <u>behind</u>. _____

10. We sat <u>behind</u> a woman with a big hat on. _____

▶ **Exercise 2**   **Adding Prepositions and Adverbs to Sentences.**   In each blank fill in a word that is appropriate for the meaning of both sentences in each pair. In the sentence in which the word is used as a preposition, underline its object.

EXAMPLE: The cake has plenty of raisins _____*throughout*_____ .

　　　　　　The baby was restless _____*throughout*_____ the <u>night</u>.

1. a. It is cooler _____ the house than outside.

　 b. Please take these packages _____ .

2. a. The diver had enough air to stay _____ the water for hours.

　 b. The sailors stayed _____ during the storm.

3. a. We heard strange noises _____ .

　 b. That information is to be kept strictly _____ the family.

4. a. Jeanne had never seen a movie star _____ .

　 b. The cast arrived at the theater an hour _____ the play.

5. a. Timmy often comes _____ for a visit with my grandmother.

　 b. Have you read any other books _____ that author?

19.1 Preposition or Adverb? • Practice 2

▶ **Exercise 1** **Distinguishing Between Prepositions and Adverbs.** Label each underlined word as a *preposition* or an *adverb*.

EXAMPLE: The car was rusted <u>underneath</u> in three places. _____*adverb*_____

1. Please take your coat <u>off</u> the table. _____
2. After I sent the letter <u>off</u>, I remembered the stamp. _____
3. The crowd would not allow him <u>through</u>. _____
4. Alicia skied easily <u>through</u> the dense pine trees. _____
5. Three beautiful boats sank slowly <u>in</u> the waves. _____
6. Although the space was tight, Dave fit his car <u>in</u>. _____
7. The crew went <u>below</u> after they heard the order. _____
8. <u>Below</u> the surface, I saw green and blue fish. _____
9. Entering the apartment, she turned the radio <u>on</u> to catch the news. _____
10. Bill enjoys water skiing <u>on</u> one ski. _____

▶ **Writing Application** **Writing Sentences with Prepositions.** Use each prepositional phrase in a sentence of your own.

EXAMPLE: before school

_____*I usually do my homework in the morning before school.*_____

1. into the water

   _____

2. above the clouds

   _____

3. except for one student

   _____

4. toward my house

   _____

5. until next Saturday

   _____

6. in addition to soccer

   _____

7. outside the window

   _____

8. without any fear

   _____

9. in front of the post office

   _____

10. in spite of the rain

   _____

Name _____ Date _____

19.2 Conjunctions and Interjections (Different Kinds of Conjunctions) • Practice 1

Different Kinds of Conjunctions A conjunction is a word used to connect other words or groups of words. Coordinating conjunctions and correlative conjunctions join similar kinds of words or word groups. Subordinating conjunctions connect two ideas by making one of them less important than the other.

COORDINATING CONJUNCTIONS			
and	for	or	yet
but	nor	so	

CORRELATIVE CONJUNCTIONS	
both ... and	not only ... but also
either ... or	whether ... or
neither ... nor	

FREQUENTLY USED SUBORDINATING CONJUNCTIONS					
after	as long as	before	since	till	whenever
although	as soon as	even though	so that	unless	where
as	as though	if	than	until	wherever
as if	because	in order that	though	when	while

▶ **Exercise 1** **Identifying Conjunctions.** Underline the conjunction in each sentence. Write whether it is *coordinating*, *correlative*, or *subordinating* in each blank at the right.

EXAMPLE: After the race, we were <u>not only</u> tired <u>but also</u> thirsty. _____*correlative*_____

1. Mr. Kellogg phoned while you were out. _____

2. Alison knew the answer, yet she did not volunteer. _____

3. The swimmer was exhausted but proud. _____

4. We need both cucumbers and tomatoes for the salad. _____

5. I waited in the car while Ted got his bathing suit. _____

6. Katie is a better swimmer than I am. _____

7. Neither Pete nor Carol solved the last problem correctly. _____

8. We will leave as soon as the car is loaded. _____

9. Dad leaves an hour early so that he can avoid traffic. _____

10. Put the packages down wherever there is room for them. _____

▶ **Exercise 2** **Adding Conjunctions in Sentences.** Fill in each blank with a conjunction of the kind given in parentheses.

EXAMPLE: Aunt Joan came with us, _____*but*_____ Uncle Jack stayed home. (coordinating)

1. _____ you need any help, please call me. (subordinating)

2. The food was _____ delicious _____ appealing to the eye. (correlative)

3. The fans were clapping _____ cheering wildly. (coordinating)

4. Al's last book has made him _____ rich _____ famous. (correlative)

5. _____ the cake looked delicious, it was not on my diet. (subordinating)

6. The bus broke down, _____ many students were late. (coordinating)

7. _____ she has the time, Mom volunteers at the hospital. (subordinate)

8. Please type _____ print clearly. (coordinating)

9. The shortstop is good at _____ hitting _____ fielding. (correlative)

10. _____ you pass the high school, turn left. (subordinating)

19.2 Conjunctions and Interjections (Different Kinds of Conjunctions) • Practice 2

Exercise 1 **Identifying Conjunctions.** Underline the conjunction in each sentence. Then label each as *coordinating*, *correlative*, or *subordinating*.

EXAMPLE: As the rain ended, a rainbow appeared. _____*subordinating*_____

1. Either Elizabeth or Susanne would make a good class president. _____
2. Janet will never agree to that plan, nor will she support anyone who does. _____
3. When the bus was late, Carlos became impatient. _____
4. The pilot of the airplane waited until he received the signal for takeoff. _____
5. You must either leave for the movies immediately or forget about going. _____
6. Wherever the child went, she left cookie crumbs. _____
7. The runner was exhausted but happy. _____
8. Sandy ate not only her own dinner but also mine. _____
9. We waited for hours, yet no one came. _____
10. You will have to call after lunch because she is in a meeting now. _____
11. Both Kevin and Jennifer are working on the ticket committee. _____
12. As soon as he heard about the sale, he rushed to the department store. _____
13. Would you rather have a hot dog or a hamburger? _____
14. Neither the tomatoes nor the peppers are ripe yet. _____
15. If you hear of a part-time job, please let me know. _____
16. Would you please set the table for dinner while I finish the salad. _____
17. We had to take a detour because the bridge had been washed out. _____
18. The town has cleaned up Jones Park, so it is now a safe place to play. _____
19. We all went out for pizza after we finished painting the house. _____
20. The visiting team played hard and well. _____

Exercise 2 **Using Conjunctions in Sentences.** Fill in each blank with the kind of conjunction indicated in parentheses.

EXAMPLE: The day started out normally, (1) *but* (coordinating) soon things began to change.

Jason had always wanted to visit the Capitol, (1) _____ (coordinating) he signed up for the 1:00 tour. At the appointed time, the tourists (2) _____ (coordinating) their guide set out on the tour of the famous building. The guide pointed out interesting items (3) _____ (subordinating) the group got close to them.

It was (4) _____ hot _____ (correlative) extremely humid, (5) _____ (coordinating) Jason could barely concentrate.

(6) _____ (subordinating) he had looked forward to the tour, he was now eager for it to end.

Jason looked at his watch, (7) _____ (coordinating) he was wondering how much longer the tour would continue. It was 3:00, (8) _____ (coordinating) the tour was supposed to be over. It seemed (9) _____ (subordinating) the tour guide would never stop talking. (10) "_____ this guide ends the tour immediately _____ (correlative) I will have to be rude and leave," thought Jason.

19.2 Conjunctions and Interjections • Practice 1

Conjunctive Adverbs   A conjunctive adverb is an adverb that acts as a conjunction to connect complete ideas.

FREQUENTLY USED CONJUNCTIVE ADVERBS		
accordingly	finally	nevertheless
again	furthermore	otherwise
also	however	then
besides	indeed	therefore
consequently	moreover	thus

Interjections   An interjection is a word that expresses feeling or emotion and functions independently of a sentence.

SOME COMMON INTERJECTIONS		
aha	goodness	tsk
alas	hurray	well
darn	oh	whew
golly	ouch	wow

▸ **Exercise 1**   **Recognizing Conjunctive Adverbs.**   Underline each conjunctive adverb in the sentences below. If a sentence does not have a conjunctive adverb, write *none* in the blank at the right.

EXAMPLE: We waited for the bus; not a single one came by. _____*none*_____

1. Ellen's new bike was a bargain; besides, she needed one. _____
2. I overslept this morning; therefore, I was late for school. _____
3. The phone rang ten times; no one answered. _____
4. It is not unusual for Phil to be late; indeed, he is seldom on time. _____
5. Louise had never eaten snails; nevertheless, she was willing to try. _____
6. Please eat your potatoes; they are getting cold. _____
7. The third batter struck out; again, the Pirates had not scored. _____
8. Len finished his homework; then, he was ready to relax. _____
9. One twin is extremely cautious; the other is impulsive. _____
10. We were caught in traffic; consequently, we missed the overture. _____

▸ **Exercise 2**   **Adding Interjections to Sentences.**   Fill in each blank with an interjection that shows the feeling or emotion given in parentheses.

EXAMPLE: _____ This tastes terrible! (disgust)

1. _____ I just bit my tongue. (pain)
2. _____ The stain will not come out. (regret)
3. _____ What a terrific car that is! (delight)
4. _____ It's just what I always wanted. (surprise)
5. _____ What a close game this is! (excitement)
6. _____ I'm trapped in here! (fear)
7. _____ I knew I got that one wrong. (annoyance)
8. _____ The game has been rained out. (disappointment)
9. _____ Our team is winning. (enthusiasm)
10. _____ What a workout that was! (exhaustion)

19.2 Conjunctions and Interjections • Practice 2

▶ **Exercise 1** **Recognizing Conjunctive Adverbs.** Read each sentence to see whether or not it has a conjunctive adverb. If it does, underline the conjunctive adverb. If it does not, write a conjunctive adverb in the blank and mark where it belongs in the sentence.

EXAMPLE: Eat your breakfast; ∧ go to school. _____*then,*_____

1. Several accidents have occurred on that ride; nevertheless, people wait in line for their turn on it.

_____

2. I saw that movie; however, I did not enjoy it. _____

3. The train arrived late; we missed the concert. _____

4. The book was exciting; I read it all evening. _____

5. Her car broke down; consequently, she had to walk home. _____

6. Finish your dinner; you will have no dessert. _____

7. Al is reliable; moreover, he is never late. _____

8. The fans waited for hours; finally, the star arrived. _____

9. Your appointment was at 6:00; you arrived at 7:00. _____

10. We ran out of gas; we had a flat tire. _____

▶ **Exercise 2** **Supplying Interjections.** Complete each sentence by writing an interjection that shows the indicated emotion.

EXAMPLE: _____*Whew!*_____ This has been a long day. (weariness)

1. _____ I lost my keys. (annoyance)

2. _____ I was hoping for that. (surprise)

3. _____ I stubbed my toe. (pain)

4. _____ What a beautiful cake you made. (delight)

5. _____ It's starting to rain. (disappointment)

▶ **Writing Application** **Using Conjunctions and Conjunctive Adverbs to Combine Sentences.** Turn each pair of sentences into a single sentence by using the kind of conjunction or conjunctive adverb indicated.

EXAMPLE: I keep fit. I swim every day. (subordinating conjunction)

_____*I keep fit because I swim every day.*_____

1. The team practiced hard all week. They did not win the match. (coordinating conjunction)

_____

2. We yanked the door open. Jody stumbled out. (coordinating conjunction)

_____

3. I will go. I will stay. (correlative conjunction)

_____

4. He insisted on driving. He had never driven a truck before. (subordinating conjunction)

_____

5. It rained. The game was canceled. (conjunctive adverb)

_____

20.1 # The Sentence (Complete Subjects and Predicates)
• Practice 1

Complete Subjects and Predicates   A sentence is a group of words with two main parts: a complete subject and a complete predicate. Together these parts express a complete thought.

Complete Subjects	Complete Predicates
Everyone in our family	likes Mexican food.
The house down the street	has been for sale for months.
Fish	swim.

▶ **Exercise 1**   **Recognizing Complete Subjects and Predicates.**   On the blank after each sentence, write *S* or *P* to tell whether the underlined word or group of words is the complete subject or the complete predicate.

EXAMPLE: The bike with the missing reflector <u>is mine.</u>   _P_

1. <u>Azaleas</u> do well in acid soil.   _S_
2. <u>The last essay question</u> was really challenging.   _S_
3. <u>Most of the students in my class</u> study hard.   _P_
4. The player with the most points at the end of the game <u>loses.</u>   _P_
5. Weather forecasters <u>predict another storm front from the west.</u>   _P_
6. <u>The first volunteer fire company in the United States</u> was in Philadelphia.   _S_
7. Benjamin Franklin <u>organized it.</u>   _P_
8. <u>Franklin</u> was once ambassador to France.   _S_
9. <u>Many American towns and cities</u> are named for places in England.   _S_
10. You <u>may have a little trouble with the lock.</u>   _P_

▶ **Exercise 2**   **Identifying Complete Subjects and Predicates.**   In each sentence underline the complete subject once and the complete predicate twice.

EXAMPLE: <u>The tall ships</u> <u>sailed up the Atlantic Coast.</u>

1. Several members of that family have served in the armed forces.
2. Louise borrowed my sweater last week.
3. A pane in one of the bedroom windows cracked.
4. Lemmings follow their leader to their death.
5. A portrait of my grandmother hangs above the mantel.
6. The first pianist on the program seemed nervous.
7. All the children in the neighborhood enjoyed the new playground.
8. Searchlights from the rescue ships flashed across the water.
9. The fans of the losing team groaned.
10. Philip or his brother will surely help you.

20.1 The Sentence (Complete Subjects and Predicates)
• Practice 2

▶ **Exercise 1** **Recognizing Complete Subjects and Predicates.** In each sentence, underline each complete subject once and each complete predicate twice.

EXAMPLE: The tall pine trees swayed in the wind.

1. The car swerved away from the child.
2. My favorite radio station plays all of the hit songs.
3. Grandfather Kim owns an art gallery in Chicago.
4. Mexico City was built on a lake.
5. The evening news summarizes the day's events.
6. Shakespeare's father was a glove maker.
7. Computers process information very quickly.
8. My older brother has a telephone shaped like Mickey Mouse.
9. The bags of coins were placed in an armored truck.
10. Damascus, the capital of Syria, has been continuously inhabited for over four thousand years.
11. Mr. Axelrod worked for years as a traveling salesman.
12. The magma in a volcano is called lava when it reaches the air.
13. The ancient Greeks were the first people to have free public museums.
14. People in ancient times used the abacus to compute numbers.
15. Some museums are devoted entirely to computers.
16. Some species of bats are very beneficial to the environment.
17. More than five hundred volcanoes have erupted over the centuries.
18. Our sun is a typical, medium-sized star.
19. The gravity of the sun is almost twenty-eight times the gravity of Earth.
20. Some planets have one or more moons.

▶ **Exercise 2** **Recognizing Complete Subjects and Predicates.** In each sentence underline the complete subject once and the complete predicate twice.

EXAMPLE: The blue-eyed Siamese cat curled up on the oak desk.

(1) The giant panda lives in the remote mountains of southern China. (2) This animal is a frustrating mystery to zoologists. (3) The Chinese name for the panda is *xiong-mao*, or "bear-cat". (4) However, the animal is not a cat. (5) Zoologists do not agree about its identity. (6) Some call it a bear. (7) Others place it in the same family as the raccoon. (8) Sadly, the panda is becoming rare. (9) The reason for this is the scarcity of bamboo, its main food. (10) The panda populations can be saved only through worldwide efforts.

Name _____ Date _____

Sentence or Fragment?   A fragment is a group of words that does not express a complete thought.

Fragments	Complete Sentences
Early Sunday afternoon	Our weekend guests left early Sunday afternoon.
The beautiful phoenix	The beautiful phoenix was a mythical bird.
Rose from its own ashes	The phoenix rose from its own ashes.

Fragments as Sentence Parts   To turn fragments into sentences, add whatever sentence parts are needed to express a complete thought. The chart below explains what sentence parts were added to the fragments in the chart above.

SENTENCE PARTS ADDED
Complete subject and predicate areas were added.
A predicate area was added.
A subject area was added.

▶ **Exercise 1**   **Distinguishing Between Sentences and Fragments.**   In the blanks below, write *S* for each sentence and *F* for each fragment.

EXAMPLE: throughout the day and into the night. ___*F*___

1. Without any trouble at all. __F__
2. Played quietly after dinner. __F__
3. Pete plays the piccolo. __S__
4. Beyond our wildest expectations. __F__
5. Yellowstone Park attracts many tourists. __S__
6. People from all parts of the world. __F__
7. The contestant with the most unusual costume. __8 F__
8. Has traveled widely throughout the United States. __8 F__
9. The prospector struck oil. __S__
10. Robins fly south for the winter. __S__

▶ **Exercise 2**   **Adding Words to Make Sentences from Fragments.**   Rewrite five of the fragments above as complete sentences.

EXAMPLE: _Snow fell throughout the day and into the night._

1. She did it without any trouble at all.
2. The children played quietly after dinner.
3. The prom was beyond our wildest expectations.
4. People from all parts of the world come here to visit.
5. Giovanni has traveled widely throughout the United States.

20.1 The Sentence (Sentence or Fragment?) • Practice 2

▶ **Exercise 1** **Distinguishing Between Sentences and Fragments.** Identify each item as a *sentence* or a *fragment*.

EXAMPLE: Worked for many hours ____*fragment*____

1. In the woods almost until dawn. _____

2. A few inches of snow. _____

3. The grizzly bear needs large territories undisturbed by people. _____

4. Have been unusually high because of the very heavy rains this season. _____

5. Herds of thousands of caribou. _____

6. Haste makes waste. _____

7. Dived in search of food. _____

8. Cousteau believes artificial islands could be built off the coast. _____

9. About a great white shark, one of the largest ones ever caught. _____

10. Cougars have become increasingly rare. _____

11. Is the last frontier. _____

12. There he sat, totally content. _____

13. In the day in order to hunt at night. _____

14. Ice-covered Mount McKinley in Alaska attracts many tourists. _____

15. Wolves, jaguars, and grizzly bears once numerous in North America. _____

▶ **Writing Application** **Using Fragments to Make Sentences.** Combine each of the ten complete subjects on the left with one of the ten complete predicates on the right to make ten logical sentences.

EXAMPLE: The umpire at yesterday's game   told me to watch my temper.

_____The umpire at yesterday's game told me to watch my temper._____

1.	His Roman costume	took the wrong bus.
2.	The children	stuck to the stage.
3.	The girl with butterflies in her stomach	wandered into the tack room.
4.	The curious horse	can fool people.
5.	The boy with the confused expression	was tangled in the stage scenery.
6.	Lemon jello inside empty eggshells	put sugar at the bottom of her sleeping bag.
7.	Their cousins coming for dinner	was wearing his shirt inside out.
8.	The man standing on the corner	scored a goal for the opposing team.
9.	Her long, pointed putty nose	thought the raccoon was a ghost.
10.	Her friends at the slumber party	spoke to the flag instead of to the class.

1. _____

2. _____

3. _____

4. _____

5. _____

6. _____

7. _____

8. _____

9. _____

10. _____

20.1 # Subjects and Verbs (Simple Subjects and Predicates) • **Practice 1**

Simple Subjects and Predicates The simple subject is the essential noun, pronoun, or group of words acting as a noun that cannot be left out of the complete subject. The simple predicate is the essential verb or verb phrase that cannot be left out of the complete predicate. In the chart below, each simple subject and simple predicate is in darker type.

Complete Subjects	Complete Predicates
Tired of arguing, **Maria**	finally **agreed** to the plan.
Like many others in my class, **I**	**do** not especially **like** homework.
Many **citizens** in town	**oppose** higher taxes.
Others	**agree**.

Focusing on Subjects and Verbs Being able to locate subjects and verbs quickly in sentences will help you to determine that a sentence is clear and grammatically correct.

FINDING SUBJECTS AND VERBS
To find the subject, ask "What word is the sentence telling about?" To find the verb, look for a word or word group that expresses action, existence, or a linking relationship.

▶ **Exercise 1** **Recognizing Complete and Simple Subjects and Predicates.** Draw a line between the complete subject and the complete predicate in each sentence. Then circle each simple subject and predicate.

EXAMPLE: That tall (girl) in the red dress | usually (gets) the best grades.

1. The album with the original cast is now available in most stores.

2. Senator Billings will propose the new law.

3. The fourth Thursday in November is celebrated as Thanksgiving Day.

4. The skydiver landed safely.

5. Youngsters sometimes jump from those high rocks.

6. Dignitaries from all over the world attended the reception.

7. The children's elaborate skyscraper collapsed.

8. Ghosts are popular Halloween characters.

9. Several students from Europe are staying with local families.

10. The mysterious figure in black vanished.

▶ **Exercise 2** **Adding Sentence Parts.** Each word group below is missing either a complete subject or a complete predicate. On the line write a missing part to create a complete sentence. Circle the simple subject and simple predicate in the final sentence.

EXAMPLE: (Most) of the people passing by (did) not (offer) to help.

1. From among the many entries, only one _____ .

2. Every visitor to our school _____ .

3. _____ gradually overcame the fear of heights.

4. My younger brother _____ .

5. _____ has misplaced a library book.

20.1 Subjects and Verbs (Simple Subjects and Predicates) • Practice 2

▶ **Exercise 1** **Recognizing Simple Subjects and Predicates.** Draw a line between the complete subject and complete predicate. Then underline each simple subject once and each simple predicate twice.

EXAMPLE: A <u>friend</u> of mine | <u>plays</u> chess with me.

1. A sixteen-year-old girl from California gave the best dramatic interpretation.
2. A muddy dog of unknown breed ran away with Bernard's lunch.
3. Her friends at school helped her get a job.
4. The weary commuters were angry about the delay.
5. The freshman with the most unusual hat won the contest.
6. The boxes under the sink are empty.
7. The frightened witnesses wrote reports for the police.
8. The speaker caught his fishing pole on the light fixture.
9. Students going on the trip left early this morning.
10. The forward with the knee brace made ten baskets.

▶ **Exercise 2** **Finding Subjects and Verbs.** Underline the subject once and the verb twice.

EXAMPLE: Many <u>people</u> <u>visit</u> the Grand Canyon.

(1) A tourist gets a spectacular view at the Grand Canyon. (2) Curious visitors can take nature walks along the trails on the edge of the canyon. (3) Hikers may want to venture down the steep trails into the canyon. (4) However, the crumbling walls of the canyon's sides make mountain climbing dangerous. (5) A guided mule trip is a safer way to see the canyon. (6) Trips down the Colorado River also enable tourists to see the canyon from the inside.

(7) Tourists can also take a helicopter or an airplane ride over the canyon. (8) From the helicopter or plane, passengers can see the different branches of the canyon. (9) The aircraft can fly into the canyon for a closer view of the river and rock formations. (10) With all of these approaches, tourists can see the canyon from above, from the inside, or from the edge.

▶ **Writing Application** **Using Subjects and Verbs to Write Sentences.** Use each subject and verb in a sentence of your own.

EXAMPLE: robins   chirped

In the nest baby robins chirped for food.

1. truck   is stopping _____
2. girl   jumped _____
3. steak   shriveled _____
4. wind   was shrieking _____
5. radio   blared _____
6. lawnmower   sputtered _____
7. automobile   is wobbling _____
8. water   feels _____
9. waiter   dropped _____
10. newscaster   hiccupped _____

20.1 Compound Subjects and Verbs • Practice 1

Compound Subjects   A compound subject is two or more subjects that have the same verb and are joined by a conjunction such as *and* or *or*.

COMPOUND SUBJECTS
Mother or Dad will pick us up after the movie.
Lobsters, shrimp, and crabs are popular shellfish.

Compound Verbs   A compound verb is two or more verbs that have the same subject and are joined by a conjunction such as *and* or *or*.

COMPOUND VERBS
The waves crested and broke against the rocks.
The passers-by did not move on but stopped to watch the mime.
Paul and Andrew write, direct, and star in their own plays.

▶ **Exercise 1**   **Recognizing Compound Subjects.**   Underline the nouns or pronouns that make up each compound subject below.

EXAMPLE: High winds and freezing rain caused the power failure.

1. Carrots or small tomatoes would make an attractive garnish.
2. Cheese and whole-wheat crackers are a healthful snack.
3. Nancy, Darryl, and I worked on the decorations.
4. Time and the tide wait for no one.
5. In the forest, ferns and wildflowers abound.
6. Neither my brother nor I felt comfortable with those people.
7. Without your help, the table and the food would not have been ready.
8. Jason and Ulysses are characters from Greek mythology.
9. Pueblos, hogans, and tepees were common Indian dwellings.
10. In colonial times, stocks and pillories were used for punishment.

▶ **Exercise 2**   **Recognizing Compound Verbs.**   Underline the verbs that make up each compound verb below.

EXAMPLE: The masked stranger mounted his horse and galloped away.

1. The baby eats and sleeps on a regular schedule.
2. The photographer checked the lighting, posed the subject, and snapped the picture.
3. The paramedic did not hesitate but acted at once.
4. The captain hoisted the sail and pulled up the anchor.
5. The sick puppy neither ate nor drank.
6. The whole family baked and cooked for days before the holiday.
7. Brenda organized her note cards and began her rough draft.
8. Mike pruned and fertilized the grapefruit plant.
9. The departing dignitary neither waved nor looked back.
10. Some students seldom study but still do well.

20.1 # Compound Subjects and Verbs • Practice 2

▶ **Exercise 1** **Recognizing Compound Subjects.** Underline the nouns that make up each compound subject.

EXAMPLE: The <u>windows</u> and <u>doors</u> are locked.

1. Both flowers and perfume cause her to sneeze.
2. David and Marie both failed to win the prize.
3. Neither pets nor pianos are allowed in the apartment.
4. Lettuce, tomatoes, peppers, and cucumbers grew in the garden.
5. Hurricanes and tornadoes cause much damage to property every year.

▶ **Exercise 2** **Recognizing Compound Verbs.** Underline the verbs that make up each compound verb.

EXAMPLE: I <u>studied</u> hard and <u>passed</u> the test.

1. The car suddenly skidded on the ice and hit the curb.
2. Winds howled through the night but died down at dawn.
3. Hercules lifted Antaeus from the ground and crushed him.
4. Sports medicine is a relatively new field and offers many opportunities for careers.
5. The duck waddled down the bank, splashed into the water, and paddled to safety.
6. My brother and I built a rowboat in 1979 and used it on the lake the next year.
7. We washed the dishes and put them away.
8. He survived the war but died soon after.
9. The Romans erected buildings in brick and then faced them with marble.
10. We rehearsed the play for three weeks, had a dress rehearsal, and then gave a performance.

▶ **Writing Application** **Writing Sentences with Compound Subjects and Verbs.** Use the following items to write ten sentences of your own. Use the first three items as compound subjects, the next three as compound verbs, and the last four as compound subjects and verbs.

EXAMPLE: dog   squirrel
_____ *Our dog and a squirrel raced around the yard.* _____

1. jumper   sprinter _____
2. beaches   docks _____
3. guitarist   drummer   composer _____
4. stamped   screamed _____
5. dribbled   tossed _____
6. nods   smiles _____
7. orchestra   conductor   bowed   disappeared

   _____
8. horses   riders   galloped   trotted

   _____
9. clown   acrobat   stumbled   fell   rose

   _____
10. vans   trucks   cost   carry

   _____

20.2 Hard-to-Find Subjects (in Orders and Directions, in Questions) • Practice 1

Subjects in Orders and Directions   In sentences that give orders or directions, the subject is understood to be *you*.

Orders or Directions	With Understood Words Added
Return your library books immediately.	[You] return your library books immediately.
David, answer the door.	David, [you] answer the door.

Subjects in Questions   In questions the subject often follows the verb. To find the subject in a question, mentally rephrase the question as a statement.

Questions	Reworded as Statements
Is this your address?	This is your address.
Can we eat now?	We can eat now.
Where are you going ?	You are going where.

▶ **Exercise 1**   **Finding the Subject in Orders or Directions.**   Write the subject of each sentence in the blank at the right. Put a caret (^) where the subject belongs in the sentence.

EXAMPLE: André,^ please clear the table. _____you_____

1. A block past the First Bank, turn left. _____
2. Whatever the difficulties, do your best. _____
3. Please take out the trash. _____
4. Alison, don't forget your lunch. _____
5. Blacken in the grid with a soft pencil. _____
6. Derek, please give your mother a message. _____
7. Meet me at the library after school. _____
8. Mandy, please let me copy that recipe. _____
9. Before starting out, buckle your safety belt. _____
10. Help yourself, everyone. _____

▶ **Exercise 2**   **Finding the Subject in Questions.**   Underline the simple subject in each question below.

EXAMPLE: How much do these shoes cost?

1. Do you know the combination to this lock?
2. Have your parents given their permission for the class trip?
3. How is that casserole prepared?
4. What color did you paint the kitchen walls?
5. Did anyone bring directions to the farm?
6. Where are the Claytons going for the weekend?
7. Didn't Shakespeare write sonnets as well as plays?
8. Who brought the sandwiches?
9. Whom did Sue invite on the picnic?
10. Whose story should we believe?

20.2 # Hard-to-Find Subjects (in Orders and Directions, in Questions) • Practice 2

> **Exercise 1** **Finding Subjects in Orders or Directions.** Rewrite each sentence, inserting the understood subject in brackets.

EXAMPLE: During your break, take the dog out.

<u>During your break, [you] take the dog out.</u>

1. After school, come straight home.

   _____

2. Joanne, give me a quarter.

   _____

3. Now tell me what happened.

   _____

4. When using that machine, always wear safety goggles.

   _____

5. Sue, order me a milkshake, please.

   _____

6. After class, meet me at the library.

   _____

7. Pete, during takeoff, keep your seatbelt fastened.

   _____

8. Before leaving, pack a good lunch.

   _____

9. Dad, turn left at the end of the exit ramp.

   _____

10. When filling out that form, use ink.

    _____

> **Exercise 2** **Finding Subjects in Questions.** Underline the subject of each sentence.

EXAMPLE: Where did <u>they</u> spend their last winter vacation?

1. Have you seen the new horror movie?
2. When will Sally be home?
3. Who baked this cake?
4. About what will Andy write?
5. Are the final reports complete?
6. Is the story ready for publication?
7. Why hasn't Judy answered my note?
8. What did Jack wear to the game?
9. Has Joyce finished her term paper yet?
10. Which team won the championship?

20.2 Hard-to-Find Subjects (in Sentences Beginning with *There* or *Here*, in Sentences Inverted for Emphasis)
• Practice 1

Subjects in Sentences Beginning with *There* or *Here* The subject of a sentence is never *there* or *here*. Like inverted questions, such sentences can usually be rephrased as statements to find the subject.

Sentences Beginning with *There* or *Here*	Reworded with Subjects First
There goes my best friend.	My best friend goes there.
Here is your tennis racquet.	Your tennis racquet is here.

Subjects in Sentences Inverted for Emphasis In some sentences the subject is placed after the verb in order to receive greater emphasis. Such sentences can be mentally rephrased in normal subject-verb order to find the subject.

Inverted Word Order	Rephrased in Subject-Verb Order
After the elephants came the *clowns*.	The *clowns* came after the elephants.
Beyond the river lay the *cliffs*.	The *cliffs* lay beyond the river.

▶ **Exercise 1** **Finding the Subject in Sentences Beginning with *There* or *Here*.** Underline the subject in each sentence below.

EXAMPLE: Here comes the circus parade.

1. There is the new mayor.
2. Here are the proofs from the photographer.
3. There has seldom been a more beautiful sunset.
4. There is little undeveloped land in this part of town.
5. Here comes the custodian with the keys.
6. There must be a better restaurant in town than this one.
7. Here is the newest book by my favorite author.
8. There is no doubt about the outcome.
9. There went our last chance at the championship.
10. Here comes the President's helicopter.

▶ **Exercise 2** **Finding the Subject in Inverted Sentences.** Underline the subject in each sentence below.

EXAMPLE: Over the mantel hangs a beautiful landscape.

1. Right before our eyes appeared a white rabbit.
2. Between the creek and the dirt road stretches a lush meadow.
3. Throughout the town flew rumors about the bank manager.
4. Outside my bedroom window blooms a beautiful lilac bush.
5. On the front page appeared a story about the student of the year.
6. Into the stadium filed the throng of eager fans.
7. Through these halls have passed generations of dedicated lawmakers.
8. In the center of the harbor stands the Statue of Liberty.
9. From every window streamed tons of ticker tape and confetti.
10. Along the cobblestone streets stood restored colonial houses.

Name _____ Date _____

▶ **Exercise 1** Finding Subjects in Sentences Beginning with *There* or *Here*. Underline the subject of each sentence.

EXAMPLE: Here she is.

1. There are your keys on the table.
2. Here comes the bus.
3. There was no excuse for his behavior.
4. There goes the kite into the tree.
5. Here is your pizza with mushrooms and extra cheese.
6. There is the rest of the strawberry pie.
7. There are last week's papers.
8. Here are the poppy-seed rolls from the bakery.
9. There went my sister in her new car.
10. There were only three seeds left in the birdfeeder.

▶ **Exercise 2** Finding Subjects in Inverted Sentences. Underline the subject of each sentence.

EXAMPLE: In her hand was the missing letter.

1. After the rain came a beautiful rainbow.
2. All about us rang the bells of the village's three churches.
3. To the south rose the snow-covered peaks of the lofty mountains.
4. Ahead of the couple ran four noisy children.
5. All around them lay the scattered leaves.
6. With their safe arrival came a feeling of great happiness and relief.
7. Among the people in the crowd were our neighbors.
8. Beside the fire sat an old man.
9. On a raft floating down the river were their treasured possessions.
10. From the distance came the sound of thunder.

▶ **Writing Application** Writing Sentences with Hard-to-Find Subjects. Write four sentences of your own. The first sentence should give an order; the second should ask a question; the third should be an inverted sentence that begins with *there* or *here*; and the fourth sentence should be inverted for emphasis.

EXAMPLE: _____Lisa, leave right away._____

1. _____

   _____

2. _____

   _____

3. _____

   _____

4. _____

   _____

20.3 Direct Objects (The Direct Object, Compound Direct Objects) • Practice 1

The Direct Object A direct object is a noun, pronoun, or group of words acting as a noun that receives the action of a transitive verb.

DIRECT OBJECTS
DO Mom bought new |curtains| for my bedroom.
DO What |color| did she buy ? (Reworded: She did buy what |color|?)

Compound Direct Objects A compound direct object is more than one noun, pronoun, or group of words acting as a noun that receives the action of the same transitive verb.

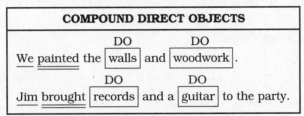

COMPOUND DIRECT OBJECTS
DO   DO We painted the |walls| and |woodwork| .
DO   DO Jim brought |records| and a |guitar| to the party.

Exercise 1 **Recognizing Direct Objects.** Draw a box around the direct object in each sentence.

EXAMPLE: Please set this \|vase\| in the center of the table.

1. What tapes did you bring?
2. Everyone enjoyed the performance.
3. Who will teach classes during Mr. Roper's leave of absence?
4. The owner of the missing dog has offered a reward.
5. Too much sugar may promote tooth decay.
6. Did you make this long-distance call to Denver?
7. Tanya likes basketball better than I do.
8. The campers took a wrong turn.
9. On the day of the test, bring two sharpened pencils.
10. Phyllis's parents surprised her with a new bike.

Exercise 2 **Recognizing Compound Direct Objects.** Draw a box around the nouns or pronouns that make up each compound direct object.

EXAMPLE: Would you rather have \|sausage\| or \|pepperoni\| on your pizza?

1. Mandy plays both basketball and soccer.
2. The new album brought fame and fortune to the young singer.
3. Should we serve the soup or the salad first?
4. The contestant won not only the car but also a cash jackpot.
5. Would you rather play chess or checkers?
6. Did the painter use a roller or a brush?
7. The chef will prepare pancakes or omelets.
8. The shopper bought both the knee-high boots and the matching purse.
9. For a bedtime snack, Fran has a sandwich and milk every night.
10. Are you taking biology or chemistry next term?

20.3 Direct Objects (The Direct Object, Compound Direct Objects) • **Practice 2**

▶ **Exercise 1**   **Recognizing Direct Objects.**   Underline the direct object in each sentence.

EXAMPLE: Most people own <u>umbrellas</u>.

(1) Umbrellas have a long history. (2) Even the ancient Egyptians used them. (3) The umbrella symbolized royal and religious power to the Egyptians. (4) Assyrian tablets from 1350 B.C. show an umbrella-shaded king. (5) The early Greeks also used the umbrella symbol. (6) Religious festivals and parades featured it prominently. (7) The later Greeks used the umbrella shape more practically. (8) They invented the sunshade. (9) They even developed a sunshade hat. (10) Later still, the Romans used parasols.

▶ **Exercise 2**   **Recognizing Compound Direct Objects.**   Underline the nouns or pronouns that make up each compound direct object.

EXAMPLE: Maggie knitted a <u>hat</u> and <u>mittens</u>.

1. Don't forget the hammer and nails.
2. Mike bought a new jacket, shirt, and trousers.
3. The fire destroyed both the main house and the barn.
4. Who invited Joan and Jack?
5. That factory produces cars and trucks.
6. The baby doesn't eat fruit or cereal yet.
7. Which shrubs and bushes did the gardener trim?
8. The recipe requires cinnamon and sugar.
9. The waiter overlooked you and me.
10. Mom planted cabbage, tomatoes, lettuce, and peppers.
11. We read the bulletin board and the pamphlets carefully.
12. Susan had salad and soup for lunch.
13. The dog chased woodchucks and rabbits all over the field.
14. Caroline bought roses and carnations for the centerpiece.
15. My duties that summer included filing and word processing.
16. On our road trip, we visited Montana and Idaho.
17. William Shakespeare wrote sonnets and plays.
18. The mechanic replaced the points and plugs in the car.
19. Mabel added sprouts and radishes to the salad.
20. Winifred is studying history and literature.

20.3 Direct Objects (Direct Object or Object of a Preposition?) • Practice 1

Direct Object or Object of a Preposition A direct object is never the noun or pronoun at the end of a prepositional phrase.

DIRECT OBJECTS AND PREPOSITIONAL PHRASES
DO Marge and Steve played │croquet│ . (played *what?* croquet)
DO   PREP PHRASE They played │croquet│ in the back yard. (played *what?* croquet)
PREP PHRASE They played in the back yard. (played *what?* no answer)

▷ **Exercise 1** **Distinguishing Between Direct Objects and Objects of Prepositions.** Draw a box around only direct objects in the sentences. Do not box any objects of prepositions.

EXAMPLE: We joined │Kelly│ and │Tim│ for a picnic.

1. Please put the fruit into the refrigerator.
2. Several new families moved into our neighborhood.
3. A true story inspired the novel about Robinson Crusoe.
4. Alexander Selkirk survived on a desert island.
5. We changed planes in Chicago.
6. Betsy chose fruit instead of ice cream for dessert.
7. Linus carries his blanket everywhere.
8. We watched the sunset from the porch.
9. Eventually the cowboy overcame his fear of horses.
10. The guest of honor arrived in time for dinner.

▷ **Exercise 2** **Writing Sentences with Direct Objects.** Add words to each sentence beginning below to make a complete sentence. Be sure each sentence ending includes a direct object.

EXAMPLE: The singer performed _____*an old-time favorite*_____ .

1. My sister broke _____ .
2. The teacher gave Ian _____ .
3. We all enjoyed _____ .
4. Some of the children followed _____ .
5. Have you read _____ .
6. My friend Jessica wrote _____ .
7. The guests ate _____ .
8. Robins built _____ .
9. Our team won _____ .
10. Please put _____ .

20.3 Direct Objects (Direct Object or Object of a Preposition?) • Practice 2

Exercise 1 **Distinguishing Between Direct Objects and Objects of Prepositions.** Write the direct object in each sentence. If a sentence does not have one, write *none*.

EXAMPLE: People have used umbrellas for a long time. _____*umbrellas*_____

(1) The word umbrella has come to us from the Romans. (2) The Latin word *umbra* translates into our word "shade." (3) The Romans used umbrellas for protection against the sun. (4) People often carried them to chariot races. (5) Romans sometimes dyed the umbrellas with the colors of their favorite chariot team. (6) Eventually umbrellas at chariot races caused a public uproar. (7) They often blocked the view of other spectators. (8) The Roman emperor Domitian finally settled the dispute about umbrellas. (9) By his decree only sunshade hats could be used at the public games. (10) No one with an umbrella could attend the games.

1. _____   5. _____   8. _____
2. _____   6. _____   9. _____
3. _____   7. _____   10. _____
4. _____

Writing Application **Writing Sentences with Direct Objects.** Use each subject and verb to write a sentence with a direct object. Then circle each direct object.

EXAMPLE: kittens   played

_____The kittens played (tag) with each other._____

1. police   will escort _____
2. truck   dented _____
3. Mr. Lopez   described _____
4. elephant   trampled _____
5. water   ruined _____
6. Eileen   organized _____
7. Craig   should have won _____
8. grasshoppers   destroy _____
9. detectives   found _____
10. noise   shook _____

20.3 Indirect Objects (Indirect Objects, Compound Indirect Objects) • Practice 1

Indirect Objects   An indirect object is a noun or pronoun that appears with a direct object and names the person or thing that something is given to or done for.

INDIRECT OBJECTS
IO   DO The clerk sold me the wrong size . (sold *to whom?* to me)
IO   DO I gave the car a coat of wax. (gave *to what?* to the car)

Compound Indirect Objects   A compound indirect object is two or more nouns or pronouns that appear with a direct object and name the people or things that something is given to or done for.

COMPOUND INDIRECT OBJECTS
IO   IO   DO Jason did Anna and me a big favor . (did *for whom?* for Anna and me)
IO   IO   DO The cleaner gave the slacks and jacket special care . (gave *to what?* to the slacks and jacket)

▶ **Exercise 1**   **Recognizing Indirect Objects.**   Draw a box around each indirect object.

EXAMPLE: My parents gave me an allowance for doing chores.

1. Grandma offered us another piece of pie.
2. The baby sitter read the children another story before bedtime.
3. Warren gave the teacher his first draft this morning.
4. The testing service will send the school our grades in a few weeks.
5. The prisoner passed the warden his empty cup.
6. The famous chef served the guests an elegant meal.
7. Who told you that secret?
8. Jimmy's parents allowed him one more chance.
9. Doris dealt each player thirteen cards.
10. Has anyone given the dog a bath this week?

▶ **Exercise 2**   **Recognizing Compound Indirect Objects.**   Draw a box around the nouns or pronouns that make up each compound indirect object.

EXAMPLE: Brenda showed her brother and me pictures from her vacation.

1. We fixed Mom and Dad a special anniversary dinner.
2. The PTA gave the teachers and aides an end-of-year luncheon.
3. Hannah brought the painter and his helper a cold drink.
4. The magician showed me and the others the secret compartment.
5. The principal handed Doug and Karen their diplomas first.
6. We gave Mom and Grandma corsages.
7. Aunt Paula always makes my cousins and me a special dessert.
8. The city gave the players and their families a ticker tape parade.
9. The mechanic gave the chain, sprocket, and axles a coat of oil.
10. The child left Santa and his reindeer a snack.

20.3

Indirect Objects (Indirect Objects, Compound Indirect Objects) • Practice 2

▷ **Exercise 1** **Recognizing Indirect Objects.** Underline the indirect object in each sentence.

EXAMPLE: He gave <u>me</u> his old tennis racquet.

1. He told his parents the news.
2. Greg ordered us seconds.
3. The receptionist gave the messenger an envelope.
4. The sitter read Paul two stories at bedtime.
5. I lent Amanda my pink sweater.
6. Ms. Hall showed us slides of Venice.
7. Who sent you these flowers?
8. Sandy hasn't written me a letter for weeks.
9. Mom left the painters a note.
10. Mr. Poirot teaches his students French.
11. You owe me a more complete explanation than that.
12. Please do Sylvia this favor.
13. Give James a call about your plans for the trip.
14. The federal government sent the flooded city aid.
15. Henry gave the school a memorial bench.
16. The coach handed the team members their new jerseys.
17. Mr. Costanza bought his daughter a new bicycle for her birthday.
18. Emma knitted her granddaughter a lavender blanket.
19. The store owner sold the young child a defective toy.
20. The politician told the people his plans for the future.

▷ **Exercise 2** **Recognizing Compound Indirect Objects.** Underline the nouns or pronouns acting as indirect objects in each sentence. Then circle the nouns or pronouns that make up each compound indirect object.

EXAMPLE: We wrote (Sue) and (Al) letters about our trip.

(1) Bart showed us the route for the trip. (2) Mr. Perkins rented Joyce and me bikes. (3) My mother packed us a snack. (4) I had already given the group the other food supplies. (5) I had also given Helen and Max the sleeping bags. (6) Our families wished us a pleasant trip. (7) At the campsite Bart showed Helen, Joyce, and Max the best way to make a fire. (8) We cooked ourselves a fine meal. (9) No one left the raccoons and other animals even a nibble. (10) Then Joyce told us ghost stories around the campfire.

20.3 # Indirect Objects and Objective
Complements • Practice 1

Indirect Object or Object of a Preposition   An indirect object never follows the word *to* or *for*.

INDIRECT OBJECT VERSUS PREPOSITIONAL PHRASE
IO · · · DO · · · · · · · · · · · · · · · IO · · · DO
The caller left │you│ a │message│ .   We gave │mother│ a │corsage│ .
· · · · · · · · · DO · · · PREP PH · · · · · · · · · · DO · · · PREP PH
The caller left a │message│ for you.   We gave a │corsage│ to mother.

The Objective Complement   An objective complement is an adjective, noun, or group of words acting
as a noun that follows a direct object and describes or renames it.

OBJECTIVE COMPLEMENTS
· · · · · · · DO · · OC
The gift made │me│ │happy│ . (made me *what?* happy)
· · · · · · · · DO · · · · OC
We chose │Paula│ │captain│ . (chose Paula *what?* captain)

▶ **Exercise 1**   **Distinguishing Between Indirect Objects and Objects of Prepositions.**   In each
blank at the right, write whether the underlined word is an *indirect object* or an *object of a preposition*.

EXAMPLE: Volunteers offered each passer-by a flyer. _____*indirect object*_____

1. The realtor showed the family several houses. _____

2. The child brought an apple for the teacher. _____

3. Lana told us a funny joke. _____

4. A volunteer brought the patient a newspaper. _____

5. The messenger handed the envelope to the secretary. _____

6. Please give this note to Phillip. _____

7. Ms. Nelson gave us a surprise quiz. _____

8. The principal read the notice to the entire school. _____

9. The defendant told the judge his story. _____

10. Luis made his father a bookcase. _____

▶ **Exercise 2**   **Recognizing Objective Complements.**   Underline the objective complement in each
sentence below. Then write whether it is a *noun* or an *adjective* in the blank to the right.

EXAMPLE: The race left us exhausted. _____*adjective*_____

1. The team made the coach proud. _____

2. The class elected Harry treasurer. _____

3. The jury found the defendant not guilty. _____

4. The mechanical swing kept the baby quiet for hours. _____

5. Everyone in his family calls Jeremy "Jem." _____

20.3 # Indirect Objects and Objective
Complements • Practice 2

▶ **Exercise 1** **Distinguishing Between Indirect Objects and Objects of Prepositions.** In the
following sentences, change each indirect object into a prepositional phrase. Change each prepositional
phrase that you can into an indirect object.

EXAMPLE: Janet left a message for you.

_____ *Janet left you a message.* _____

1. Last night at the restaurant, the chef prepared a special dessert for us.

   _____

2. The sitter handed the baby the rattle.

   _____

3. The realtor showed us four apartments.

   _____

4. Alex sold his farm to the county.

   _____

5. Did you bring some ice cream for the children?

   _____

▶ **Exercise 2** **Recognizing Objective Complements.** Underline the objective complement in each
sentence.

EXAMPLE: The movie made him very <u>sad</u>.

1. The third-period class nominated him treasurer.
2. The continuous rain made them depressed.
3. The cousins called their talented uncle a wizard.
4. The actor dyed his blond hair red.
5. My parents' rules sometimes make me angry.

▶ **Writing Application** **Using Indirect Objects to Combine Sentences.** Turn each pair of
sentences into a single sentence with an indirect object.

EXAMPLE: I bought the album. I bought it for Mark.

_____ *I bought Mark the album.* _____

1. The sitter prepared a snack. He prepared it for Paul.

   _____

2. The waiter served my order. He served it to Ann.

   _____

3. I made a macramé belt. I made it for my mother.

   _____

4. The realtor rented the apartment. She rented it to us.

   _____

5. The principal gave an award. He gave it to our class.

   _____

Subject Complements (Predicate Nominative, Predicate Adjective) • **Practice 1**

Subject Complements A predicate nominative is a noun or pronoun that follows a linking verb and renames, identifies, or explains the subject of a sentence.

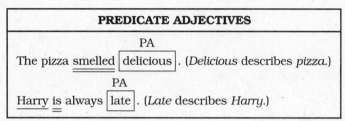

PREDICATE NOMINATIVES
PN
Jackson became a |superstar|. (*Superstar* renames *Jackson*.)
PN
The better player is |Tim|. (*Tim* identifies *player*.)

The Predicate Adjective A predicate adjective is an adjective that follows a linking verb and describes the subject of the sentence.

PREDICATE ADJECTIVES
PA
The pizza smelled |delicious|. (*Delicious* describes *pizza*.)
PA
Harry is always |late|. (*Late* describes *Harry*.)

▶ **Exercise 1** **Recognizing Predicate Nominatives.** Underline each predicate nominative.

EXAMPLE: Helen has been my best <u>friend</u> since kindergarten.

1. The Tigers are the team to beat.
2. Math and science are my best subjects.
3. My sister became a lawyer after years of study.
4. The former President remained a prominent figure after leaving office.
5. The specialty of the house is cheese fondue.
6. Judy's plan seemed a workable one.
7. The understudy became an overnight success.
8. He is the best choice for the job.
9. The executive remained an officer even after her retirement.
10. Nero Wolfe is a famous fictional detective.

▶ **Exercise 2** **Recognizing Predicate Adjectives.** Underline each predicate adjective.

EXAMPLE: The movie sounds <u>ridiculous</u>.

1. The first plan seemed unworkable.
2. The color of that blouse is unbecoming.
3. Paul was disappointed with his strikeout.
4. Audrey sounded quite cheerful on the phone.
5. The crowd grew restless because of the long delay.
6. That centerpiece looks beautiful on the table.
7. The singer appeared nervous before the concert.
8. You will surely feel better after a nap.
9. The patient grows stronger every day.
10. The weather stayed sunny throughout the weekend.

20.3 **Subject Complements** (Predicate Nominative, Predicate Adjective) • **Practice 2**

▶ **Exercise 1** **Recognizing Predicate Nominatives.** Underline the predicate nominative in each sentence.

EXAMPLE: Carl is my <u>brother</u>.

1. Hawkins remained the best player on the team.
2. Some people stay children throughout their lives.
3. The first speaker was I.
4. Which of those records is a classic?
5. A hamburger seemed the safest thing to order.
6. The puppies in the corner are the ones for sale.
7. Our state senator may soon become governor.
8. The special today is broiled swordfish.
9. The girls have remained friends for years.
10. Ellen appears the strongest candidate.
11. Florence is Albert's youngest sister.
12. The result of the revolution was chaos.
13. The best item on the menu has always been the salmon.
14. The aroma in the air was clearly cinnamon.
15. Ramona is Rachel's best friend.

▶ **Exercise 2** **Recognizing Predicate Adjectives.** Underline the predicate adjective in each sentence.

EXAMPLE: Jean seems <u>tired</u> this afternoon.

1. The flowers smell heavenly.
2. I look awful in this shade of green.
3. Some of the cheese is moldy.
4. The pineapple tasted delicious.
5. The music sounds better from farther away.
6. The sky became cloudy toward evening.
7. I felt angry after our argument.
8. The weather remained hot all week.
9. The team's fans became more unhappy with each new setback.
10. The children grew tan from the summer sun.
11. The path is extremely treacherous.
12. The oatmeal seemed much too hot.
13. The moon was full last night.
14. The children looked very unhappy.
15. The price of the couch is much too high.

20.3 Subject Complements (Compound Subject Complements) • Practice 1

Compound Subject Complements   A compound predicate nominative is two or more nouns or pronouns that follow a linking verb and rename the subject of the sentence. A compound predicate adjective is two or more adjectives that follow a linking verb and describe the subject of the sentence.

COMPOUND SUBJECT COMPLEMENTS
PN   PN
The new officers are │Kate│ and │Tom│. (*Kate* and *Tom* identify *officers*)
PA   PA
The puppy was │hungry│ and │dirty│. (*Hungry* and *dirty* describe *puppy*.)

▶ **Exercise 1**   **Recognizing Compound Subject Complements.**   Underline the nouns or adjectives that make up each compound subject complement. On the line at the right, write *PN* for predicate nominative or *PA* for predicate adjective to describe each one.

EXAMPLE: The chair is neither <u>attractive</u> nor <u>sturdy</u>.   *PA*

1. The twins are Kim and Karen. _____
2. The main-course choices are steak, shrimp, or chicken. _____
3. That blazer is neither attractive nor affordable. _____
4. Cory will become either a lawyer or a politician. _____
5. When annoyed, the dog becomes mean and vicious. _____
6. After the long drought, the ground looks hard and dusty. _____
7. My favorite breakfast is pancakes and sausage. _____
8. The pizza will be ready and waiting in ten minutes. _____
9. Monsieur Henri is the owner and chef of that restaurant. _____
10. Without proper care, the plant may become bent or discolored. _____

▶ **Exercise 2**   **Writing Sentences with Compound Subject Complements.**   Each sentence below contains a subject complement. On each line to the right, add a conjunction and a noun or adjective to make the subject complement compound. Be sure the word you add is the same part of speech as the subject complement given.

EXAMPLE: The child became tired _____*and cranky*_____.

1. That remark sounded rude _____.
2. The stew tastes both rich _____.
3. Every visitor to their home feels comfortable _____.
4. The winner will surely be either Hank _____.
5. The best math students are Ellen _____.
6. All the fans felt proud _____.
7. A good snack would be fruit _____.
8. That star is both intelligent _____.
9. The losing team felt neither discouraged _____.
10. Her favorite months are January _____.

20.3 Subject Complements (Compound Subject Complements) • Practice 2

▶ **Exercise 1** **Recognizing Compound Subject Complements.** Underline the nouns or adjectives that make up each compound subject complement. Then label each compound complement as a *predicate nominative* or *predicate adjective*.

EXAMPLE: The museum is beautiful and interesting.   *predicate adjective*

(1) The most frequent visitors to the museum are foreign visitors or other out-of-towners. (2) The museum's treasures are mainly furniture and paintings. (3) Its collection grows larger and better every year. (4) The paintings are old and valuable. (5) Most of them are pastels, watercolors, or oils. (6) The majority of paintings are Dutch or Italian. (7) The museum's furnishings are graceful and elegant. (8) The most interesting pieces in the foyer are a colonial table, a Philadelphia clock, and a silver lamp. (9) Other museum highlights are its beautiful rugs and its formal gardens. (10) The museum is free to the public and open daily except holidays.

1. _____   6. _____
2. _____   7. _____
3. _____   8. _____
4. _____   9. _____
5. _____   10. _____

▶ **Writing Application** **Writing Sentences with Subject Complements.** Use each subject and verb to write a sentence with the kind of subject complement indicated.

EXAMPLE: Liz   seems   (predicate adjective)   *Liz seems excited about the trip.*

1. friends   are   (compound predicate nominative)

   _____

2. dogs   became   (predicate adjective)

   _____

3. baby   grew   (compound predicate adjective)

   _____

4. Eric   became   (predicate nominative)

   _____

5. singer   was   (predicate nominative)

   _____

6. leaves   turned   (compound predicate adjective)

   _____

7. vegetables   are   (compound predicate nominative)

   _____

8. guests   looked   (predicate adjective)

   _____

9. voice   sounded   (predicate adjective)

   _____

10. Agnes   remained   (predicate nominative)

21.1 # Prepositional Phrases • Practice 1

Adjective Phrases   A phrase is a group of words, without a subject and verb, that acts as one part of speech. An adjective phrase is a prepositional phrase that modifies a noun or pronoun by telling what kind or which one.

ADJECTIVE PHRASES
The woman *with the tan briefcase* is the mayor. (*Which* woman?)
We have always liked the big house *on the hill.* (*Which* house?)

Adverb Phrases   An adverb phrase is a prepositional phrase that modifies a verb, adjective, or adverb by pointing out where, when, in what manner, or to what extent.

ADVERB PHRASES
After the game, we went *into town.* (*Went* when? *Went* where?)
Tanya felt good *about her report card.* (*Good* to what extent?)

▶ **Exercise 1**   **Identifying Adjective Phrases.**   Underline the adjective phrase in each sentence below. Circle the noun or pronoun it modifies.

EXAMPLE: Someone should water the flower (bed) in the front yard.

1. Only one of us can play the guitar.
2. Several houses on our street have decks.
3. Each student will write a report about a different capital.
4. Louise gave a surprise party for Mary.
5. My grandmother collects teacups from different countries.
6. The bike in the shop window is expensive.
7. The only difference between Gerri and her twin sister is their names.
8. Someone just bought that empty lot down the street.
9. Eddy made a statue of a bird.
10. The top of the wall is barbed wire.

▶ **Exercise 2**   **Identifying Adverb Phrases.**   Underline the adverb phrase in each sentence below. Circle the word it modifies.

EXAMPLE: After our long workout, we (collapsed).

1. This coupon is good for another month.
2. Our next-door neighbors moved to New Mexico.
3. After all your hard work, you deserve a vacation.
4. With your help, I finished the job.
5. After high school, my sister became a computer programmer.
6. We arrived at the theater early.
7. With only slight hesitation, Diane approached the microphone.
8. Peter quickly slipped under the gate.
9. Outside the theater a large crowd watched the arriving celebrities.
10. We sometimes drive far into the country.

21.1 Prepositional Phrases • Practice 2

▶ **Exercise 1** **Identifying Adjective Phrases.** Underline the adjective phrase or adjective phrases in each sentence. Then draw an arrow from each phrase to the word it modifies.

EXAMPLE: Their house in the mountains is spectacular.

1. The price of the car was much too high.

2. Put that box of books down here.

3. My sister is the one in the yellow sweater.

4. The house on the corner of our street needs paint.

5. The cry of the wounded animal haunted us.

6. This is another book by the same author.

7. The shapes of the two objects are very similar.

8. Something in the corner of the room moved.

9. Did you close the window behind the couch?

10. I enjoyed your article about Mr. Hill.

▶ **Exercise 2** **Identifying Adverb Phrases.** Underline the adverb phrase or adverb phrases in each sentence. Then draw an arrow from each phrase to the word it modifies.

EXAMPLE: After school we went to the soccer game.

1. Simmer the stew over low heat.

2. The coach is always tougher on newcomers.

3. Louis delivered their anniversary present to the wrong house.

4. Lightning hit the barn during the storm.

5. The frightened squirrel ran across the roof and jumped into the tree.

6. Allie swam away from us.

7. The couple sailed their boat around the world.

8. They returned before dark.

9. The flood waters rose over the breakwater and onto the roadway.

10. Run into the backyard and take the lawnmower out of the rain.

Appositives and Appositive Phrases
• Practice 1

Appositives   An appositive is a noun or pronoun placed next to another noun or pronoun to identify, rename, or explain it.

+---+
| **APPOSITIVES** |
+---+
| Robert Frost wrote the poem "*Birches*." |
| |
| My new dog, *Max*, has a pedigree. |
+---+

Appositive Phrases   An appositive phrase is an appositive with modifiers.

+---+
| **APPOSITIVE PHRASES** |
+---+
| Robert Frost, *a New England poet*, wrote "Birches." |
| |
| The dog, *a standard poodle with a brown coat*, has a pedigree. |
+---+

▶ **Exercise 1**   **Identifying Appositives.**   Underline the appositive in each sentence. Circle the noun or pronoun it renames.

EXAMPLE: My ⟨uncle⟩, a dentist, favors fluoridating the water supply.

1. The play *Cats* is based on poems by T. S. Eliot.
2. Our first president, George Washington, was a native Virginian.
3. The story appeared in the popular magazine *Time*.
4. The film was nominated for Hollywood's top award, the Oscar.
5. The new park, Hammer Field, has three baseball diamonds.
6. I invited my best friend, Dora, to spend the weekend.
7. Please give this note to the principal, Mrs. Spiegel.
8. April 19, Patriots' Day, commemorates Paul Revere's famous ride.
9. Lou told only his brother Mike the secret.
10. The site of the fair will be Minnesota's capital, St. Paul.

▶ **Exercise 2**   **Identifying Appositive Phrases.**   Underline the appositive phrase in each sentence. Circle the noun or pronoun it renames.

EXAMPLE: The ⟨centerpiece⟩, an arrangement of roses, was beautiful.

1. Norma Ellis, a local TV reporter, was the first to report the fire.
2. My personal favorite is Talmadge, the candidate with the best record.
3. The unicorn, a creature with one horn, is a mythical animal.
4. That word comes from Natick, a Native American language.
5. Chinese cooking is often done in a wok, a large pan with a rounded bottom.
6. The movie, another in the popular science-fiction series, was awful.
7. Those flowers, members of the same family, grow in the woods.
8. The new road, a link between the two largest cities in the state, will be completed soon.
9. Please take this message to Judy, the girl in the last row.
10. My cousin, a senior at Eastern High, plans to become a nurse.

21.1 # Appositives and Appositive Phrases
• Practice 2

▷ **Exercise 1** **Identifying Appositives.** Underline the appositive in each sentence. Then circle the word or words each appositive renames.

EXAMPLE: This (book), a <u>novel</u>, is extremely fast-paced.

 1. Mr. Smith, a lawyer, is away on vacation.

 2. My sister Alice is a medical student.

 3. Our house, a saltbox, is typical of colonial New England architecture.

 4. The reporter, Ms. Hughes, confirmed the story.

 5. John Greenleaf Whittier wrote the poem "Snowbound."

 6. My favorite teacher, Ms. Jenkins, will retire next year.

 7. The artist Mary Cassatt painted mothers and their children.

 8. Dad's special dessert, cheesecake, won a blue ribbon.

 9. The poet Shelley drowned in a boating accident.

10. Ed ordered his favorite dinner, pizza.

11. My cousin Dorothy is coming to visit in December.

12. One candidate, Sharon, is the only one with a chance to win.

13. Rodin's work *The Thinker* is his most well-known sculpture.

14. A river, the Thames, runs through London.

15. The suspect, Bill Carlton, was arrested last night.

▷ **Exercise 2** **Identifying Appositive Phrases.** Underline the appositive phrase in each sentence. Then circle the word or words each appositive phrase renames.

EXAMPLE: Our new (pet), a <u>frisky puppy</u>, loves to play.

 1. They hope to win the prize, a trip for two to Hawaii.

 2. Mrs. Konevich fixed the car, an old station wagon.

 3. Shelley's sister, a track star at UCLA, runs three miles daily.

 4. He took her to a movie, a comedy about army life.

 5. Two boys, friends of ours, gave us a ride.

 6. The youngest player, a pitcher on the second team, received an award at the dinner.

 7. We gave Mrs. Hunt, our noisy neighbor, a warning.

 8. Amy's father, a federal court judge, will be the speaker.

 9. Chess, her favorite game, can take hours to play.

10. He is an artist, a genius with a paint brush.

11. The story takes place in Thebes, an ancient city in Greece.

12. Stevie, a talented skateboarder, won a contest on Saturday.

13. The Morrises' house, a restored Victorian, needs a new paint job.

14. *Moby-Dick*, a novel by Herman Melville, is highly regarded by many critics.

15. The Amazon, the longest river in South America, is 4,000 miles in length.

21.1 Appositives and Appositive Phrases
(Compound Appositives) • Practice 1

Compound Appositives A compound appositive is two or more appositives or appositive phrases connected by a conjunction and used to identify the same noun or pronoun.

COMPOUND APPOSITIVES
Two cities, *Venice and Genoa*, were great rivals at one time.
Any new car, whether *a small compact* or *a fancy sport model*, will be an improvement over this one.

▶ **Exercise 1** **Identifying Compound Appositives.** Underline each compound appositive in the sentences below. Then circle the word or words it renames.

EXAMPLE: The (puppies), a tiny hound and a winsome terrier, stared up at us.

1. I could not choose between the two desserts, cheesecake and brownies.
2. Which Shakespearean tragedy, *Hamlet* or *Macbeth*, is longer?
3. Our two newest states, Alaska and Hawaii, do not border other states.
4. The star added a Grammy to her other awards, a Tony, an Oscar, and an Emmy.
5. Sacajawea was a guide for the explorers Lewis and Clark.
6. The family could not decide between the houses, a small Cape Cod or a rambling ranch-style.
7. The battery, the pitcher and catcher, conferred on the mound.
8. We had a party for the new couple next door, a man and woman from Utah.
9. I like all movies by the Marx Brothers, Harpo, Groucho, Chico, Zeppo, and Gummo.
10. The ball was held for the visiting dignitaries, the King and Queen of Spain.

▶ **Exercise 2** **Writing Sentences with Appositives, Appositive Phrases, and Compound Appositives.** Turn each pair of sentences into a single sentence with an appositive, an appositive phrase, or a compound appositive.

EXAMPLE: The play was very amusing. The play was a farce.

    The play, a farce, was very amusing.

1. Ed Jenkins went to college with my father. He is a local disc jockey.

_____

2. Scrooge is a symbol of miserliness. He is the main character in Dickens' A Christmas Carol.

_____

3. Mom had several choices for the main course. The choices were stuffed chicken, lasagna, or baked fish.

_____

4. Both home teams were high in the standings. The teams are the Bears and the Cubs.

_____

5. Their new apartment is quite spacious. It was once a loft with fourteen-foot ceilings.

_____

21.1 Appositives and Appositive Phrases
(Compound Appositives) • Practice 2

▶ **Exercise 1**   **Identifying Compound Appositives.**   In each sentence, underline each part of each compound appositive. Then draw an arrow from each part to the word or words it renames.

EXAMPLE: Viewing ocean creatures, fish and other animals, is one reason that underwater diving is popular.

1. As early as 4500 B.C., people were diving in the ocean to bring up food, both fish and plants.

2. Early Greek and Roman divers also dived to retrieve the ocean's riches, pearls, sponges, and shells.

3. The most common diving method, skin diving or breath-hold diving, has been practiced the longest.

4. Skin diving, a very simple type of diving and a popular form of recreation today, requires little or no equipment.

5. The basic equipment, fins, masks, and snorkels, is easy to use.

6. Years ago, divers used natural equipment, hollow reeds for snorkels and tortoise shells for goggles.

7. Now, however, this equipment is made from more modern materials, glass and plastic.

8. In 1943, two Frenchmen, Cousteau and Gagnan, developed practical independent breathing equipment.

9. Improved equipment gives today's divers great advantages, more mobility and increased time under water.

10. Today, divers often use special gear, compressed-air tanks and wet suits, which allows them to swim underwater for long periods.

▶ **Writing Application**   **Using Appositives and Appositive Phrases to Combine**
Sentences.   Turn each pair of sentences into one with an appositive or appositive phrase.

EXAMPLE: Sam typed his paper. It was a book report.

_____Sam typed his paper, a book report._____

1. The book was published in many languages. It was an autobiography.

_____

2. A neighbor's tree became the graveyard for their colorful kite. The kite was a large dragon with a silver tail.

_____

3. Candice completed the race in spite of her injury. She had a twisted ankle.

_____

4. The memorial honors the people who died while in service during World War II. It is a simple, symbolic structure made of white stone.

_____

5. Mount Shasta towers thousands of feet above the surrounding valleys and plateaus. The mountain is a volcano.

_____

21.1 Participles and Participial Phrases
(Participles; Verb or Participle?) • Practice 1

Participles   A participle is a form of a verb that acts as an adjective and modifies a noun or pronoun.

Present Participles	Past Participles
A *bubbling pot* sat on the stove. *Purring*, the kitten settled into my lap.	A *typed* report looks neater. *Pleased*, Kimberly sat down.

Verb or Participle?   A verb phrase always begins with a helping verb, but a participle acting as an adjective stands by itself.

Verb Phrases	Participles
The crowd *was laughing* at the street corner clown. The taxpayers *were dismayed* at the latest increases.	*Laughing*, the children raced away. *Dismayed*, the librarian began to pick up the books.

▶ **Exercise 1**   **Identifying Participles.**   Underline the participle in each sentence and circle the word it modifies. On each line at the right, write *present* or *past* to tell which kind it is.

EXAMPLE: An underline{amused} (smile) played across her face. ____*past*____

1. Marilyn wished on the falling star. _____

2. Keith is the leading hitter on our team. _____

3. The detective had a puzzled expression on his face. _____

4. Can you repair this broken vase? _____

5. My favorite dessert is baked apples. _____

6. Marc auditioned for the casting director. _____

7. The dry cleaner had a pressing appointment. _____

8. The sitter soothed the frightened child. _____

9. In Davy's dream, he rode on a flying carpet. _____

10. Laura returned the borrowed book this morning. _____

▶ **Exercise 2**   **Distinguishing Between Verbs and Participles.**   On each line at the right, write whether each underlined word is a *verb* or a *participle*.

EXAMPLE: The annoyed customer spoke rudely to the clerk. ____*participle*____

1. The plane has been delayed by the weather. _____

2. The delayed game will be played next week. _____

3. A growing child needs nutritious food. _____

4. Queen Anne's lace was growing by the roadside. _____

5. You will find the information on the following pages. _____

6. Someone has been following me for the last block. _____

7. Some spots are becoming worn. _____

8. That dress is a very becoming color. _____

9. This restaurant has an interesting but limited menu. _____

10. My parents have limited my nights out to weekends. _____

21.1 Participles and Participial Phrases
(Participles; Verb or Participle?) • Practice 2

▶ **Exercise 1** **Identifying Participles.** Underline the participle in each sentence. Then label each as *present* or *past*.

EXAMPLE: The <u>frightened</u> cat ran up a tree. ___*past*___

1. The howling coyotes woke the neighborhood. _____
2. Raoul brought the injured hawk to a veterinarian. _____
3. The child gave his mother a crumbling cookie. _____
4. Stumbling, Nicole dropped her books in the hall. _____
5. A falling star streaked across the clear sky. _____
6. The frozen ice cream was too hard to eat. _____
7. The disappointed team vowed to practice harder. _____
8. Hurt, Vivian ate lunch by herself. _____
9. Howard turned off the blaring radio. _____
10. The torn tent was no protection against the wind. _____
11. The freezing rain made the roads quite treacherous. _____
12. The exhausted climbers were rescued after three days. _____
13. The dwindling water supply worried the city's residents. _____
14. Cornered, the thief finally gave up. _____
15. The carpenter fixed the child's broken toy. _____

▶ **Exercise 2** **Distinguishing Between Verbs and Participles.** Identify each underlined word as a *V* (verb) or *P* (participle). If the word is used as a participle, also write the word it modifies.

EXAMPLE: The cat <u>frightened</u> the bird. ___*V*___

1. The train is <u>arriving</u> on track 7. _____
2. Reporters interviewed the <u>arriving</u> delegation. _____
3. My little brother loves <u>frozen</u> yogurt. _____
4. Usually, by this time of year, the pond has <u>frozen</u>. _____
5. The theatrical company has been <u>touring</u> major cities. _____
6. The <u>touring</u> company will perform here next week. _____
7. The Baskins are <u>moving</u> to Toronto. _____
8. The <u>moving</u> truck arrived an hour late. _____
9. Have the police recovered the <u>stolen</u> jewels? _____
10. Someone has <u>stolen</u> a valuable painting from the museum. _____
11. Michael has <u>grown</u> at least three inches taller this year. _____
12. Axelrod, a fully <u>grown</u> poodle, is groomed regularly. _____
13. Kurt has <u>written</u> his thank-you notes already. _____
14. Jo memorized six of Shakespeare's beautifully <u>written</u> sonnets. _____
15. The speech was made to honor our <u>fallen</u> soldiers. _____

21.1 Participles and Participial Phrases
(Participial Phrases) • Practice 1

Participial Phrases   A participial phrase is a participle modified by an adverb or adverb phrase or accompanied by a complement. The entire phrase acts as an adjective.

PARTICIPIAL PHRASES

The man *holding the baby* is my uncle.

Feeling better, the patient ate some soup.

The boy *running down the street* is Eddy.

The woman *singing now* has a good voice.

Balancing himself carefully, the aerialist walked across the wire.

▶ **Exercise 1**   **Recognizing Participial Phrases.**   Underline the participial phrase in each sentence. Then circle the word it modifies.

EXAMPLE: (Games) played before opening day do not count toward the championship.

1. The train arriving on track 10 is an hour late.
2. A first-edition book signed by the author may become valuable.
3. Looking hot and tired, the tennis players rested in the shade.
4. All the seafood cooked in that restaurant is fried.
5. Found in an abandoned barn, the painting was in excellent condition.
6. Mandy is the girl passing out the programs.
7. Anyone wishing an application may get one in the office.
8. Frightened by the horror movie, the child had nightmares for weeks.
9. The bush growing beside the front steps is an azalea.
10. The dog, chained to a stake, barked loudly.

▶ **Exercise 2**   **Writing Sentences with Participial Phrases.**   Turn each pair of sentences into a single sentence with a participial phrase.

EXAMPLE: The money was stolen from First Bank. It was later recovered.

   The money stolen from First Bank was later recovered.

1. The small boy sits at the end of the pier. He has caught nothing all day.

   _____

2. The sun sets behind the mountains. It is a beautiful sight.

   _____

3. Many books have been written by that author. Many of them have been bestsellers.

   _____

4. The speaker appeared somewhat nervous. The speaker approached the microphone.

   _____

5. The players sat on the bench. They cheered for their teammates.

   _____

21.1 Participles and Participial Phrases
(Participial Phrases) • Practice 2

▷ **Exercise 1**   **Recognizing Participial Phrases.**   Underline the participial phrase in each sentence. Then draw an arrow from each participial phrase to the word it modifies.

EXAMPLE: Frightened by the cat, the bird flew away.

1. Our house, shaded by trees, stays cool in the summer.

2. Kicking stones, the children ran down the street.

3. They boarded the subway packed with people.

4. Frightened by the smoke, they called the fire department.

5. Ms. Foley served a pie steaming from the oven.

▷ **Writing Application**   **Using Participial Phrases to Combine Sentences.**   Turn each pair of sentences into one with a participial phrase. Then underline each participial phrase and draw an arrow from it to the word it modifies.

EXAMPLE: The palms sway in the wind. They are like dancers.

Swaying in the wind, the palms are like dancers.

1. The tollbooth would not accept the coins. It buzzed.

_____

2. The soft music flows out of the restaurant. It invites passersby to enter.

_____

3. The outrigger canoe sprayed water onto the faces of the crew. It raced along the tops of the waves.

_____

4. The telephone poles had been snapped by the hurricane. They hung dangerously over the road.

_____

5. Dolores placed her shot carefully. She hit the ball to her opponent's backhand.

_____

▷ **Writing Application**   **Writing Sentences with Participial Phrases.**   Use the following instructions to write five sentences with participial phrases.

EXAMPLE: Use *paint* as a past participle.

A picture painted on wet plaster is called a fresco.

1. Use *write* as a present participle.

_____

2. Use *laugh* as a present participle.

_____

3. Use *cook* as a past participle.

_____

4. Use *stamp* as a past participle.

_____

5. Use *amuse* as a present participle.

_____

Name _____   Date _____

 21.1 # Gerunds and Gerund Phrases (Gerunds; Verb,
Participle, or Gerund?) • Practice 1

Gerunds   A gerund is a form of a verb that acts as a noun.

GERUNDS
Subject: *Running* has become very popular.
Direct Object: Unfortunately, Susan adored *singing*.
Indirect Object: Uncle Lew gave *skiing* a single try.
Predicate Nominative: Her favorite activity was *riding*.
Object of a Preposition: Steve was not very fond of *raking*.
Appositive: Her hobby, *shopping*, tires me out.

Verb, Participle, or Gerund?   Words ending in *-ing* that act as nouns are gerunds. They do not have helping verbs, nor do they act as adjectives.

Verb	Participle	Gerund
Who *is cooking* tonight?	*Cooking* smells filled the house.	Paul enjoys *cooking*. (DO)

▶ **Exercise 1**   **Recognizing Gerunds.**   Underline the gerund in each sentence. Then write whether each one is used as a *subject, direct object, indirect object, predicate nominative, object of a preposition,* or *appositive* on each line to the right.

EXAMPLE: Bill improved by practicing. _____*object of a preposition*_____

1. Winning is less important than sportsmanship. _____

2. Since childhood, Tony has shown a love of learning. _____

3. The doctor recommended exercise instead of dieting. _____

4. Alice's knitting is quite remarkable. _____

5. Jody won several medals for swimming. _____

6. Jogging is a popular form of exercise. _____

7. During her free time, Michelle enjoys reading. _____

8. Chris turned his hobby, painting, into a profession. _____

9. The sound of drilling disturbed our sleep. _____

10. Dad's favorite sport is fishing. _____

▶ **Exercise 2**   **Distinguishing Between Verbs, Participles and Gerunds.**   Write *V, P,* or *G* on each line to the right to indicate whether the underlined word in each sentence is a verb, a participle, or a gerund.

EXAMPLE: A <u>rolling</u> stone gathers no moss. _____*P*_____

1. Who is <u>pitching</u> today? _____

2. He has a strong <u>pitching</u> arm. _____

3. <u>Pitching</u> is our weakness. _____

4. Her great love is <u>acting</u>. _____

5. Who is <u>acting</u> in the play? _____

6. Portia was her first <u>acting</u> role. _____

7. The <u>moving</u> van was late. _____

8. <u>Moving</u> is always troublesome. _____

9. The Halls are <u>moving</u> away. _____

10. I am afraid of <u>flying</u>. _____

21.1 Gerunds and Gerund Phrases (Gerunds; Verb, Participle, or Gerund?) • Practice 2

▷ **Exercise 1** **Identifying Gerunds.** Underline the gerund or gerunds in each sentence. Label each one as a *subject, direct object, indirect object, predicate nominative, object of a preposition,* or *appositive.*

EXAMPLE: <u>Swimming</u> is her favorite activity. ____*subject*____

1. She expanded her vocabulary by reading. _____
2. At the age of five, Winston began acting. _____
3. Dribbling requires coordination and dexterity. _____
4. On summer nights, the family enjoys picnicking. _____
5. One of Lenore's hobbies is sewing. _____
6. The parakeet's main pastime, chirping, prevents loneliness. _____
7. Loving is trusting. _____
8. Stephanie loved excitement and dancing. _____
9. Weeding has improved the appearance of the yard. _____
10. The team excelled in batting and running. _____
11. Swimming is an excellent way to stay in shape. _____
12. Unfortunately, studying is Raymond's least favorite activity. _____
13. Have you ever done any mountain climbing? _____
14. The judges gave Mel's skating a score of nine. _____
15. You'll never get anywhere by simply dreaming. _____

▷ **Exercise 2** **Distinguishing Between Verbs, Participles, and Gerunds.** Identify each underlined word as a *verb, participle,* or *gerund.*

EXAMPLE: The girls are <u>swimming</u> in the lake. ____*verb*____

1. The <u>losing</u> team put up a good fight. _____
2. No one enjoys <u>losing</u>. _____
3. The home team was <u>losing</u> at the half. _____
4. The contractors are <u>painting</u> the exterior today. _____
5. <u>Painting</u> is more than a hobby to Chuck. _____
6. Have you seen my <u>painting</u> clothes? _____
7. Our <u>meeting</u> at the station was a surprise. _____
8. Hayes was a member of the delegation <u>meeting</u> the plane. _____
9. You will be <u>meeting</u> many new people at camp. _____
10. Why are you <u>reading</u> that book? _____
11. <u>Reading</u> is Ralph's favorite activity. _____
12. Once a month, the <u>reading</u> group meets for a book discussion. _____
13. The <u>laughing</u> children encouraged the clown to continue. _____
14. The children were <u>laughing</u> at the clown's antics. _____
15. The clown enjoys <u>laughing</u>. _____

Name _____ Date _____

Gerunds and Gerund Phrases (Gerund Phrases) • Practice 1

Gerund Phrases   A gerund phrase is a gerund with modifiers or a complement, all acting together as a noun. In the chart, notice the words before the gerunds in the second and third examples. Remember that the possessive form of a noun or pronoun is used before a gerund.

GERUND PHRASES
Working hard usually pays off.
We were grateful for *Mary's careful planning.*
Our arriving so late caused a stir.
Paul surprised us by *hitting the ball so far.*

▶ **Exercise 1**   **Recognizing Gerund Phrases.**   Underline the gerund phrase in each sentence. Then write whether each one is used as a *subject, direct object, indirect object, predicate nominative, object of a preposition,* or *appositive* on each line to the right.

EXAMPLE: The comedian told the joke without cracking a smile. _____*object of a preposition*_____

1. Debby enjoys working in the garden. _____
2. Darryl's hobby is collecting old coins. _____
3. Practicing for several hours a day is not unusual for a musician. _____
4. Until the day before, we continued changing the menu. _____
5. Driving along the mountain road was a frightening experience. _____
6. This ice pack will reduce the swelling around the injury. _____
7. The candidate was gracious in thanking all her campaign workers. _____
8. Tonight's homework is writing a rough draft. _____
9. Her great love, cooking gourmet meals, delights her friends. _____
10. Damian dreams about becoming a rock star. _____
11. Tess entered the house without disturbing anyone. _____
12. His honesty gave running for office a new respectability. _____
13. Recognizing shapes and colors is important for preschoolers. _____
14. Everyone rose for the singing of the national anthem. _____
15. My chores include setting the table before each meal. _____
16. All the guests raved about his exquisite cooking. _____
17. She was reprimanded for taking far too much time on the project. _____
18. Decorating the gym was one thing the committee looked forward to. _____
19. Beyond everything else, she liked working crossword puzzles. _____
20. He was intensely annoyed by her yawning so openly. _____

▶ **Exercise 2**   **Writing Nouns and Pronouns Before Gerunds.**   Fill in each blank with the correct word from the parentheses at the right.

EXAMPLE: _____*Her*_____ singing the lullaby put the baby to sleep. (She, Her)

1. Everyone appreciated _____ working so hard. (we, our, us)
2. _____ reading of the poem gave it new meaning. (He, His, Him)
3. We were surprised by _____ repeating that comment. (Tom, Tom's)
4. _____ snoring so loudly kept us all awake. (She, Her)
5. _____ being ready early amazed the family. (I, My, Me)

21.1 Gerunds and Gerund Phrases (Gerund Phrases) • Practice 2

▶ **Exercise 1**   **Identifying Gerund Phrases.**   Underline the gerund phrase or gerund phrases in each sentence. Label each one as a *subject, direct object, predicate nominative,* or *object of a preposition.*

EXAMPLE: During our vacation last summer, we all enjoyed <u>swimming in the lake</u>.

        ___*direct object*___

1. The pilot of a hang glider generally takes off by running down a hill. _____
2. Holly's favorite activity is climbing mountains in state parks. _____
3. Thousands of spectators showed their interest by following the pro golfers around the course. _____
4. After one night of mosquito attacks the Percivals regretted camping by the river. _____
5. In the 1800's some miners made as much as $5,000 in a few days of panning gold. _____
6. Flying an airplane in bad weather requires extensive training. _____
7. Running out of gas is a horrible experience. _____
8. Some body surfers use styrofoam boards for riding the waves. _____
9. Going to bed late and getting up early may lead to exhaustion. _____
10. Given the choice between hearing a story and playing a game, the children chose hearing a story. _____
11. Visiting the art museum was not Wesley's idea of fun. _____
12. Derek is an expert at flying kites. _____
13. Our music teacher enjoys conducting the choir. _____
14. One of the most dangerous sports is jumping from airplanes. _____
15. Watching television all day is not the best use of your time. _____

▶ **Writing Application**   **Writing Sentences with Gerund Phrases.**   Use the following instructions to write five sentences with gerund phrases. Then underline the gerund phrase in each.

EXAMPLE: Use *sneezing* as a subject.

        ___*Her violent sneezing startled me.*___

1. Use *staring* as a subject.

_____

2. Use *joking* as a predicate nominative.

_____

3. Use *driving* as the object of a preposition.

_____

4. Use *whispering* as a direct object.

_____

5. Use *sliding* as a direct object.

_____

21.1 # Infinitives and Infinitive Phrases (Infinitives;
Prepositional Phrase or Infinitive?) • Practice 1

Infinitives   An infinitive is a form of a verb that comes after the word *to* and acts as a noun, adjective, or adverb.

INFINITIVES
Subject: *To succeed* is not always easy.
Direct Object: They promised *to remember*.
Predicate Nominative: Her goal was *to act*.
Object of a Preposition: He had no choice but *to relent*.
Appositive: Andrea's decision, *to leave*, was a difficult one.
Adjective: Her latest mystery is the book *to read*.
Adverb: He struggled *to rise*. The loss was not easy *to accept*.

Prepositional Phrase or Infinitive?   A prepositional phrase always ends with a noun or pronoun. An infinitive always ends with a verb.

Prepositional Phrase	Infinitive
Will you drive me *to the store*?	I need *to shop*.

> **Exercise 1**   **Identifying Infinitives.**   Underline the infinitive in each sentence. Then write the part of speech it is used as on each line to the right.

EXAMPLE: The music began to play.   _____noun_____

1. The Bombers are the team to beat. _____
2. The offer was hard to refuse. _____
3. His greatest desire, to win, caused his ruthlessness. _____
4. Is this the right road to take? _____
5. This recipe is easy to make. _____
6. The whole class recognized Julie's ability to lead. _____
7. Dora always plays to win. _____
8. That will be a difficult promise to keep. _____
9. The new game is easy to learn. _____
10. Where is the best place to sit? _____

> **Exercise 2**   **Distinguishing Between Prepositional Phrases and Infinitives.**   Write *PP* for prepositional phrase or *Inf.* for infinitive on each line to the right to describe each underlined group of words.

EXAMPLE: I take the bus to school.   _____PP_____

1. Would you like to play? _____
2. Bud is kind to everyone. _____
3. Ben went to bed early. _____
4. This is no time to stop. _____
5. Please come to dinner. _____
6. It is too early to eat. _____
7. I need to rest. _____
8. Please give this to Jan. _____
9. Please try to relax. _____
10. This belongs to Pat. _____

21.1 Infinitives and Infinitive Phrases (Infinitives; Prepositional Phrase or Infinitive?) • Practice 2

▷ **Exercise 1** **Identifying Infinitives.** Underline the infinitive in each sentence. Then label each as a *noun, adjective,* or *adverb.*

EXAMPLE: My friend started to laugh. _____noun_____

1. He wanted to protest. _____
2. Her only thought was to win. _____
3. She had no alternative except to drive. _____
4. Eager to succeed, he studied every night. _____
5. The ghost town to visit is on a deserted road. _____
6. Rob likes to swim. _____
7. Nadine told me what book to read. _____
8. To write takes more time than I have. _____
9. That is the most economical car to buy. _____
10. The bus to take stops only at major towns. _____
11. At eight o'clock exactly, the curtains began to open. _____
12. Paula must have forgotten to invite James to the party. _____
13. The push to reach the North Pole was dangerous and exciting. _____
14. Dean knows the best way to cook burgers. _____
15. Too scared to continue, Bill turned back toward the cave entrance. _____

▷ **Exercise 2** **Distinguishing Between Prepositional Phrases and Infinitives.** Underline the prepositional phrase or infinitive beginning with *to* in each sentence. Then label each as a *prepositional phrase* or *infinitive.*

EXAMPLE: He had an essay to write. _____infinitive_____

1. Because the music was so loud, Pat found it hard to study. _____
2. To win was our only desire. _____
3. Have you ever been to Seattle? _____
4. My sister likes to ski. _____
5. When do we go back to school? _____
6. My grandparents are coming to visit. _____
7. Who phones in the message about the lost children to headquarters? _____
8. Have you shown her the pictures of your trip to Alaska? _____
9. Is it time to go? _____
10. Our neighbors have gone to Europe. _____
11. What would you like to say? _____
12. Speak directly to the audience. _____
13. Darryl did not want to lend Freddie any money. _____
14. Jane gave her favorite sweater to Pam. _____
15. When she grows up, Isabel plans to teach. _____

21.1 # Infinitives and Infinitive Phrases (Infinitive Phrases) • Practice 1

Infinitive Phrases   An infinitive phrase is an infinitive with modifiers, complements, or a subject, all acting together as a single part of speech. Notice that the infinitives in the first two chart examples do not include the word *to*. When an infinitive or infinitive phrase is used as the direct object of certain verbs, *to* is often omitted.

INFINITIVE PHRASES
Please help *set the table.*
I watched Pam *prepare the salad.*
To plan carefully is a good beginning.
That job is hard *to do without help.*

▷ **Exercise 1**   **Recognizing Infinitive Phrases.**   Underline the infinitive phrase in each sentence below. Then write the part of speech it is used as on the line to the right.

EXAMPLE: Dana's desire <u>to help people</u> led to her career in medicine. ___*adjective*___

1. Elise is a good person to ask for directions. _____

2. Did you get the message to call home? _____

3. The new law requires infants to ride in special seats. _____

4. The whole family was eager to see the new car. _____

5. Pam wants to invite her to the party. _____

6. The carpenters were unable to finish the job in time. _____

7. The troops found the fort impossible to defend against the enemy. _____

8. Do you need a volunteer to help with refreshments? _____

9. Who is the candidate to vote for? _____

10. I helped Phil to rake the yard. _____

▷ **Exercise 2**   **More Work with Infinitive Phrases.**   Underline the infinitive phrase in each sentence. On the line at the right, write the infinitive itself. If *to* has been omitted, add it in parentheses.

EXAMPLE: Let me <u>help you with that.</u> ___*(to) help*___

1. We saw the Olympic torch bearer pass by. _____

2. The teacher offered to give me extra help. _____

3. I heard him sing in person at the coliseum. _____

4. We watched the sun rise over the ocean. _____

5. The owner allows visitors to tour the house during the week. _____

6. We wouldn't dare ask for another piece of pie. _____

7. No one can make Linda change her mind. _____

8. I warned you to read the directions carefully. _____

9. Alice arranged for Clare to visit for the weekend. _____

10. Let's find a good place for dinner. _____

21.1 Infinitives and Infinitive Phrases (Infinitive Phrases) • Practice 2

▶ **Exercise 1** **Identifying Infinitive Phrases.** Underline the infinitive phrase or infinitive phrases in each sentence. Label each one as a *subject, direct object, predicate nominative, object of a preposition, adjective,* or *adverb.*

EXAMPLE: To become an astronaut requires special training.   *subject*

(1) To carry out their missions, astronauts undergo years of preparation. (2) At first only experienced pilots were able to become astronauts. (3) They needed to have a degree in engineering, physical science, or mathematics. (4) Since 1965 "mission specialists" have been recruited to perform scientific experiments. (5) They also needed to complete flight training. (6) To prepare for missions, astronauts study subjects ranging from rocket engines to geology. (7) Astronauts use full-size spacecraft models and simulators (devices that reproduce conditions of space flight) to train for missions. (8) Astronauts have no choice but to work hard. (9) We admire their ability to succeed at difficult tasks. (10) They make us feel proud of their accomplishments.

1. _____   6. _____
2. _____   7. _____
3. _____   8. _____
4. _____   9. _____
5. _____   10. _____

▶ **Writing Application** **Writing Sentences with Infinitive Phrases.** Use the following instructions to write ten sentences with infinitive phrases. Then underline the infinitive phrase in each.

EXAMPLE: Use *to help* as a direct object.   *He wanted to help the lost child.*

1. Use *to change* as a predicate nominative.

_____

2. Use *to build* as an adjective.

_____

3. Use *to paint* as a subject.

_____

4. Use *to refuse* as an adjective.

_____

5. Use *to leap* as a direct object.

_____

6. Use *to know* as a predicate nominative.

_____

7. Use *to send* as an adjective.

_____

8. Use *to spoil* as a subject.

_____

9. Use *to meet* as a direct object.

_____

10. Use *to advise* as a subject.

_____

21.2 # Adjective Clauses • Practice 1

The Adjective Clause   A clause is a group of words containing its own subject and verb. A clause that can stand by itself as a sentence is an independent clause. A clause that can only be part of a sentence is a subordinate clause. An adjective clause is a subordinate clause that modifies a noun or pronoun, telling what kind or which one. Adjective clauses usually begin with a relative pronoun — *that, which, who, whom,* or *whose*.

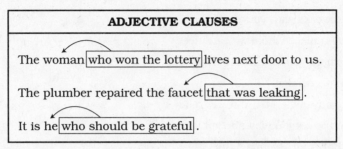

Exercise 1   **Recognizing Adjective Clauses.**   Underline the adjective clause in each sentence.

EXAMPLE: The mayor praised the girl who rescued the drowning child.

1. The candidate who led in the polls became overconfident.
2. Items that are on sale are marked by a red sticker.
3. The contest is open to anyone who lives in this state.
4. The President that was elected four times was Franklin D. Roosevelt.
5. My uncle has a parrot that can say several sentences.
6. The person whom the police arrested turned out to be innocent.
7. The mill that once stood here was torn down long ago.
8. The treasure map, which was crumpled and torn, was hard to make out.
9. Fleetfoot, who was favored to win the race, came in last.
10. Dad needs a secretary who can speak Portuguese.

Exercise 2   **Identifying Adjective Clauses and the Words They Modify.**   Underline the adjective clause in each sentence. Then circle the word the clause modifies.

EXAMPLE: The (book) that was missing had turned up at last.

1. Only people who have experience with lions and tigers need apply.
2. The carton that contained the dishes was undamaged.
3. A trapper who knew the woods well led the rescue party.
4. Grandpa still has the first dollar that he ever earned.
5. The author dedicated the book to his uncle, who had been kind to him.
6. The beggar whom the poor farmer helped was really the king.
7. We need a treasurer who can add and subtract.
8. The judges awarded the prize to the girl who made the dragon kite.
9. The page that has the brownie recipe on it is too smudged to read.
10. Alicia finally met the woman whom she had admired for so long.

21.2 # Adjective Clauses • **Practice 2**

▶ **Exercise 1** **Identifying Adjective Clauses.** Underline the adjective clause in each sentence. Then circle the relative pronoun or relative adverb in each.

EXAMPLE: The town (where) I live is peaceful.

1. I met a woman who works with your mother.

2. Have you thought of a place where we can meet?

3. Is this the person whom you saw in the library?

4. I found the book that I needed.

5. She remembers the days when there were trolley cars.

6. Did Harriet tell you the reason why she left?

7. I lost the sweater that Aunt Sue made me.

8. Have they found the girl who was lost?

9. Most people who visit the museum are impressed.

10. The pictures that I took are not ready yet.

11. James Fenimore Cooper, who wrote *The Last of the Mohicans*, died in 1851.

12. The baseball cards that Peter bought last year have increased in value.

13. My aunt, whom you met last week, is on vacation now.

14. The restaurant, which is near the river, has an outdoor patio.

15. Carol grows vegetables in the backyard, where she also grows flowers.

▶ **Exercise 2** **Identifying Adjective Clauses and the Words They Modify.** Underline the adjective clause in each sentence. Then write the word the adjective clause modifies.

EXAMPLE: The town where she lives is hectic.   *town*

1. Crocuses are usually the first flowers that bloom. _____

2. She works in the town where the movie was filmed. _____

3. The boys who play handball with me go to Central. _____

4. Is this the weekend that you are leaving? _____

5. The scene that reveals the hero's secret is the best. _____

6. The dessert that I ordered never came. _____

7. Did you find all of the tools that you needed? _____

8. They can subpoena anyone who refuses to testify. _____

9. The books that you ordered will be in next week. _____

10. Is he the one who told you about the meeting? _____

11. The advice that my dad gave me could apply to you as well. _____

12. The poem, which is written in iambic pentameter, is quite lovely. _____

13. The three girls who tried out for the team all made it. _____

14. The space under the porch, where the dog rests during the day, is very cool. _____

15. The yarn that the cat is playing with is made of fine wool. _____

21.2 # Adjective Clauses (Relative Pronouns and Relative Adverbs) • Practice 1

Relative Pronouns   Relative pronouns connect adjective clauses to the words the clauses modify. Relative pronouns act as subjects, direct objects, adjectives, or objects of prepositions within the clause. Putting the clause in normal word order can help you see how the word acts within the clause.

RELATIVE PRONOUNS
I bought the dictionary *which* was recommended. (*which* was recommended)
This is the house *that* Jack built. (Jack built *that*)
She is a poet *whose* work I greatly admire. (I greatly admire *whose* work)
The person with *whom* I spoke was the boss. (I spoke with *whom*)

Relative Adverbs   Adjective clauses are sometimes introduced by a relative adverb such as *where*, *when*, *why*, *before*, or *since*. The relative adverb connects the clause to the word the clause modifies and acts as an adverb within the clause.

RELATIVE ADVERBS
This is the spot *where* we stopped to rest. (we stopped to rest *where*)
We will come again another time *when* we can stay. (we can stay *when*)

▶ **Exercise 1**   **Recognizing the Use of Relative Pronouns.**   Underline the adjective clause in each sentence. Circle the relative pronoun. On each line at the right, write the use of the pronoun within the clause.

EXAMPLE: The person (who) called you has hung up. _____*subject*_____

1. The book that I wanted to read had been checked out. _____

2. Betsy wrote to the man who returned her lost dog. _____

3. The play in which those lines appear is *Hamlet*. _____

4. The player who has the fewest points wins. _____

5. Columbus is a person whose name everyone knows. _____

6. The page that should follow this one is missing. _____

7. The plane in which the President flies is *Air Force One*. _____

8. Dorris is a critic whose opinions are usually sound. _____

9. The book that I am reading now is about mountain climbing. _____

10. Nick is the partner with whom I usually play doubles. _____

▶ **Exercise 2**   **Recognizing Adjective Clauses with Relative Adverbs.**   Underline the adjective clause in each sentence. Circle the relative adverb.

EXAMPLE: Those were the days (when) every city had trolley cars.

1. Areas where flooding was severe have been evacuated.

2. We couldn't imagine the reason why Laura was so late.

3. An *x* marks the spot where the treasure is buried.

4. In the days before the telegraph was invented, news traveled slowly.

5. No one was in the building at the time when the fire occurred.

21.2 Adjective Clauses (Relative Pronouns and Relative Adverbs) • Practice 2

> **Exercise 1** **Recognizing the Uses of Relative Pronouns.** Underline the adjective clause in each sentence, circling the relative pronoun. Then label the use of the relative pronoun within the clause as *subject, direct object, object of a preposition,* or *adjective.*

EXAMPLE: Leonardo, (who) is greatly admired, was an artist. _____*subject*_____

(1) Leonardo da Vinci, whose paintings are among the most famous in the world, was born in 1452 in Italy. (2) As a teenager Leonardo was apprenticed to a painter, with whom he worked for several years. (3) Later, Leonardo moved to Milan to work for a duke who needed the services of an artist. (4) There he designed artillery and planned ways to change the course of rivers, tasks that were usually the jobs of an engineer. (5) Leonardo also designed revolving stages, on which plays were performed.

1. _____   4. _____

2. _____   5. _____

3. _____

> **Exercise 2** **Recognizing the Use of Relative Adverbs.** Underline the adjective clause in each sentence, circling the relative adverb. Then draw an arrow from the relative adverb to the word or words it modifies.

EXAMPLE: The street (where) Joyce lives is near the library.

1. Anna wouldn't tell us the reason why she quit.

2. In the week since the report was filed, many of the facts have been changed.

3. It was a day when we all enjoyed every minute.

4. The stands where the dignitaries would sit were draped with bunting.

5. In the twelve years since I visited Greece, I have learned to speak German.

> **Writing Application** **Using Adjective Clauses to Combine Sentences.** Turn each pair of sentences into one with an adjective clause. Then underline each adjective clause and draw an arrow from it to the word it modifies.

EXAMPLE: The letter will be mailed today. I wrote the letter.

We arrived at the airport | as our plane was taking off |.

1. Give this package to the person. The person is at the door.

   _____

2. Tomorrow is the day. School starts then.

   _____

3. The player struck out. He is everyone's favorite.

   _____

4. The book is about Africa. I got the book from the library.

   _____

5. The candidate has withdrawn for some reason. No one knows the reason.

   _____

21.2 Adverb Clauses • Practice 1

The Adverb Clause An adverb clause is a subordinate clause that modifies a verb, adjective, adverb, or verbal. An adverb clause always begins with a subordinating conjunction. Adverb clauses tell *when, where, how,* or *why.*

ADVERB CLAUSES
We arrived at the airport as our plane was taking off.
Because we had to be up at five, we went to bed early.

Elliptical Adverb Clauses An elliptical adverb clause is one in which the verb or the subject and verb are understood but not actually stated.

ELLIPTICAL CLAUSES
My brother is taller *than I (am).*
Please send your payment as early as *(it is) possible.*

▶ **Exercise 1**   **Identifying Adverb Clauses.**   Underline the adverb clause in each sentence. Then circle the subordinating conjunction in each.

EXAMPLE: The movie had already started (when) we arrived.

1. The elevator will not move unless both doors are closed.
2. You will find the almanacs where the other reference books are shelved.
3. Betsy plays golf whenever she gets the chance.
4. After you have beaten the eggs, slowly add the dry ingredients.
5. The washer will stop if the door is opened.
6. Residents are urged to conserve water until the shortage ends.
7. The pictures came out badly because the lighting was poor.
8. We had a good time at the picnic even though it rained off and on.
9. No one may enter the studio while the red light is on.
10. A tire blew out as the jet taxied to the runway.

▶ **Exercise 2**   **Completing Elliptical Clauses.**   Write each adverb clause, adding any understood words that have been left out.

EXAMPLE: Wherever possible, the guide planted trees.   _Wherever it was possible_

1. When younger, Edison worked for the railroad. _____
2. The contestants valued the honor more than the prize money. _____
3. They walked unsteadily, as if dazed. _____
4. The Penguins are a better all-round team than the Seals. _____
5. I would like to see Dr. Richard this afternoon, if possible. _____
6. An adverb clause is a subordinate clause that acts as an adverb. _____
7. We believe our climate is much better than theirs. _____
8. George goes surfing as often as Glenda. _____
9. If ready, the new chairs will be delivered on Tuesday. _____
10. Julie's dog is more aggressive than Van Winkle. _____

21.2 Adverb Clauses • Practice 2

Exercise 1   **Identifying Adverb Clauses.**   Underline the adverb clause in each sentence. Then circle the subordinating conjunction in each.

EXAMPLE: We arrived (after) the band had left.

1. Will you move the couch when you have time?

2. Because the music was so loud, I got a headache.

3. No one came since I forgot to mail the invitations.

4. Did you see Alex when you were in Bloomington?

5. My ride came before I had finished breakfast.

6. Even though it was raining, we enjoyed the day.

7. Mimi takes her dog wherever she goes.

8. Have you heard from James since I saw you last?

9. She stayed there until the report was finished.

10. Before you leave, please stop by my office.

Exercise 2   **Identifying Adverb Clauses and the Words They Modify.**   Underline the adverb clause in each sentence. Then circle the word or words the adverb clause modifies.

EXAMPLE: When I was three, I (lived) in Dallas.

1. I called you before I fell asleep.

2. I will not be able to finish while you are here.

3. Will you wait until I get a sweater?

4. Mom likes skating when the ice is thick.

5. Put those books where the others are.

6. The old house was quiet after the guests had left.

7. Though it was still early, many of the picnickers were leaving.

8. I feel better than I did yesterday.

9. Jay stood in the wings while he waited for his cue.

10. Daisy plans to work as soon as we leave.

Exercise 3   **Recognizing Elliptical Adverb Clauses.**   Write each adverb clause, adding the missing words in any elliptical clause. Then circle any words you have added.

EXAMPLE: I like cake more than candy.

             than (I like) candy.

1. The other members were more restless than I. _____

2. We found our backpacks where we had left them. _____

3. The thieves acted as if no one knew their whereabouts. _____

4. The San Mateo Matadors are ranked higher in football than our team. _____

5. The actors wanted the new spotlights more than a videotape machine. _____

21.2 **Noun Clauses • Practice 1**

The Noun Clause   A noun clause is a subordinate clause that acts as a noun. It can be used in any of the functions common to single-word nouns.

NOUN CLAUSES
Subject: What she said was worth remembering. *Direct Object:* I don't know *where the library is.* *Indirect Object:* The judges will award *whoever finishes last* a prize. *Predicate Nominative:* His problem was *how he could earn a living.* *Object of a Preposition:* The pirates quarreled over *why they were lost.*

Introductory Words   Some of the words that introduce noun clauses function as the subject, direct object, or some other important part of their clause. Other introductory words have no function in the clause.

USE OF INTRODUCTORY WORDS WITHIN NOUN CLAUSES
Subject: The police officer asked <u>who</u> had witnessed the accident. *Adverb:* We argued about <u>where</u> we should eat. *Adjective:* Jody couldn't decide <u>which</u> job she should take. *Direct Object:* You are <u>what</u> you eat. *No function in clause:* Do you know <u>whether</u> the train has gone?

▶ **Exercise 1**   **Identifying Noun Clauses.**   Underline the noun clause in each sentence. In the space provided, indicate the function of the clause within the sentence.

EXAMPLE: We wondered <u>what we should do next</u>.   *direct object*

1. When the next meeting will be held has not been announced. _____

2. We have to do our best with what we have. _____

3. Aaron modestly admitted that he had driven in the winning run. _____

4. All of Elaine's friends believed what she said. _____

5. Angie's dream was that she could have a horse of her own. _____

6. The witnesses disagreed about how tall the robber had been. _____

7. What happened next surprised us all. _____

8. The economist predicted that the cost of living would keep rising. _____

9. The real surprise is how the movie ends. _____

10. Do you know if the Penguins won this afternoon? _____

▶ **Exercise 2**   **Recognizing the Use of Introductory Words.**   Underline the noun clause in each sentence. Circle the introductory word. Then in the space provided, write the use of the introductory word within the clause.

EXAMPLE: Do you remember (where) we parked the car?   *adverb*

1. "Whose woods these are, I think I know,"—Robert Frost _____

2. The *x* shows where the treasure is buried. _____

3. Betsy doesn't know who will be playing tennis next week. _____

4. Whoever leaves last should turn off the lights. _____

5. We will never forget what she said next. _____

21.2 Noun Clauses • Practice 2

▶ **Exercise 1** **Identifying Noun Clauses.** Underline the noun clause in each sentence. Then label the clause as a *subject, direct object, predicate nominative,* or *object of a preposition.*

EXAMPLE: Andy wished <u>that they would leave</u>.   *direct object*

1. No one understands why Tim is afraid of the dark. _____

2. Jean chose to write about how bees communicate. _____

3. Where the treasure is buried remains a mystery. _____

4. He wrote to whoever promised to write back. _____

5. Our biggest worry was where we would end up. _____

6. My sister has not decided what she wants to study. _____

7. That he didn't ask his neighbors to the party suggests his dislike of them. _____

8. The most difficult question was whether the land should be re-zoned. _____

9. He gave whoever flattered him his friendship. _____

10. They consulted about who would do the job. _____

11. We wondered which route was shorter. _____

12. Her excuse was that she had lost the assignment. _____

13. Why he dropped the class isn't clear. _____

14. Whoever you hire must speak French. _____

15. They worried about how they would cross Death Valley. _____

▶ **Exercise 2** **Recognizing the Uses of Introductory Words.** Underline the noun clause in each sentence, circling the introductory word. Then label the use of the introductory word in the clause as *subject, direct object, object of a preposition, adjective, adverb,* or a word with *no function.*

EXAMPLE: Ellen knew (that) she would be late.   *no function*

1. Do you know whether Ms. Hall will be in today? _____

2. What she wanted to speak about was Judy's decision. _____

3. Just leave a message with whoever answers the phone. _____

4. Pete feared that he would forget his lines. _____

5. The university catalog lists which professor gives each course. _____

6. Whether you go or stay makes no difference. _____

7. Do you know whose keys these are? _____

8. The governor said that she would not run again. _____

9. The real issue is who would do a better job. _____

10. We began without knowing where we were headed. _____

11. Whoever draws the short straw must do the dishes. _____

12. No one told us what we were looking for. _____

13. The rumor is that the house is haunted. _____

14. Someone should have told us how he would react. _____

15. No one could remember where the keys were. _____

21.2 # Sentences Classified by Structure
• Practice 1

The Four Structures of Sentences   Sentences can be classified by the number and kind of clauses they contain.

Kind of Sentence	Number and Kind of Clauses	Examples (subjects underlined once, verbs twice)
Simple	One independent clause (subject or verb or both may be compound)	Hawks hunt mice. Hawks and owls hunt mice. Owls catch mice and eat them.
Compound	Two or more independent clauses	Football is a good game, but I prefer soccer.
Complex	One independent clause and one or more subordinate clauses	┌── IND. CL. ──┐ ┌── SUBORD. CL. ──┐ The train whistled as it neared the tunnel.
Compound-Complex	Two or more independent clauses and one or more subordinate clauses	┌── IND. CL. ──┐┌ SUBORD. CL. ┐ Paul ate a sandwich when he got home, ┌── IND. CL.──┐ but he still felt hungry.

▷ **Exercise 1**   **Distinguishing Between Simple and Compound Sentences.**   In the space provided, identify each sentence as *simple* or *compound*.

EXAMPLE: The ball hit the foul pole and bounced into the stands. _____*simple*_____

1. The detour was clearly marked, but we still missed it. _____

2. Rangers and volunteers fought the forest fire together. _____

3. The bull pawed the ground, lowered his head, and charged. _____

4. Whales and porpoises are mammals, but sharks are not. _____

5. The surface should be clean, or the paint will not stick. _____

▷ **Exercise 2**   **Identifying the Structure of Sentences.**   Identify each sentence as (*1*) simple, (*2*) compound, (*3*) complex, or (*4*) compound-complex by writing the proper number on the line.

EXAMPLE: The bolt that holds the handlebar in place is loose. _____*3*_____

1. The club has not decided when the picnic will take place. _____

2. Coach Gaudioso warned his team against overconfidence. _____

3. The runners were on their marks, and the race was about to begin. _____

4. Members must give the password, or they will not be admitted. _____

5. Algebra and biology are my favorite subjects. _____

6. Alicia took an earlier bus than she needed to, for she didn't want to be late. _____

7. Jenny raised herself from the chair and took a tentative step. _____

8. Although it is old and battered, Uncle Jack's car runs well. _____

9. A driver who is entering traffic should yield. _____

10. The ripcord that opens the chute must be strong, or it could break. _____

21.2 Sentences Classified by Structure
• Practice 2

▷ **Exercise 1**   **Identifying the Structure of Sentences.**   Identify each sentence as *simple*, *compound*, *complex*, or *compound-complex*.

EXAMPLE: I got the one that I wanted. _____*complex*_____

1. We chose one way; they chose another. _____

2. They learned a dance with a variety of steps. _____

3. Whenever Angelo gets to school early, he talks to his friends. _____

4. The vibrations from the jet caused the vase to fall and crack. _____

5. The gum stuck to his face; it looked like glue. _____

6. Stuck to his face, the gum looked like glue. _____

7. The gum that stuck to his face looked like glue. _____

8. My uncle planned to drive to work, but he couldn't until the snowplows cleared the roads. _____

9. She wanted to go on the study tour, yet she could not bring herself to spend all of her savings. _____

10. Because Kelly forgot to water her plants, they wilted. _____

▷ **Writing Application**   **Writing Application: Writing Sentences with Different Structures.**   Use the following instructions to write ten sentences of your own.

EXAMPLE: Write a compound sentence about hiking.
          Sara wore good hiking shoes, but her socks were not heavy enough.

1. Write a simple sentence about a story you have read.

    _____

2. Write a compound sentence about dancing.

    _____

3. Write a complex sentence about snow.

    _____

4. Write a compound-complex sentence about photography.

    _____

5. Write a simple sentence about computers.

    _____

6. Write a compound sentence about a dog.

    _____

7. Write a complex sentence about a cat.

    _____

8. Write a compound-complex sentence about traveling.

    _____

9. Write a simple sentence about a family get-together.

    _____

10. Write a compound-complex sentence about the area in which you live.

    _____

Sentences Classified by Function • Practice 1

The Four Functions of Sentences   Sentences can also be classified by their function.

Kind of Sentence	Function	Examples	End Mark
Declarative	States an idea	Water freezes at 0 C.	period (.)
Interrogative	Asks a question	What is the longest day of the year?	question mark (?)
Imperative	Gives an order or a direction	Abandon ship! Please close the window.	period or exclamation mark (. or !)
Exclamatory	Conveys strong emotion	How wrong you are! You must be joking!	exclamation mark (!)

▶ **Exercise 1**   **Identifying the Function of Sentences.**   Identify each sentence as *declarative*, *interrogative*, *imperative*, or *exclamatory*.

EXAMPLE: Sauté the onions until they are soft. _____*imperative*_____

1. Be sure to enclose a stamped, self-addressed envelope. _____

2. Has anyone ever photographed the Loch Ness monster? _____

3. Which is longer, a meter or a yard? _____

4. The phoenix and the unicorn are mythical creatures. _____

5. Sand the surface lightly before applying the second coat. _____

6. What a dreadful sight that was! _____

7. Go directly to JAIL. _____

8. Natives in Borneo once used human skulls as money. _____

9. The eggs laid in a single nest are called a clutch. _____

10. Is it bigger than a breadbox? _____

▶ **Exercise 2**   **Choosing the Correct End Mark by Function.**   Supply an appropriate end mark for each sentence on the line provided. When you are through, you should have four periods, two question marks, and four exclamation marks.

EXAMPLE: Arabian camels have one hump; Bactrian camels have two ____.____

1. Stop in the name of the law _____

2. Did the caller leave a number _____

3. What a weird coincidence that was _____

4. Run for your lives _____

5. Currents are fast-flowing streams within larger bodies of water _____

6. Who won the Oscar for best actor last year _____

7. Now that's what I call hot chili _____

8. Penguins keep their eggs warm by holding them next to their bodies _____

9. Be sure to let us know what you decide _____

10. Americans spend a great deal of money on pet food _____

22.1 Sentences Classified by Function • Practice 2

▶ **Exercise 1** **Identifying the Function of Sentences.** Write the end mark for each sentence. Then, identify each sentence as *declarative, interrogative, imperative,* or *exclamatory.*

EXAMPLE: I decided to run for class president(.) _____declarative_____

(1) When my friends asked how they could help me campaign for class president, the answer was simple (2) "Make some posters for me" (3) Having little artistic talent, I needed all the help with posters that I could get (4) The next challenge I had to face really worried me—making a campaign speech (5) Should I talk about my previous experience as secretary of the Spanish Club (6) Perhaps I should talk about my ability to get along with my classmates (7) The day of the speech was I nervous (8) I knew what I had to do, and I repeated my task to myself again and again (9) "Go out there and convince them" (10) I guess I succeeded because when the results were announced, I was the new class president.

1. _____   6. _____
2. _____   7. _____
3. _____   8. _____
4. _____   9. _____
5. _____   10. _____

▶ **Writing Application** **Writing Sentences with Different Structures and Functions.** Use the following instructions to write ten sentences of your own.

EXAMPLE: Write a compound interrogative sentence about dogs.

_____Should we get a poodle, or should we get a dachshund?_____

1. Write a simple declarative sentence about food.

   _____

2. Write a compound declarative sentence about music.

   _____

3. Write a complex declarative sentence about homework.

   _____

4. Write a compound-complex declarative sentence about politics.

   _____

5. Write a simple interrogative sentence about next weekend.

   _____

6. Write a compound interrogative sentence about a friend.

   _____

7. Write a complex interrogative sentence about a friend.

   _____

8. Write a compound-complex interrogative sentence about a sports event.

   _____

9. Write a simple imperative sentence about something that needs cleaning.

   _____

10. Write a simple exclamatory sentence about the results of the action in Sentence 9.

   _____

22.2 Sentence Combining • Practice 1

Combining Ideas   Combine short sentences by using compound subjects or verbs, phrase modifiers, compound sentences, complex sentences, or compound-complex sentences.

Separate Sentences	Combined Sentences
The tide came up. It washed away our sand castle.	The tide came up and washed away our sand castle.
It was a huge sand castle. It had a moat around it.	It was a huge sand castle with a moat around it.
We had hoped to visit the rock. The Pilgrims had landed there. The area was blocked off.	We had hoped to visit the rock where the Pilgrims had landed, but the area was blocked off.

 **Exercise 1**   **Combining Sentences.**   Combine the sentences in each item into a single, longer sentence.

EXAMPLE: Our neighbor was the first one on the scene. She is a paramedic.

Our neighbor, a paramedic, was the first one on the scene.

1. Arthur asked a question. The teacher couldn't answer it.

_____

2. We visited the house. Abraham Lincoln had lived there.

_____

3. Did you see the exam schedule? It is on the bulletin board.

_____

4. Several students requested a class newspaper. They are good writers. No advisor was available.

_____

5. The cake is easy to make. Follow the recipe.

_____

Exercise 2   **More Work with Combining Sentences.**   Follow the directions for Exercise 1.

1. We tried to make a gingerbread house. We had seen it in a magazine. The walls collapsed.

_____

2. Alvin entered the competition. His coach advised against it.

_____

3. He is a very popular musician. Thousands of people showed up to buy tickets for one of his concerts.

_____

4. Marc Chagall created those stained-glass windows. Chagall is a famous painter. The windows are in a chapel. The chapel is in the south of France.

_____

5. I need that book for my report. The librarian ordered it for me. She said it has not come in yet.

_____

22.2 Sentence Combining • Practice 2

▶ **Exercise 1** **Combining Sentences.** Combine the sentences in each item.

EXAMPLE: Wes and Ted bicycled about twenty-five miles a day. They stayed in youth hostels.

Wes and Ted bicycled about twenty-five miles a day and stayed in youth hostels.

1. The dazed guests stumbled out of the house. The host called the police to report the fire.

_____

_____

2. Last year, farmers turned the soil in the north field. Then they planted soybeans and corn.

_____

_____

3. The moon rose over the hills. It cast long shadows across the valley.

_____

_____

4. A hand is a unit of measure used to specify the height of a horse. It equals four inches.

_____

_____

5. At the picnic we had some special games. We had an egg toss, a pie-eating contest, a bake-off, and a three-legged race.

_____

_____

_____

▶ **Writing Application** **Further Practice in Combining Sentences.** Combine the sentences in each item. Try to use a variety of methods.

EXAMPLE: The goalie darted to the left. He almost blocked the goal.

Darting to the left, the goalie almost blocked the goal.

1. The eruption of a volcano can be destructive. Volcanic eruptions also enrich the soil and bring water up to the surface.

_____

_____

2. Mount Pelée is in Martinique. Kilhauea is in Hawaii. They are both active volcanoes.

_____

_____

3. Snow began to fall in the morning. Six inches had accumulated by evening.

_____

_____

4. A reporter for a newspaper is very busy. However, the city desk editor is even busier.

_____

_____

5. A reporter tracks down the details of a story and then writes an article. The editor must be familiar with all of the developing stories to choose which ones to print.

_____

_____

22.3 Varying Your Sentences (Expanding Short Sentences, Shortening Long Sentences) • Practice 1

Expanding Short Sentences Short sentences can be expanded by adding details that develop the subject, verb, or complement.

Short Sentences	Expanded Sentences
The woman addressed the convention.	The woman, *a lawyer from Chicago*, addressed the convention.
The delegates applauded her remarks.	The delegates *loudly and enthusiastically* applauded her remarks.
She nominated a candidate.	She nominated a *popular presidential* candidate *from her home state*.

Shortening Long Sentences Long, involved sentences can be broken into shorter, simpler sentences.

Long, Involved Sentence	Shorter, Clearer Sentences
The puppy, which was a honey-colored cocker spaniel, was frisky and loved to romp around the living room, which caused problems such as a broken antique vase, tears in the slipcovers, and scratches on the table legs.	The frisky puppy, a honey-colored cocker spaniel, loved to romp around the living room. The results included a broken antique vase, tears in the slipcovers, and scratches on the table legs.

▶ **Exercise 1** **Adding Details to Short Sentences.** Add details to improve each sentence.

EXAMPLE: Len had but one dream.

Len had but one dream, to win the marathon.

1. That plant has magnificent flowers.

   _____

2. The same menu is served every New Year's Eve.

   _____

3. The athletes prepared well.

   _____

4. The story aroused her curiosity.

   _____

5. They learned more about chess.

   _____

▶ **Exercise 2** **Shortening Sentences.** Divide each long sentence into two or more sentences.

1. A whole group of us had arranged to work together on a huge banner which we would carry to the pep rally, but it didn't take long for us to begin to disagree about how to design it.

   _____

   _____

2. Having rehearsed several weeks both in the classroom and on the stage, we felt quite confident when the day of the dress rehearsal finally came and were firmly convinced that all would go well.

   _____

   _____

22.3 # Varying Your Sentences (Expanding Short Sentences, Shortening Long Sentences) • Practice 2

▶ **Exercise 1**   **Adding Details to Short Sentences.**   Improve each sentence by adding the phrase in parentheses.

EXAMPLE: The river flooded the streets. (swollen by rain)

The river, swollen by rain, flooded the streets.

1. We must develop new sources of energy. (to provide for the future as well as the present)

_____

2. The teller counted one-dollar bills. (slowly and tediously)

_____

3. The bicycle rider crossed the finish line. (followed closely by an enthusiastically cheering crowd)

_____

4. The noise came from beneath the water. (of the scuba divers salvaging the downed submarine)

_____

5. The hikers returned. (eager to tell about their adventure)

_____

▶ **Exercise 2**   **Shortening Long Sentences.**   Divide each long sentence into two or more shorter, clear sentences.

EXAMPLE: When Jerry turned the ignition key in the car, it made a clicking noise, but the motor did not start because, as the mechanic later explained, the battery was dead.

When Jerry turned the ignition key in the car, he heard a clicking noise, but the motor did not start. As the mechanic later explained, the car's battery was dead.

1. Ants are warlike creatures, and they are natural empire builders, so they attack weaker insects to increase the numbers of their slaves and the size of their territory.

_____

_____

_____

2. The boat's crew located the sound and used radar to track its course through the harbor but could not identify the sound, and whatever lurked beneath the surface circled the area for almost thirty minutes.

_____

_____

_____

3. Gale-force winds buffeted the tiny seacoast village, including Judd Beere's old, single-masted sloop, which was tied to the rotting town dock, and the sloop's lines strained against rusty cleats until first one and then another gave way.

_____

_____

_____

4. Helen was determined to compete in the marathon and had been training for the race for several months by exercising and running one mile each morning and five miles each afternoon.

_____

_____

_____

22.3 # Varying Your Sentences (Using Different

Sentence Openers, Using Different Sentence Structures)
• Practice 1

Using Different Sentence Openers   Vary sentence openers, using one-word modifiers, phrases, and clauses.

WAYS TO BEGIN SENTENCES
Subject First: The whole *family* drove Grandma to the station.
Modifier First: Eventually, we found a parking place.
Phrase First: Peering through the train window, Grandma waved good-bye.
Clause First: Although we hated to see Grandma leave, we knew she would come for another visit soon.

Using Different Sentence Structures   Use a variety of sentence structures in your writing.

Monotonous Sentences	Varied Sentence Structures
My cousin enjoys her job. She is a counselor at a summer camp. She teaches crafts during the day. She sleeps in a cabin with the ten-year-olds. She says that some of them are homesick at first. They usually get over it after a couple of days.	My cousin enjoys her job as a counselor at a summer camp. During the day, she teaches crafts, and at night she sleeps in a cabin with the ten-year-olds. Many of the youngsters, she says, are homesick at first but usually recover after a couple of days.

▶ **Exercise 1**   **Using Different Sentence Openers.**   Rewrite each sentence to make it begin with a one-word modifier, a phrase, or a clause.

EXAMPLE: We will meet you at the library as soon as school is over.

_____*As soon as school is over, we will meet you at the library.*_____

1. The train occasionally makes whistle stops to discharge passengers.

   _____

2. We allowed plenty of time to be sure of seeing the kick-off.

   _____

3. My parents ask us to serve and clean up when they entertain.

   _____

4. I usually have no problem with math.

   _____

5. We watched fireflies in the backyard at night.

   _____

▶ **Exercise 2**   **Using Different Sentence Structures.**   On separate paper, rewrite the following paragraph, combining sentences and using a variety of sentence structures.

   (1) Thomas Jefferson was a great public leader. (2) He was an architect and an inventor, too. (3) He bought land on a small mountain. (4) He named the place Monticello. (5) That means "little mountain." (6) Jefferson built a home there. (7) He was his own architect and builder. (8) He invented the dumbwaiter. (9) It was used in Monticello. (10) He invented revolving bookshelves for his library. too.

22.3 Varying Your Sentences (Using Different Sentence Openers, Using Different Sentence Structures) • Practice 2

▶ **Exercise 1** **Identifying Sentence Openers.** Label each sentence opener as a *subject*, a *one-word modifier*, a *phrase*, or a *clause*.

EXAMPLE: Like a carefree seagull, the hang glider hovered over the waves. _____*phrase*_____

1. When the storm ended, we inspected the barn for damage. _____
2. Proudly, the marchers strutted down the boulevard waving their flags. _____
3. The mayor feared a drop in the city's mass transit income. _____
4. To do somersaults on a trampoline, you need good balance. _____
5. Hissing loudly, the cat backed away from the curious puppy. _____
6. Lost, the three-year-old sat down on the curb and cried. _____
7. Pedro earned letters in three varsity sports. _____
8. In the street eight floors below, the taxis darted to and fro like yellow bugs. _____
9. While Angie entertained the guests, Karl made dinner. _____
10. Usually, the local bus runs on schedule on weekdays. _____

▶ **Exercise 2** **Using Different Sentence Openers.** Rewrite each sentence to make it begin with a one-word modifier, a phrase, or a clause.

EXAMPLE: You should pass the test if you review your notes.

___*If you review your notes, you should pass the test.*___

1. You should read the instructions carefully before you assemble a model.

_____

2. Carol, insulted, turned on her heel and stalked out.

_____

3. The cars on the highway were backed up for miles because of a jackknifed tractor-trailer.

_____

4. The auditorium was filled with the sound of cheering at the end of the graduation ceremony.

_____

5. The spacecraft encountered the other ship at 1300 hours.

_____

6. The governess happily waved to Meg on the Ferris wheel.

_____

7. See the dentist at least twice a year to check for cavities and other problems.

_____

8. A mid-afternoon solar eclipse predictably drew hundreds of onlookers into the street.

_____

9. Chicago was a thriving young city when the great fire erupted.

_____

10. The actor enthusiastically campaigned for the senator.

_____

Name _____ Date _____

Fragments   A fragment is a group of words that does not express a complete thought. Part of a sentence should not be presented as a full sentence ending with a period or other end mark.

Fragments	Sentences
Because we missed the train	We were late *because we missed the train.*
After the rainfall	*After the rainfall*, the river rose.
Without looking back	Sue got on the train *without looking back.*
The boy wearing the green shirt	*The boy wearing the green shirt* is Tim.
Hope to return to New York someday	They *hope to return to New York someday.*

▶ **Exercise 1**   **Identifying Sentence Fragments.**   Write whether each group of words is a *sentence* or a *fragment*.

EXAMPLE: Riding on the *Orient Express.* _____*fragment*_____

1. To see the new museum was a real thrill. _____

2. Which Cindy got for her birthday. _____

3. Who won? _____

4. The player with the lowest score. _____

5. Enjoys working out at the gym. _____

6. Stop. _____

7. The smell of buttery popcorn. _____

8. The most amazing thing about Andrew. _____

9. Playing musical chairs. _____

10. My bike is missing. _____

11. What time is it? _____

12. After searching high and low. _____

13. The combination of diet, rest, and exercise. _____

14. Surrounded by a line of poplars. _____

15. The movie is hilarious. _____

16. Bagels used to be found only in the East. _____

17. Whoever you want. _____

18. After the circus had come to our town. _____

19. Beyond the ridge lay another valley. _____

20. Known for good service, the restaurant prospered. _____

▶ **Exercise 2**   **Identifying Fragments in a Paragraph.**   Underline each sentence fragment in the paragraph below.

EXAMPLE: We gathered all our equipment. <u>Before setting out on our camping trip.</u>

(1) We each had a sleeping bag and backpack. (2) Which we would carry ourselves. (3) Dad would drag the tent behind him on poles. (4) As some Indians had dragged their tepees. (5) The day before the expedition. (6) We had done our food shopping. (7) Our main purchases had been lightweight, dried foods. (8) Including rice, nuts and dried fruit, and beans. (9) After one last check of our list. (10) We were ready to start out on our adventure.

22.4 # Fragments (Recognizing Fragments) • Practice 2

> **Exercise 1**   **Identifying Sentence Fragments.**   Identify each item as a *fragment* or *sentence*.

EXAMPLE: Leaving early in the morning. _____*fragment*_____

1. A bouquet of freshly cut flowers. _____
2. Will arrive between one and two o'clock. _____
3. In the jar on top of the refrigerator. _____
4. Swimming, skiing, or boating on the lake. _____
5. That hurts. _____
6. Wanting to write to you. _____
7. To know her is to admire her. _____
8. Broke all speed records in the last race. _____
9. After you sit down, I will begin. _____
10. A doctor of great skill and devotion to her patients. _____
11. While we were swimming. _____
12. Please be seated. _____
13. Seeing my friend at the concert. _____
14. If the train is not late. _____
15. John was angry with us. _____
16. Because the rain has stopped. _____
17. Someone left a mess behind. _____
18. Everyone had voted. _____
19. Which hangs on the wall. _____
20. Until the next time we meet. _____

> **Exercise 2**   **Identifying Fragments in a Paragraph.**   Underline each sentence fragment in the
paragraph below.

EXAMPLE: (1) The football game would begin in less than five minutes. (2) <u>Weren't in our seats yet.</u>

(1) Basketball is the only major sport that originated in the United States. (2) Invented by a Canadian,
James Naismith, who was teaching at the Y.M.C.A. in Springfield, Massachusetts, at the time. (3) The
students there were studying to become secretaries and physical education instructors. (4) Bored with the
marching, calisthenics, and gymnastics that made up their gym classes. (5) The head of the department
had a talk with Naismith. (6) In the fall of 1891. (7) Asking the Canadian teacher to develop a game that
could be played in a gym. (8) Had no physical contact. (9) Lightweight ball. (10) to make it safe for the
students and also for the school's gym. (11) Each player was to have an equal chance to handle the ball.
(12) And to make plays. (13) By December, Naismith had developed what he called "the game."
(14) Intended to nail up some boxes to serve as targets. (15) No boxes being available, they nailed up some
half-bushel peach baskets instead. (16) The game was soon called *basket ball.* (17) By 1902 the word was
often hyphenated. (18) Becoming *basket-ball.* (19) It wasn't until about 1912 that the name of the game was
written as one word. (20) It's interesting to note that if the school had had some boxes, we might be playing
boxball today.

22.4 Fragments (Correcting Fragments) • Practice 1

Correcting Fragments   A phrase should not be capitalized and punctuated as if it were a sentence.

Phrase Fragments	Completed Sentences
a person with great integrity	A person *with great integrity* is needed.
followed us home	A stray dog *followed us home.*
throughout the house	We searched *throughout the house.*
fed by the spring	The river *fed by the spring* is cold.

A subordinate clause should not be capitalized and punctuated as if it were a sentence.

Clause Fragments	Completed Sentences
whom I greatly respect	Lee is someone *whom I greatly respect.*
just as we began our picnic	The rain started *just as we began our picnic.*
what I asked	*What I asked* was impossible to do.

Words in a series should not be capitalized and punctuated as if they were a sentence.

Series Fragment	Completed Sentence
blueberry pie, strawberry shortcake, and cherry cheesecake	The dessert choices include *blueberry pie, strawberry shortcake, and cherry cheesecake.*

▶ **Exercise 1**   **Identifying Kinds of Sentence Fragments.**   After each item below, write *phrase, clause, series,* or *sentence* to describe the word group.

EXAMPLE: Wherever you want them. _____*clause*_____

1. To make friends in a new place. _____
2. A wide meadow, a babbling brook, and bright sunshine. _____
3. Please wait for me. _____
4. That you invited to the party. _____
5. You succeeded. _____
6. Without a second thought. _____
7. Whenever you are ready. _____
8. Offered by the dog's owner. _____
9. Take your mark. _____
10. The action during the first scene. _____

▶ **Exercise 2**   **Correcting Fragments.**   Turn five of the fragments in Exercise A into sentences.

EXAMPLE: *I will put these boxes wherever you want them.*

1. _____
2. _____
3. _____
4. _____
5. _____

22.4 Fragments (Correcting Fragments) • Practice 2

▷ **Exercise 1** **Using Phrase Fragments to Write Sentences.** Use each fragment in a complete sentence.

EXAMPLE: Among the clouds.

   Our hot-air balloon rose higher and higher until it floated among the clouds.

1. on the front page

   _____

2. to sing folk songs professionally

   _____

3. many beautiful birds

   _____

4. drinking from a green glass

   _____

5. a dark, menacing cloud

   _____

▷ **Exercise 2** **Using Clause Fragments to Write Sentences.** Use each fragment in a complete sentence.

1. when I awoke this morning

   _____

2. that my class likes best

   _____

3. unless you practice each day

   _____

4. if it is cold tomorrow

   _____

5. who waited in line

   _____

▷ **Exercise 3** **Using Series Fragments to Write Sentences.** Use each of the following fragments in a complete sentence.

1. calico kittens, green parakeets, and dachshund puppies

   _____

2. ran, skipped, and jumped

   _____

3. in the drawer, on the top shelf of the closet, or under the sink

   _____

4. deep orange, yellow, or red

   _____

5. slowly, methodically, and quite gracefully

   _____

22.4 Run-ons (Recognizing Run-ons) • Practice 1

Recognizing Run-ons   A run-on sentence is two or more complete sentences that are not properly joined or separated; that is, they are not separated by an end mark, or they are separated only by a comma.

RUN-ONS
The coals are ready now we can begin cooking.
The lettuce is thriving, the broccoli is straggly.

▶ **Exercise 1**   **Identifying Run-ons.**   Identify each item as a *run-on* or a *sentence* in each space to the right.

EXAMPLE: David has a new camera, but he forgot to bring it. _____*sentence*_____

1. Emily Dickinson wrote most of her poems without leaving her room. _____

2. The children played in the back yard, the swings and sandbox amused them. _____

3. We got three easy outs our team was up. _____

4. Louise did a wonderful job, we knew she would. _____

5. Amanda stepped through the gate and into a beautiful garden. _____

6. The TV series was excellent, but it never found its audience. _____

7. Billy wanted to be an actor, jobs were hard to get. _____

8. Languages are not easy for me I do better in math. _____

9. Several new families live on our block, we have been here longer. _____

10. Lisa left early, but no one knew why. _____

11. Although we all were hungry, we waited patiently. _____

12. The architects have worked hard the lowest bid will get the job. _____

13. The cove is quite pretty, it is rocky at low tide. _____

14. The audience applauded when the curtain fell. _____

15. The boat docked, all the passengers got off. _____

16. The family reunion was a much greater success than we had expected. _____

17. No one liked our new neighbors, they made incredible noises. _____

18. Jack listens to the radio all the time except when Laura turns it off. _____

19. Kurt didn't know what he wanted to do; however, Carla had plans. _____

20. She loved science, nevertheless she failed the test. _____

▶ **Exercise 2**   **Identifying Run-ons in a Paragraph.**   Underline each run-on in the paragraph below.

EXAMPLE: Our new house is finally finished, we moved in last week. There is still much to be done.

(1) Some rooms still need painting not all the light fixtures are in. (2) However, even more work needs to be done outside. (3) In clearing the lot, the builders razed all the trees. (4) We have ordered new trees and shrubs, they will be delivered this weekend. (5) After the nursery has planted them, we can begin thinking about flowers. (6) Rick and I have picked out a perfect spot for a vegetable garden, Dad has other ideas. (7) Mom plans a flower bed in front there is a perfect sunny spot for it. (8) We have already put in grass seed, it needs to be watered every day. (9) Soon we will have a beautiful yard. (10) It is hard work every bit is worth it.

22.4 # Run-ons (Recognizing Run-ons) • Practice 2

▶ **Exercise 1**　　**Identifying Run-ons.**　Identify each item as a *run-on* or a *sentence.*

EXAMPLE: Although he disliked her, he was polite. _____*sentence*_____

1. Queen Mary slowly entered the huge hall in silence the crowd gathered there gazed at the woman who was about to be executed. _____

2. Forced onto the sidelines by his torn ligament, Jack was restless and unhappy. _____

3. Keats came into the house from the garden and casually threw down some paper, on it was written "Ode on a Grecian Urn." _____

4. Lord Rosse built a telescope in Ireland in 1845, it was often inactive because of poor Irish weather. _____

5. Though billions of comets circle beyond the edges of our solar system, few come close to the earth. _____

6. Wind and water are major causes of erosion of the soil, they constantly change the appearance of the Earth's surface. _____

7. Shrimp eggs can survive for over one year in the desert sands, rainwater brings them to life. _____

8. March is the month when huge blocks of ice in the Arctic begin to melt and break up. _____

9. In drawings by young children, sizes and shapes of objects often look wrong. _____

10. Deserts turn cold at night, there is nothing to stop the heat from escaping into the atmosphere. _____

11. My grandmother loved *Gone with the Wind* she read it years ago. _____

12. Lightning turns nitrogen in the air into an oxide, it then falls with the rain and fertilizes the soil. _____

13. The famous Irish writer James Joyce left his native land in 1902 at various times he lived in the cities of Paris, Trieste, and Zurich. _____

14. For the last fifty years of his life, the poet Robinson Jeffers lived in a tower on the California coast. _____

15. When the bases are loaded and two players are already out, baseball is at its most exciting. _____

16. National parks in this country were established to protect wildlife, preserve natural resources, and provide recreational areas. _____

17. Crater Lake in the state of Oregon is a unique tourist attraction, it fills a crater on top of an inactive volcano. _____

18. The typical sonnet has fourteen lines, ten syllables make up each line. _____

19. The sun's rays striking raindrops can produce a rainbow you can see it if the sun is behind you and the rain is ahead of you. _____

20. Roosters begin to crow at dawn, they seem to bring the farm to life. _____

22.4 # Run-ons (Correcting Run-ons) • Practice 1

Correcting Run-ons   Use one of the following methods to correct run-ons.

END MARK	
What do you think will we win?	What do you think? Will we win?
COMMA AND COORDINATING CONJUNCTION	
Kelly came with us, Sue stayed home.	Kelly came with us, but Sue stayed home.
SEMICOLON	
The food was delicious the service was excellent.	The food was delicious; the service was excellent.
ONE SIMPLE SENTENCE	
The jet was a 747 it landed gracefully.	The jet, a 747, landed gracefully.
ONE COMPLEX SENTENCE	
We lost the game we had played our best.	Although we lost the game, we had played our best.

▶ **Exercise 1**   **Preparing to Correct Run-ons.**   If a word group below is a run-on sentence, insert a caret (^) between the two sentences or independent clauses. If a sentence is correct, write *C* after it.

EXAMPLE: The trick amazed the group ^ they had never seen anything like it. _____

1. Senator Hill was the graduation speaker he talked about responsibility. _____
2. The base of the Statue of Liberty is granite which came from Stony Creek, Connecticut. _____
3. Several council members opposed the tax, they voted against it. _____
4. Many cactuses are odd-looking plants they have beautiful blossoms. _____
5. The owner offered a handsome reward no trace of the show dog was found. _____
6. The troops had no defense they were completely surrounded. _____
7. Without saying a word, the messenger handed me an envelope. _____
8. Lighthouse keepers have a lonely life they do important work. _____
9. We rounded the bend, the castle came into view. _____
10. Judy recognized the bike at once it was the one she had sold last week. _____

▶ **Exercise 2**   **Correcting Run-ons.**   Rewrite five run-ons from Exercise 1. Use each method of rewriting noted in the chart.

EXAMPLE: _The trick amazed the crowd, who had never seen anything like it._ _____

1. _____
2. _____
3. _____
4. _____
5. _____

22.4 # Run-ons (Correcting Run-ons) • **Practice 2**

▷ **Exercise 1**   **Using Punctuation and Conjunctions to Correct Run-ons.**   Use an end mark, a comma and a coordinating conjunction, or a semicolon to correct each run-on. Use each method at least once.

EXAMPLE: The cash was hidden in a rusty tin can nobody thought to look inside it.

 The cash was hidden in a rusty tin can, but nobody thought to look inside it.

1. I could hardly wait to jump in the water looked so inviting.

 _____

2. They seemed to expect me to babysit again, I wouldn't do it for any price.

 _____

3. A stray dog wandered onto the field, the outfielder tried to catch it.

 _____

4. We spent hours searching for the car keys we never found them.

 _____

5. Would you care for French dressing on your salad, would you prefer it unseasoned?

 _____

▷ **Exercise 2**   **Forming Simple and Complex Sentences to Correct Run-ons.**   Form a simple or complex sentence to correct each run-on. Use each method at least two times.

EXAMPLE: The sun set, the forest was quiet.

 When the sun set, the forest was quiet.

1. Mr. Adams was a candidate for mayor, he spoke to many community organizations.

 _____

2. The iguana raced across the yard it was a family pet.

 _____

3. The snow was piled around the parked cars, it made it impossible for us to leave.

 _____

4. The child was delighted with the gift, he began to play with it right away.

 _____

5. I couldn't handle the luggage alone I had three suitcases and a small trunk.

 _____

▷ **Writing Application**   **Correcting Run-ons.**   Rewrite the following paragraphs, correcting all run-ons.

(1) After flying through a dense, seemingly endless cloud bank, the shuttle plane with its pilot, co-pilot, and three nervous passengers was lost. (2) The pilot could not recognize any landmarks, the co-pilot could not recognize any either. (3) One of the passengers, a young girl, entered the pilot's cabin and asked if she could help. (4) Although worried, the pilot smiled, he was very good-natured.

(5) The girl explained that she recognized the terrain her father had taken her camping in these hills just last summer. (6) "If you turn slightly and fly over that far ridge," explained the girl, "you will see a highway. (7) Follow it west it will lead toward Pescadora."

(8) The pilot and co-pilot thanked the girl and complimented her on her keen sense of direction. (9) Their praises pleased the girl, they also gave her an idea. (10) As soon as she finished school, she would take flying lessons.

22.4 # Misplaced Modifiers • Practice 1

Recognizing Misplaced Modifiers A modifier should be placed as close as possible to the word it modifies. A misplaced modifier appears to modify the wrong word in a sentence.

MISPLACED MODIFIERS
Joan went to meet the President <u>wearing her new white suit</u>.
We found an old olive grove <u>hiking up the mountain</u>.

Correcting Misplaced Modifiers Correct a misplaced modifier by moving the phrase or clause closer to the word it should logically modify.

Misplaced Modifiers	Corrected Sentences
Joan went to meet the president <u>wearing her new white suit</u>.	<u>Wearing her new white suit</u>, Joan went to meet the President.
We found an old olive grove <u>hiking up the mountain</u>.	<u>Hiking up the mountain</u>, we found an old olive grove.

▶ **Exercise 1** **Recognizing Misplaced Modifiers.** Underline each misplaced modifier. If a sentence is correct as written, leave it unmarked.

EXAMPLE: Uncle Al shot the tiger that sprang at him <u>with his rifle</u>.

1. The sale at Bowen's features shirts for men with minor flaws.

2. Aground on some rocks, the freighter was slowly breaking apart.

3. My sister dropped in while I was scrubbing the floor with her new baby.

4. Clare opened the package brought by the letter carrier with a cry of delight.

5. Charlie squandered all the money on new records that his uncle left him.

6. Dad had been looking for a mechanic who can repair our car without success.

7. Paul had a tomato that he had grown himself in his lunchbox.

8. Trying to stretch a single into a double, the runner was thrown out easily.

9. Ms. Dove threatened to keep the class after school many times that day.

10. In 1700, the first practical umbrella was invented by an anonymous Englishman with whalebone ribs.

▶ **Exercise 2** **Correcting Misplaced Modifiers.** Rewrite five incorrect sentences from Exercise 1, correcting the misplaced modifier. Then underline the corrected modifier and draw an arrow from it to the word it modifies.

EXAMPLE: <u>With his rifle</u>, Uncle Al shot the tiger that sprang at him.

1. _____

2. _____

3. _____

4. _____

5. _____

22.4 Misplaced Modifiers • Practice 2

▶ **Exercise 1** **Recognizing Misplaced Modifiers.** Underline each misplaced modifier. If a sentence is correct, write *correct*.

EXAMPLE: The baby crawled on the floor <u>with blue overalls</u>.

1. The messenger spoke to the receptionist who delivered the package. _____
2. The golfer won the trophy wearing green golf shoes. _____
3. Our desire grew smaller to win the prize. _____
4. Reading the menu, Hugh decided to have steak again. _____
5. Finishing the dishes, we were ready to relax. _____
6. The kitten drank the milk that was hungry. _____
7. I hurried to open the gift happily surprised. _____
8. Sailing into port, my grandfather stood at the wheel of his beautiful new boat. _____
9. Soaring gracefully over the treetops, I watched the hawk disappear from view. _____
10. Badly frightened, the puppy cowered under the porch. _____

▶ **Exercise 2** **Correcting Misplaced Modifiers.** Rewrite each of the following sentences, correcting each misplaced modifier. Then underline the correct modifier and draw an arrow from it to the word it modifies.

EXAMPLE: The child ran into the house crying loudly. <u>*Crying loudly*</u>, *the child ran into the house.*

1. A sundae was served to each guest, dripping with chocolate sauce.

_____

2. Wilkins realized the mistake he had made after a few minutes.

_____

3. The dean spoke to the boys about loitering in the principal's office.

_____

4. We gave the scraps of meat to the dog that had been left on our plates.

_____

5. Michelle bought an umbrella after shopping carefully with red and yellow stripes.

_____

6. The ballad singer heard most of the songs he later sang wandering through the hill country.

_____

7. The hunter crouched behind a tree waiting for a bear to come along with a bow and arrow.

_____

8. The bloodhound picked up the fugitive's scent sniffing in the bushes.

_____

9. We saw many beautiful homes driving through the South.

_____

10. Wilma put the trophies into a glass cabinet that she had won in golf tournaments.

_____

Name _____ Date _____

 22.4 # Dangling Modifiers • **Practice 1**

Recognizing Dangling Modifiers   A dangling modifier seems to modify the wrong word or no word at all because the word it should logically modify is missing.

DANGLING MODIFIERS

Flying over the Alps, the view was breathtaking.

Sailing out into the ocean, a tropical island appeared.

Correcting Dangling Modifiers   Correct a dangling modifier by rewriting the sentence to include the missing word.

Dangling Modifiers	Corrected Sentences
Flying over the Alps, the view was breathtaking.	*Flying over the Alps*, we found the view breathtaking.
Sailing out into the ocean, a tropical island appeared.	*Sailing out into the ocean*, they saw a tropical island.

▶ **Exercise 1**   **Recognizing Dangling Modifiers.**   Underline each dangling modifier. If a sentence has no dangling modifier, leave it unmarked.

EXAMPLE: <u>Rowing through the swamp at night</u>, many weird sounds were heard.

1. Born into a poor family, college seemed an impossible dream.

2. Speeding through a red light, the cyclist nearly hit an old man.

3. Taking the stairs two at a time, the bell rang.

4. After stepping into the shower, the telephone rang.

5. Descending by a different trail, the hazardous slope was avoided.

6. After walking across the hot sand, the clump of trees offered welcome relief.

7. Practicing for weeks, the difficult sonata was finally mastered.

8. While Mary was greeting her guests, her dog was eating the sandwiches.

9. Sympathizing with the flood victims, donations flowed in from all over.

10. Arriving a day late, the tickets were worthless.

▶ **Exercise 2**   **Correcting Dangling Modifiers.**   Rewrite five incorrect sentences from Exercise 1, correcting the dangling modifiers. Underline the modifier in the corrected sentence and draw an arrow from it to the word it modifies.

EXAMPLE: <u>Rowing through the swamp at night</u>, we heard many weird sounds.

1. _____

2. _____

3. _____

4. _____

5. _____

© Prentice-Hall, Inc.   Dangling Modifiers • 111

22.4 Dangling Modifiers • Practice 2

▶ **Exercise 1** **Recognizing Dangling Modifiers.** Underline each dangling modifier. If a sentence is correct, write *correct*.

EXAMPLE: Carrying so many packages, the path was hard to follow.

1. Skating across the pond, the ice was very slick. _____
2. Studying for weeks, the test was easy. _____
3. Considering my small allowance, the tickets were expensive. _____
4. Writing letters at camp all afternoon, home seemed far away. _____
5. Finishing the dishes, we were ready to relax. _____

▶ **Exercise 2** **Correcting Dangling Modifiers.** Rewrite each sentence, correcting the dangling modifier. Then underline the correct modifier and draw an arrow from it to the word it modifies.

EXAMPLE: Losing hope, the mountains rose in the distance.

> *Losing hope, we saw the mountains rise in the distance.*

1. Trying to get to town quickly, the highway seemed best.

   _____

2. Jogging one morning, the solution to the problem was obvious.

   _____

3. When she was five, Paula's mother graduated from the university.

   _____

4. Wandering aimlessly in the woods, the first sight of camp was welcome.

   _____

5. Hearing of the refugees' plight, emergency funds were made available.

   _____

6. Getting up much earlier than usual, the house seemed strangely quiet.

   _____

7. When he developed measles, Dan's father called the school.

   _____

8. Absorbed in the crossword puzzle, the time passed quickly.

   _____

9. Waiting for a ride, the rain pounded down all around.

   _____

10. Sailing far from shore, a squall suddenly arose.

   _____

▶ **Writing Application** **Correcting Misplaced and Dangling Modifiers.** Rewrite the following paragraph, correcting all misplaced or dangling modifiers.

(1) Washington Irving's stories often contain elements of fantasy. (2) In one story, Rip van Winkle slept through the whole American Revolution that Irving wrote. (3) Waking up, his rusted musket should have indicated that something unusual had happened. (4) Rip was greeted by other puzzling things strolling into town. (5) The faces of the people were all strange that he met. (6) Hanging over the door of the inn, Rip noticed George Washington's portrait. (7) King George's portrait had always hung there before. (8) Rip then looked for his old friend, the innkeeper. (9) Rip questioned an old man trying to find the innkeeper. (10) The old man replied, "He is dead these eighteen years."

Verb Tenses (Six Tenses of Verbs, Four Principal Parts of Verbs) • Practice 1

The Six Tenses of Verbs   A tense is a form of a verb that shows the time of an action or a condition. Each tense has a basic and a progressive form.

Tenses	Basic Forms	Progressive Forms
Present	I *work*.	I *am working*.
Past	I *worked*.	I *was working*.
Future	I *will work*.	I *will be working*.
Present Perfect	I *have worked*.	I *have been working*.
Past Perfect	I *had worked*.	I *had been working*.
Future Perfect	I *will have worked*.	I *will have been working*.

The Four Principal Parts of Verbs   A verb has four principal parts: the present, the present participle, the past, and the past participle.

THE FOUR PRINCIPAL PARTS			
Present	**Present Participle**	**Past**	**Past Participle**
cook	cooking	cooked	(have) cooked
steal	stealing	stole	(have) stolen
make	making	made	(have) made

▶ **Exercise 1**   **Recognizing Tenses and Forms of Verbs.**   Underline the verb or verb phrase in each sentence below. Then write the tense on each line to the right. If the form is progressive, write the word *progressive* after the tense.

EXAMPLE: Vinnie will be working on Saturday night. ____*future progressive*____

1. Caroline arranged the flowers for the centerpiece. _____
2. The TV was working fine last night. _____
3. I have ordered the pizza already. _____
4. In December Dad will have been working there thirty years. _____
5. We often stay in that cottage on vacation. _____
6. Grandma will visit us next week. _____
7. Someone has been snooping through my things. _____
8. The fans had hoped for a win. _____
9. The chemist had been experimenting with a new formula. _____
10. The train will have left without us. _____

▶ **Exercise 2**   **Identifying Principal Parts.**   On the lines below, write the principal part of the main verb used in each sentence above. Then write the name of that principal part.

EXAMPLE: ____*working, present participle*____

1. _____   6. _____
2. _____   7. _____
3. _____   8. _____
4. _____   9. _____
5. _____   10. _____

23.1 # Verb Tenses (Six Tenses of Verbs, Four Principal Parts of Verbs) • **Practice 2**

▷ **Exercise 1**   **Recognizing Basic and Progressive Forms.**   Identify the form of each verb as *basic* or *progressive*.

EXAMPLE: He has been swimming. _____*progressive*_____

1. He is leaving. _____

2. I was singing. _____

3. She has rested. _____

4. They had tried. _____

5. He has been waiting. _____

6. I will have been working. _____

7. He spoke. _____

8. They will help. _____

9. He had been sleeping. _____

10. You will have gone. _____

▷ **Exercise 2**   **Recognizing the Six Tenses.**   Write the tense of each verb in Exercise 1. If the tense is a progressive form, add the word *progressive*.

EXAMPLE: He has been swimming. _____*present perfect progressive*_____

1. _____   6. _____

2. _____   7. _____

3. _____   8. _____

4. _____   9. _____

5. _____   10. _____

▷ **Exercise 3**   **Recognizing Principal Parts.**   Identify the principal part used to form each verb in Exercise 1.

EXAMPLE: He has been swimming. _____*present participle*_____

1. _____   6. _____

2. _____   7. _____

3. _____   8. _____

4. _____   9. _____

5. _____   10. _____

23.1 Verb Tenses (Regular and Irregular Verbs)
• Practice 1

Regular and Irregular Verbs   A regular verb is one whose past and past participle are formed by adding *-ed* or *-d* to the present form.

PRINCIPAL PARTS OF REGULAR VERBS			
Present	**Present Participle**	**Past**	**Past Participle**
learn	learning	learned	(have) learned
carry	carrying	carried	(have) carried
promise	promising	promised	(have) promised
drip	dripping	dripped	(have) dripped

An irregular verb is one whose past and past participle are not formed by adding *-ed* or *-d* to the present form.

PRINCIPAL PARTS OF IRREGULAR VERBS			
Present	**Present Participle**	**Past**	**Past Participle**
cost	costing	cost	(have) cost
put	putting	put	(have) put
bring	bringing	brought	(have) brought
sleep	sleeping	slept	(have) slept
draw	drawing	drew	(have) drawn
freeze	freezing	froze	(have) frozen
rise	rising	rose	(have) risen

▶ **Exercise 1**   **Writing the Principal Parts of Irregular Verbs.**   Add the missing principal parts.

EXAMPLE: speak ___*speaking*___ ___*spoke*___ ___*(have) spoken*___

1. _____ writing _____ _____
2. _____ _____ flew _____
3. see _____ _____ _____
4. _____ _____ _____ (have) spun
5. _____ _____ hurt _____
6. _____ fighting _____ _____
7. _____ _____ _____ (have) driven
8. spend _____ _____ _____
9. _____ _____ wound _____
10. _____ eating _____ _____

▶ **Exercise 2**   **Recognizing Principal Parts of Verbs.**   Fill in each blank with the correct verb form from those given in parentheses.

EXAMPLE: Sasha never had ____*sung*____ in public before. (sang, sung)

1. The balloon _____ suddenly. (burst, busted)
2. The sweater _____ in the wash. (shrank, shrinked)
3. They _____ all of their money out of the bank. (drew, drawed)
4. Aunt Mary _____ she would help us. (sayed, said)
5. Jack _____ up the beanstalk. (climbed, clumb)

23.1 Verb Tenses (Regular and Irregular Verbs)
• Practice 2

▷ **Exercise 1** **Learning the Principal Parts of Irregular Verbs.** Write the present participle, the past, and the past participle of each verb.

EXAMPLE: throw _____*throwing, threw, thrown*_____

1. build _____
2. find _____
3. get _____
4. hold _____
5. drink _____

6. do _____
7. bring _____
8. burst _____
9. fly _____
10. teach _____

▷ **Exercise 2** **Recognizing Principal Parts in Sentences.** Fill in each blank with the correct verb form from those given in parentheses.

EXAMPLE: He _____*brought*_____ the wrong book to class. (bring, brought)

1. The batter _____ hard but missed the ball. (swang, swung)
2. Steve _____ me home. (drived, drove)
3. Rachel _____ the cabin in the woods in only two and a half months. (built, builded)
4. We _____ the rent a week early. (payed, paid)
5. All around us fire crackers were _____. (busting, bursting)
6. The used car _____ me only a little more than two hundred dollars. (costed, cost)
7. The campers _____ on the ground. (sleeped, slept)
8. I _____ the money on the table. (layed, laid)
9. Our guide _____ us to a waterfall. (leaded, led)
10. She _____ the package with string. (binded, bound)

▷ **Exercise 3** **Correcting Principal Parts.** The paragraph below contains five errors in the choice between the past and the past participle. Cross out the errors and write corrections on the lines that follow the paragraph.

EXAMPLE: Dorothea Dix fighted for the mentally ill. *Dorothea Dix fought for the mentally ill.*

(1) Dorothea Dix played a crucial role in helping the mentally ill. (2) After visiting a jail in Massachusetts in the 1840s, she seen that they led the same life as criminals. (3) Until her visit, she had not knew that the mentally ill led such miserable lives. (4) Often, they lived in unheated housing. (5) Dix knew that she had not took enough responsibility in the past. (6) She begun to visit each place in the state where the mentally ill lived. (7) After her visits, she wrote a detailed report. (8) She convinced the state to improve the treatment of the mentally ill. (9) She also fighted in other states. (10) In all, fifteen states passed laws to help the mentally ill.

1. _____
2. _____
3. _____
4. _____
5. _____

6. _____
7. _____
8. _____
9. _____
10. _____

Name _____   Date _____

 # Verb Tenses (Conjugating the Tenses) • Practice 1

Conjugating the Tenses   A conjugation is a complete list of the singular and plural forms of a verb. A short conjugation lists just the forms that are used with a single pronoun. As you study the following short conjugations, note that the verbs used with *you* are also used with *we* and *they*. The verbs used with *she*, likewise, are also used with *he* and *it*.

SHORT CONJUGATIONS			
Basic and Progressive Forms	**do (with *I*)**	**do (with *you*)**	**do (with *she*)**
Present	I do	you do	she does
Past	I did	you did	she did
Future	I will do	you will do	she will do
Present Perfect	I have done	you have done	she has done
Past Perfect	I had done	you had done	she had done
Future Perfect	I will have done	you will have done	she will have done
Present Progressive	I am doing	you are doing	she is doing
Past Progressive	I was doing	you were doing	she was doing
Future Progressive	I will be doing	you will be doing	she will be doing
Present Perfect Progressive	I have been doing	you have been doing	she has been doing
Past Perfect Progressive	I had been doing	you had been doing	she had been doing
Future Perfect Progressive	I will have been doing	you will have been doing	she will have been doing

▶ **Exercise 1**   **Conjugating Basic and Progressive Forms.**   Complete each of the following short conjugations.

1. use (with *I*) _____

_____

2. take (with *he*) _____

_____

3. go (with *we*) _____

_____

4. see (with *they*) _____

_____

▶ **Exercise 2**   **Supplying the Correct Verb.**   Fill in each blank with the form of each verb given in parentheses.

EXAMPLE: The train _____*will be arriving*_____ soon. (*arrive*, future progressive)

1. We _____ here for ten years. (*live*, present perfect progressive)

2. Palmer _____ his way in the jungle. (*lose*, past perfect)

3. Mom _____ just the car she wants. (*find*, present perfect)

4. Aunt Betty _____ us next week. (*visit*, future progressive)

5. The owner _____ a large reward. (*offer*, present progressive)

23.1 Verb Tenses (Conjugating the Tenses) • Practice 2

▶ **Exercise 1**   **Conjugating the Basic Forms of Verbs.**   Conjugate the basic forms of the verbs below in the manner shown in the example.

EXAMPLE: spend (conjugated with *we*)

Present: we spend   Present Perfect: we have spent
Past: we spent   Past Perfect: we had spent
Future: we will spend   Future Perfect: we will have spent

1. open (conjugated with *I*)

   _____   _____
   _____   _____
   _____   _____

2. move (conjugated with *you*)

   _____   _____
   _____   _____
   _____   _____

3. know (conjugated with *he*

   _____   _____
   _____   _____
   _____   _____

▶ **Exercise 2**   **Conjugating the Progressive Forms of Verbs.**   Conjugate the progressive forms of the verbs below in the manner shown in the example.

EXAMPLE: spend (conjugated with *we*)

Present Progressive: we are spending   Present Perfect Progressive: we have been spending
Past Progressive: we were spending   Past Perfect Progressive: we had been spending
Future Progressive: we will be spending   Future Perfect Progressive: we will have been
                                              spending

1. walk (conjugated with *you*)

   _____
   _____
   _____

2. jump (conjugated with *she*)

   _____
   _____
   _____

3. say (conjugated with *they*)

   _____
   _____
   _____

23.1 Expressing Time Through Tense (Uses of Tense in Present Time) • Practice 1

Uses of Tense in Present Time   The present and the present progressive show present actions or conditions as well as various continuing actions or conditions.

USES OF TENSE IN PRESENT TIME		
Verb Forms	**Uses**	**Examples**
Present	Present action	Here *comes* Elsie.
	Present condition	Those tomatoes *are* ripe.
	Reoccurring action	I *exercise* daily.
	Reoccurring condition	Ernie *is* often late.
	Constant action	Water *freezes* at 0°C.
	Constant condition	The sun *is* our nearest star.
Present Progressive	Continuing action	Dad *is cooking* dinner.
	Continuing condition	Laura *is feeling* better.

▶ **Exercise 1**   **Identifying the Uses of Tenses in Present Time.**   On each line to the right, identify the use of the verb in each sentence, using the labels in the chart above.

EXAMPLE: The baby is learning to walk. _____*continuing action*_____

1. Paula studies in the library. _____

2. The Nile River flows from south to north. _____

3. Tasha baby-sits for the Logans every Friday night. _____

4. The new chef is here now. _____

5. I smell something sweet. _____

6. Bruce is cutting the lawn. _____

7. Cactuses grow in deserts. _____

8. Grandpa is teaching me chess. _____

9. My sister writes home once a week. _____

10. The Martins live in Virginia now. _____

▶ **Exercise 2**   **Using Present Tense Forms in Sentences.**   Complete each sentence by filling in an appropriate verb in the present time.

EXAMPLE: Mom _____*is talking*_____ on the phone at the moment.

1. The baby _____ for two hours every afternoon.

2. Those plants _____ well in the shade.

3. Aunt Janet _____ the baby a bath now.

4. Harold _____ unusually stubborn today.

5. Many people _____ to eat in restaurants.

6. The people next door _____ their house.

7. Sometimes my sister _____ my clothes.

8. Someone _____ on the door.

9. This cheese _____ strong.

10. The sun _____ at last.

23.1 # Expressing Time Through Tense (Uses of
Tense in Present Time) • Practice 2

USES OF THE PRESENT
Present action: There he *goes.* *Present condition:* The apples *are* rotten. *Regularly occurring action:* My sister *chews* her nails. *Regularly occurring condition:* They *are* never ready. *Constant action:* The sun *radiates* energy. *Constant condition:* Human blood *is* red.

USES OF THE PRESENT PROGRESSIVE
Continuing action: He *is working* on a novel. *Continuing condition:* The baby *is being* very difficult this week.

▶ **Exercise 1** **Identifying the Uses of Tense in Present Time.** Identify the use of the underlined verb in each sentence, using the labels in the charts above.

EXAMPLE: Greg plays tennis every Saturday. _____*regularly occurring action*_____

1. I leave for school at 7:30 each morning. _____

2. Gasoline is a flammable liquid. _____

3. My friends and I race home from school every afternoon. _____

4. This entire meal is delicious. _____

5. I hear a television in the other room. _____

6. My brother is doing his homework now. _____

7. Gravity pulls all objects downward. _____

8. My father is building stereo speaker cabinets. _____

9. He reads mostly biographies. _____

10. My sister Judy generally travels to work on the train. _____

11. The birds fascinate the cats in our yard. _____

12. The peaches are ready to fall from the tree. _____

13. The sun sets in the west. _____

14. The coach starts class at two o'clock sharp. _____

15. Sandra is studying violin with Mr. Stevenson. _____

16. The twins are always cheerful. _____

17. Barbara is being helpful around the house. _____

18. The United States is part of the continent of North America. _____

19. Gina is acting like a fool. _____

20. Patrice annoys people with her whining. _____

23.1 Expressing Time Through Tense (Uses of Tense in Past Time) • Practice 1

Uses of Tense in Past Time   The six forms that express past time show actions and conditions beginning in the past.

Verb Forms	USES OF TENSES IN PAST TIME	
	Uses	Examples
Past	Indefinite past time	Eleanor *studied* hard.
	Definite past time	The sunset *was* brief tonight.
Present Perfect	Indefinite past time continuing to present	I *have seen* that movie. The baby *has been* very quiet.
Past Perfect	Completed before another past event	Some guests *had arrived* before we did.
Past Progressive	Continuous past event	Ed *was acting* strangely last night.
Present Perfect Progressive	Event continuing to present	Pan *has been looking* for a job all summer.
Past Perfect Progressive	Continuous past event before another	Before you called, we *had been planning* for a quiet evening.

▶ **Exercise 1**   **Identifying the Uses of Tense in Past Time.**   Identify the use of the verb in each sentence, using the labels in the chart above.

EXAMPLE: I have been studying for that test all week. ___*event continuing to present*___

1. Up to this inning we had hoped for a win. _____

2. Grandpa was waiting for us at the station. _____

3. Dana worked for the same company for twenty years. _____

4. The realtor has shown us this same house before. _____

5. We were uncomfortable because of the heat. _____

6. That store has been offering double coupons for several weeks. _____

7. Those youngsters have waited here for hours. _____

8. Audrey had been trying to reach you earlier. _____

9. I finished the test at three o'clock. _____

10. We were painting the house last weekend. _____

▶ **Exercise 2**   **Using Tenses in Past Time.**   Write the correct form of the verb in parentheses.

EXAMPLE: I ____*had finished*____ when the bell rang. (have finished, had finished)

1. Before he retired, Uncle Al _____ cattle on his ranch. (raised, has raised)

2. For the last two years, Sue _____ our class president. (has been, was being)

3. Last night's storm _____ with the TV. (interfered, had interfered)

4. The horse _____ before we knew it. (has escaped, had escaped)

5. Joshua certainly _____ more agreeable lately. (has grown, was growing)

6. When I saw it last, my book _____ on the table. (has lain, was lying)

7. Jan _____ oddly today. (has been acting, had been acting)

8. Lou _____ me three times yesterday. (phoned, has phoned)

9. I _____ you a note when you came in. (wrote, was writing)

10. Pat _____ for you since lunch. (has been waiting, was waiting)

23.1 # Expressing Time Through Tense (Uses of
Tense in Past Time) • Practice 2

USES OF THE PROGRESSIVE FORMS THAT EXPRESS PAST TIME	
Past Progressive	*Continuous completed action:* He *was working* on a ranch that summer.
	Continuous completed condition: Mimi *was being* agreeable last week.
Present Perfect Progressive	*Action continuing to present:* Louisa *has been reading* mysteries for a month now.
Past Perfect Progressive	*Continuing action interrupted by another:* I *had been sleeping* when you called.

▶ **Exercise 1**   **Using Past, Present Perfect, and Past Perfect.**   Write the correct form of the verb in parentheses.

EXAMPLE: Mary ____*bought*____ a new dress yesterday. (bought, has bought)

1. Father _____ tomatoes in our yard last year. (grew, has grown)

2. I _____ her three times on Tuesday. (called, have called)

3. Carol _____ an hour before she left. (has waited, had waited)

4. We _____ our trip yesterday. (postponed, have postponed)

5. Ken _____ the bus to work since he moved. (rode, has ridden)

6. Sue _____ her sister at college last week. (visited, has visited)

7. I _____ terribly sleepy lately. (was, have been)

8. My sister _____ before I did. (has arrived, had arrived)

9. I _____ my report at three o'clock. (finished, have finished)

10. He _____ across the river before I started. (has swum, had swum)

▶ **Exercise 2**   **Identifying the Uses of the Progressive Forms in the Past.**   Identify the use of the underlined verb in each sentence, using the labels in the chart above.

EXAMPLE: I <u>was writing</u> my book report last night.   ____*continuous completed action*____

1. Father <u>has been building</u> a porch behind the house.

   _____

2. My brother <u>had been going</u> to college until his accident.

   _____

3. After lunch I <u>was writing</u> my report on Walt Whitman.

   _____

4. Our fruit trees <u>have been growing</u> at an amazing rate.

   _____

5. I <u>was painting</u> my bicycle when the rain started.

   _____

6. Jan <u>was being</u> unusually generous last night.

   _____

7. They <u>were eating</u> when we arrived.

   _____

8. I <u>had been working</u> nights until I inherited the money.

   _____

9. Mary <u>has been studying</u> French for two years now.

   _____

10. Linda <u>was rehearsing</u> her speech this morning.

   _____

23.1 **Expressing Time Through Tense** (Uses of Tense in Future Time) • **Practice 1**

Uses of Tense in Future Time   The four forms that express future time show future actions or conditions.

USES OF TENSES IN FUTURE TIME		
Verb Forms	**Uses**	**Examples**
Future	Future event	The storm *will arrive* soon.
Future Perfect	Future event before another future event	We *will have finished* the book by next Tuesday.
Future Progressive	Continuing future event	That group *will be performing* here for two nights.
Future Perfect Progressive	Continuing future event before another	By then, we *will have been waiting* here for two hours.

▶ **Exercise 1**   **Identifying the Uses of Tense in Future Time.**   Identify the use of the verb in each sentence, using the labels in the chart above.

EXAMPLE: This will be my third summer on the swim team.   *future event*

1. The Bergers will be traveling in Europe this summer. _____

2. The crew will have paved the road by tomorrow. _____

3. The manager will be interviewing the candidates next week. _____

4. By Tuesday, we will have been traveling for a week. _____

5. Dr. Kelsey will see you now. _____

6. Your invitation will be arriving in the mail. _____

7. I will have finished my rough draft by Monday. _____

8. At his retirement, Mr. Poli will have been teaching for years. _____

9. I will be looking for a job next summer. _____

10. In another hour the cement will have dried. _____

▶ **Exercise 2**   **Using Tenses in Future Time.**   Fill in each blank with the indicated form of the verb in parentheses.

EXAMPLE: All the networks ____*will carry*____ the speech live. (*carry*, future)

1. I _____ French this year. (*study*, future progressive)

2. Your teacher _____ you the necessary forms. (*give*, future progressive)

3. All told, we _____ on this for forty hours. (*work*, future perfect progressive)

4. The books I ordered _____ soon. (*come*, future progressive)

5. I _____ you at the library. (*meet*, future)

6. After the party, you _____ all my friends. (*meet*, future perfect)

7. Alicia _____ my favorite piece in the recital. (*play*, future progressive)

8. If the police don't hurry, the accomplice _____ the evidence. (*destroy*, future perfect)

9. The team _____ every Saturday afternoon. (*practice*, future progressive)

10. I _____ for you after the last class. (*wait*, future)

23.1 # Expressing Time Through Tense (Uses of Tense in Future Time) • Practice 2

USES OF THE FUTURE AND THE FUTURE PERFECT	
Future	*Future action:* A frost *will damage* the crop. *Future condition:* I *will be* home tomorrow.
Future Perfect	*Future action completed before another:* I *will have left* by the time you arrive. *Future condition completed before another:* I *will have been* up for hours before you call.

USES OF THE PROGRESSIVE FORMS THAT EXPRESS FUTURE TIME	
Future Progressive **Future Perfect Progressive**	*Continuing future action:* They *will be visiting* New York this fall. *Continuing future action completed before another:* When we meet next week, I *will have been practicing* tennis for a month.

▶ **Exercise 1** **Identifying the Uses of Tense in Future Time.** Identify the use of each underlined verb, using the labels in the charts above.

EXAMPLE: She will have been traveling a full year when she comes home tomorrow.

_____ *continuing future action completed before another* _____

1. The President will deliver a speech tonight.

   _____

2. The Kramers will be vacationing for two weeks.

   _____

3. Fred will move to California next summer.

   _____

4. Fred will be transferring to Oregon in two years.

   _____

5. By the time you reach Chicago, you will have been driving for eight hours.

   _____

▶ **Exercise 2** **Using Tenses in Future Time.** Write the indicated form of each verb in parentheses.

EXAMPLE: By the time we reach the summit, we ____*will have been climbing*____ for four hours.
(climb—*future perfect progressive*)

1. My aunt _____ in Brazil for a month. (travel—*future progressive*)

2. The department store _____ in an hour. (open—*future*)

3. By tomorrow, we _____ our grades. (receive—*future perfect*)

4. I _____ for Toronto at noon. (leave—*future*)

5. When I return from Puerto Rico in August, I _____ Spanish for two months.
(speak—*future perfect progressive*)

23.1 Expressing Time Through Tense (Shifts in Tense) • Practice 1

Shifts in Tense   When showing a sequence of events, do not shift tenses unnecessarily.

Unnecessary (Incorrect Shifts)	Correct Sequence
I *had meant* to get up early but accidentally *oversleep.* (shift from past perfect to present)	I *had meant* to get up early but accidentally *overslept.* (two past actions, one completed before another)
Jed *takes* the bus to school. I *rode* my bike. (shift from present to past)	Jed *takes* the bus to school. I *ride* my bike. (two regularly occurring actions)
If the car *breaks* down, we *were* late. (shift from present to past)	If the car *breaks* down, we *will be* late. (present condition leading to future outcome)

▶ **Exercise 1**   **Recognizing Unnecessary Shifts in Tense.**   Write *P* after each sentence below that has a problem in tense. If the sentence is correct as written, label it *C*.

EXAMPLE: We will leave after you finished the dishes. ____*P*____

1. We never have dinner before Dad got home from work. _____
2. My sister will miss the twins when they were away. _____
3. Marcia began writing her paper before she reads any sources. _____
4. The owner offers a reward to anyone who found the dog. _____
5. Most likely we will be happier after we started our trip. _____
6. If Jason wins the election, he revised the dress code. _____
7. Erica has lost a lot of weight since I saw her last. _____
8. Whenever you are ready, we left. _____
9. Hugo barks loudly if he heard anything unusual. _____
10. When we got to the pier, the boat is already leaving. _____

▶ **Exercise 2**   **Correcting Errors in Tense.**   Rewrite five of the sentences labeled *P* above, correcting the error by changing the tense of the second verb.

EXAMPLE: ____*We will leave after you finish the dishes.*____

1. _____
2. _____
3. _____
4. _____
5. _____

Expressing Time Through Tense (Shifts in Tense) • Practice 2

▷ **Exercise 1** **Avoiding Unnecessary Shifts in Tense.** Correct tense problems by crossing out the second verb and writing a correction in the blank.

EXAMPLE: Bill goes fishing whenever he ~~got~~ a day off.

        _____gets_____

1. I sit in the hall all day and answered the phone. _____

2. The class had read *Hamlet* before it reads *Macbeth*. _____

3. Eric talked to the newcomers before I do. _____

4. When Grandfather arrived, the whole family greets him at the airport. _____

5. As soon as you find a pleasing color, I help you. _____

6. By the time you phoned, I will have gone to bed. _____

7. Stella had eaten by the time I get there. _____

8. He will reach his goal when he got ten more orders. _____

9. I will be lonely when you will be away. _____

10. By the time I found him, he has mailed the letter already. _____

11. It has been months since the day I have seen you. _____

12. He went below deck and cleans his bunk. _____

13. Sally opens the door whenever the dog barked. _____

14. He sailed for Paris and has arrived there two weeks later. _____

15. If he goes to the rally, I joined him later. _____

16. The game was over when we leave. _____

17. Our team never wins the championship, nor did our rival from across town. _____

18. If I am elected secretary, I will have done many things. _____

19. My little sister smiled at the doctor and says hello. _____

20. He shook my hand and asks me to sit down. _____

▷ **Exercise 2** **Correcting Errors in Tense.** In the following paragraph, cross out unnecessary shifts in tense and write corrections in the blanks that follow.

    (1) An unusual feature of Quincy Market in Boston is Faneuil Hall. (2) It was built in 1742 by Peter Faneuil, who later gives it to the city. (3) Nineteen years later, it burns. (4) Soon after, however, it was rebuilt. (5) Before the Revolutionary War, it is a theater. (6) Later, it was called "The Cradle of Liberty." (7) The name was given to it because it is the scene of many important meetings during the Revolutionary War. (8) For years the first floor was a produce market. (9) The second floor is the place for meetings. (10) It now has contained many historical paintings and is exciting to visit.

1. _____   4. _____

2. _____   5. _____

3. _____   6. _____

Name _____   Date _____

 23.2 # Active and Passive Voice (Differences Between
Active and Passive Voice, Forms of Passive Verbs)
• Practice 1

Differences Between Active and Passive Voice   Voice is the form of a verb that shows whether or not the subject is performing the action. A verb is active if its subject performs the action. A verb is passive if its action is performed upon the subject.

Active Voice	Passive Voice
Alice *left* a message.	A message *was left* by Alice.
We *called* the doctor.	The doctor *was called*.

The Forms of Passive Verbs
A passive verb is made from a form of *be* plus the past participle of a transitive verb.

THE VERB *FOLLOW* IN THE PASSIVE VOICE		
Tense	Basic Forms	Progressive Forms
Present	I am followed.	I am being followed.
Past	I was followed.	I was being followed.
Future	I will be followed.	
Present Perfect	I have been followed.	
Past Perfect	I had been followed.	
Future Perfect	I will have been followed	

▶ **Exercise 1**   **Distinguishing Between the Active and Passive Voice.**   After each sentence, write *active* or *passive* to describe the verb.

EXAMPLE: That book was autographed by the author. _____*passive*_____

1. The authorities have been notified. _____

2. This lettuce was grown in our own garden. _____

3. Mom added fresh mushrooms just before serving the salad. _____

4. Delegates to the convention have already been selected. _____

5. Every scrap of food was eaten during the party. _____

6. The team will elect a new captain tomorrow. _____

7. That car was stolen from the municipal parking lot. _____

8. Lydia has been visiting us this week. _____

9. Damian has already chosen his courses. _____

10. The governor has been asked to speak. _____

▶ **Exercise 2**   **Forming the Tenses of Passive Verbs.**   Write the basic forms of each of the following verbs in the passive voice.

1. say (with *it*)   2. drive (with *they*)   3. tell (with *you*)   4. praise (with *we*)

_____   _____   _____   _____

_____   _____   _____   _____

_____   _____   _____   _____

_____   _____   _____   _____

_____   _____   _____   _____

_____   _____   _____   _____

Name _____ Date _____

23.2 Active and Passive Voice (Differences Between Active and Passive Voice, Forms of Passive Verbs)
• Practice 2

▶ **Exercise 1** **Distinguishing Between the Active and Passive Voice.** Identify each verb as *active* or *passive*.

EXAMPLE: The letter was signed by the President. _____*passive*_____

1. The bitter medicine was taken by my sister. _____

2. Delegates to the convention have been chosen by the voters. _____

3. We each purchased several new outfits for spring. _____

4. Later, the speaker wrote a letter of apology. _____

5. Bread crumbs were then sprinkled on the fish. _____

6. Many wild animals live in the forest. _____

7. Surgery was performed by a team of specialists. _____

8. Ellen grew her own fresh vegetables this summer. _____

9. In the winter snow covers the mountains. _____

10. The bad news was then given to Brad by the coach. _____

11. Representatives had been selected earlier by Congress. _____

12. Kansas City was reached by the convoy in two hours. _____

13. I always read the evening newspaper after dinner. _____

14. After a debate the report was accepted by the chairperson. _____

15. The President has appointed a new ambassador. _____

THE VERB *CALL* IN THE PASSIVE VOICE	
Present	she is called
Past	she was called
Future	she will be called
Present Perfect	she has been called
Past Perfect	she had been called
Future Perfect	she will have been called
Present Progressive	she is being called
Past Progressive	she was being called

▶ **Exercise 2** **Forming the Tenses of Passive Verbs.** Conjugate each verb in the passive voice, using the chart above as your model.

1. type (with *it*)   2. forgive (with *we*)   3. sell (with *it*)   4. alert (with *they*)

_____ _____ _____ _____

_____ _____ _____ _____

_____ _____ _____ _____

_____ _____ _____ _____

_____ _____ _____ _____

_____ _____ _____ _____

_____ _____ _____ _____

_____ _____ _____ _____

23.2 # Active and Passive Voice (Using Voice Correctly)
• Practice 1

Using Voice Correctly   Use the active voice whenever possible. Use the passive voice to emphasize the receiver of the action rather than the performer of the action. Use the passive voice to point out the receiver of an action whenever the performer is not important or not easily identified.

THE VERB IN THE PASSIVE VOICE

My term paper *was typed* by my sister.
    (Unnecessary passive; better: My sister typed my term
    paper.)
The accident victims *were rushed* to the hospital by ambulance.
    (Emphasizes the victims rather than the ambulance.)
The library *is closed* on Saturdays during the summer.
    (Performer is not important and unknown.)

▶ **Exercise 1**   **Distinguishing Between Appropriate and Inappropriate Uses of Passive Voice.**   Label the three necessary uses of the passive voice in the sentences below as *A* (appropriate). Label the other uses as *U* (unnecessary).

EXAMPLE: Jason was asked by his mother to answer the phone. ___*U*___

1. A grand slam home run was hit by the catcher. _____

2. Lincoln was elected to his first term in 1860. _____

3. This sweater was knitted for me by my favorite aunt. _____

4. In 1983 the America's Cup races were won by Australia. _____

5. Many restaurants are closed on Mondays. _____

6. That model airplane was made by Paul. _____

7. Federal income tax returns must be postmarked by midnight on April 15. _____

8. Candidates will be judged by the voters on their merits, not on their

   speeches. _____

9. I have been being followed by that dog for three blocks. _____

10. Dinner is being fixed by Mom right now. _____

▶ **Exercise 2**   **Using the Active Voice.**   Rewrite five of the sentences that you labeled *U* in Exercise 1. Change or add words as necessary to put each verb into the active voice.

EXAMPLE: ___*Jason's mother asked him to answer the phone.*___

1. _____

2. _____

3. _____

4. _____

5. _____

23.2 Active and Passive Voice (Using Voice Correctly)
• Practice 2

▶ **Exercise 1** **Correcting Unnecessary Use of the Passive Voice.** Rewrite the following paragraph, changing at least five uses of the passive voice to active.

EXAMPLE: Loch Ness *is being studied* by many scientists.

_____*Many scientists are studying Loch Ness*_____ .

(1) For years a so-called monster has been spotted by visitors to Loch Ness in Scotland. (2) The large creature has been reported by many witnesses. (3) Do lake monsters really exist? (4) These reports have been questioned by scientists. (5) According to some Canadian scientists, the sightings may be explained by temperature inversions. (6) A temperature inversion occurs when the temperature of a body of water is much lower than the temperature of the air above it. (7) Experiments were conducted by scientists on Lake Winnipeg, Canada, during a temperature inversion. (8) Two photos of an ordinary stick floating on the lake were taken only three minutes apart. (9) The bending, or refraction, of light caused by the inversion made the stick appear to be a strangely shaped "monster." (10) These photos have been accepted by some scientists as proof that the lake monsters are really ordinary objects that appear distorted because of a temperature inversion.

_____

_____

_____

_____

_____

_____

_____

_____

_____

_____

_____

_____

_____

_____

_____

▶ **Writing Application** **Using the Active and Passive Voice in Writing.** Write five sentences describing the events that happened on your way to school this morning. Include one sentence using the passive voice. Make sure all the other sentences use the active voice.

_____

_____

_____

_____

24.1 The Cases of Pronouns (The Three Cases)
• Practice 1

The Three Cases Case is the form of a noun or pronoun that indicates its use in a sentence. The three cases are the nominative, the objective, and the possessive.

CASE FORMS OF PRONOUNS		
Case	**Use in Sentence**	**Forms**
Nominative	subject, predicate nominative	I; you; he, she, it; we; they
Objective	direct object, indirect object, object of preposition	me; you; him, her, it; us; them
Possessive	to show ownership	my, mine; you, yours; his, her, hers, its; our, ours; their, theirs

▶ **Exercise 1** **Identifying Case.** Write the case of each underlined pronoun on each line to the right.

EXAMPLE: Soon after starting out, we had a flat tire.   _nominative_

1. The doctor cannot see you until next week. _____
2. Gail has misplaced her keys again. _____
3. Foster broke his bat on that hit. _____
4. The Jacksons took the dog with them on vacation. _____
5. Surely this bike is yours. _____
6. Occasionally I enjoy a horror movie. _____
7. Edison returned to his laboratory. _____
8. Louise said that someone invited her. _____
9. The boat was turned over on its side. _____
10. Kevin asked us for directions. _____

▶ **Exercise 2** **Identifying Pronoun Case and Use.** Write the case of each underlined pronoun. Then write the number that describes how the pronoun is used in the sentence: 1 (subject), 2 (predicate nominative), 3 (direct object), 4 (indirect object), 5 (object of a preposition), 6 (to show ownership).

EXAMPLE: The first guests were Donna and I.   _nominative, 2_

1. Ms. Parker read us students the directions. _____
2. Louie and he are bringing the dessert. _____
3. Did you get a postcard from Dawn or me ? _____
4. Every house in this neighborhood has its own well. _____
5. They promised to be here in time for lunch. _____
6. Because of all the other noise, no one heard us. _____
7. Grace described her plan in detail. _____
8. The best choice would be Don or you. _____
9. The judges have not explained their choice. _____
10. Mom divided the pie among us. _____

24.1 **The Cases of Pronouns** (The Three Cases)
• **Practice 2**

▶ **Exercise 1** **Identifying Pronoun Case.** Write the case of each underlined pronoun on the line to the right of each sentence.

EXAMPLE: It was clearly a case of mistaken identity. _____nominative_____

1. The antique doll with the lace dress belonged to her. _____
2. The two brothers took their responsibilities seriously. _____
3. Our doubts about getting there on time began to grow. _____
4. Until the age of thirteen, she was afraid of dogs. _____
5. His relationship with Elizabeth kept him going. _____
6. Oscar handed me the tastefully wrapped package. _____
7. We had a garage sale last weekend. _____
8. You never know what might happen. _____
9. Do not pay any attention to them. _____
10. Is this cake yours or mine? _____

▶ **Exercise 2** **Identifying Case.** Write the case of each underlined pronoun. Then write its use: subject, predicate nominative, direct object, indirect object, object of a preposition, to show ownership.

EXAMPLE: The doctor gave her the good news. _____*objective, indirect object*_____

1. After waiting an hour, we finally spoke to the coach. _____
2. Give them the present. _____
3. Their reply surprised the judge. _____
4. Betty will see you on Friday. _____
5. John waved to us on the way to the game. _____
6. There is no question that this is my wallet. _____
7. They accepted our explanation completely. _____
8. Your mother phoned from her office. _____
9. Much to my delight, Phil asked me to dance. _____
10. My mother asked for her help with the children. _____
11. General Smith gave his word to the troops. _____
12. My sister and I agreed to perform. _____
13. The chairperson is she. _____
14. The principal gave us a broad smile. _____
15. Does Father want to hear our reasons? _____
16. Their science project is the best in the class. _____
17. The winners are Joan and I. _____
18. Give your answer to him. _____
19. Dr. Smith gave us debaters a small pin. _____
20. I really want to visit the campus. _____

24.1 The Cases of Pronouns (Nominative Case, Objective Case) • Practice 1

The Nominative Case   Use the nominative case for the subject of a verb or for a predicate nominative. When a pronoun used as a subject or predicate nominative is followed by an appositive, the nominative case is still used.

USES OF NOMINATIVE CASE	
Subject	James and *I* went to summer camp. *They* were the winners. *We* members voted on the project.
Predicate Nominative	The one who answered the phone was *she*. The winners were *we* Howlers.

The Objective Case   Use the objective case for a direct object, for an indirect object, or for the object of a preposition—even if the pronoun has an appositive.

USES OF OBJECTIVE CASE	
Direct Object	David met *us* at the library. Grandma treated Jim and *me* to a movie. The theater uses *us* students as ushers.
Indirect Object	The sitter read *him* a bedtime story. The guide showed Jim and *me* the map. The teacher read *us* students the directions.
Object of a Preposition	I got a postcard from *her*. This letter is addressed to Jan and *him*. Move the microphone closer to *us* speakers.

▶ **Exercise 1**   **Identifying Pronouns in the Nominative Case.**   Circle the nominative pronoun form in parentheses. Then write *S* (subject) or *PN* (predicate nominative) to describe its use.

EXAMPLE: Florence and ((he), him) enjoyed the lobster. _____S_____

1. Ed and (I, me) came early. _____

2. The late one was (he, him). _____

3. The winners are (them, they). _____

4. (Her, She) is the coach. _____

5. Kim or (he, him) can help. _____

▶ **Exercise 2**   **Identifying Pronouns in the Objective Case.**   Circle the objective pronoun form in parentheses. Then write *DO* (direct object), *IO* (indirect object), or *OP* (object of a preposition) to describe its use.

EXAMPLE: The director told (we, (us)) campers the rules. _____IO_____

1. No one saw (she, her). _____

2. I left this for (him, he). _____

3. Leave (we, us) kids alone. _____

4. Please show (I, me) that. _____

5. Tell (we, us) a story. _____

24.1 The Cases of Pronouns (Nominative Case, Objective Case) • Practice 2

▷ **Exercise 1** **Using Pronouns in the Nominative Case.** Write a nominative pronoun to complete each sentence. Then, in the blank after the sentence, write the use of the pronoun.

EXAMPLE: Jane and _____I_____ worked late. _____subject_____

1. _____ are waiting for us at the station. _____

2. _____ is a cold and damp morning. _____

3. Are _____ serious about that offer? _____

4. The key to victory is _____ delegates from Boston. _____

5. _____ are hoping for an invitation to the party. _____

6. _____ is the uncle I love most. _____

7. You know that _____ is ill today. _____

8. I hope that _____ will go with me. _____

9. _____ is my oldest sister. _____

10. Surely _____ will accept your offer. _____

▷ **Exercise 2** **Using Pronouns in the Objective Case.** Write an objective pronoun to complete each sentence. Then, in the blank after the sentence, write the use of the pronoun.

EXAMPLE: George gave _____me_____ his old catcher's mitt. _____indirect object_____

1. Brenda gave _____ lots of unwanted advice. _____

2. The disc jockey smiled at _____ girls. _____

3. My father lent _____ his car. _____

4. Our teacher gave _____ two new baseball bats after our surprise victory. _____

5. With his record, can we really trust _____ ? _____

6. He gave _____ Little Leaguers tickets to the big game next Saturday. _____

7. That experience gave _____ boys a real scare. _____

8. Call for Elizabeth and _____ in about an hour. _____

9. I gave _____ different eye makeup to try. _____

10. I congratulated _____ and the other swimmers. _____

The Cases of Pronouns (Possessive Case)
• Practice 1

The Possessive Case   Use the possessive case before nouns to show ownership and before gerunds. Use certain possessive pronouns by themselves to indicate possession.

USES OF POSSESSIVE CASE	
Before Nouns	*My* bicycle chain needs oil.
	Joan showed us *her* new camera.
Before Gerunds	*Our* playing the music disturbed Mr. Hayes.
	Max is a darling baby, but *his* crying sometimes gets on my nerves.
Alone	Are these keys *yours* ?
	Mine is the third locker from the end.

▶ **Exercise 1**   **Using Pronouns in the Possessive Case.**   Write the correct word from the parentheses to complete each sentence.

EXAMPLE: The cat has _____*its*_____ own basket to sleep in. (it's, its)

1. _____ constant whining is very annoying. (Him, His)

2. None of the books on this table are _____ . (mine, my)

3. I'm sure Mr. Lawson appreciated _____ helping him. (our, us)

4. These are June's sneakers, but where are _____ ? (your's, yours)

5. Carol forgot _____ lunch. (her, hers)

6. Did you ask Peter about _____ playing the piano at the party? (him, his)

7. The Holts claim this picnic table is _____ . (their's, theirs)

8. _____ learning magic tricks cost the family a lot of eggs. (Me, My, Mine)

9. After you have looked it over, put the radio back in _____ original packing carton. (it's, its)

10. Everyone enjoyed _____ singing. (them, their)

▶ **Exercise 2**   **Using All Three Cases.**   Complete each sentence with the appropriate pronoun form. The code number in parentheses indicates which group of pronouns to choose from:

(1) I, me, my, mine   (3) he, him, his; it, its; she,   (4) we, us, our, ours
(2) you, your, yours   her, hers   (5) they, them, their, theirs

EXAMPLE: The first one to volunteer was _____*I*_____ . (1)

1. Surely this house must be _____ . (5)

2. Next summer _____ older campers can help the younger ones. (4)

3. When I saw Rhona, I told _____ about the party. (3)

4. _____ practicing the drums sometimes disturbs the neighbors. (1)

5. Which of these duffel bags is _____ ? (2)

6. Bobby asked the sitter to sing _____ a song. (3)

7. Happily the argument between Don and _____ didn't last very long. (1)

8. The coach urged _____ players to do our best. (4)

9. The boat slipped loose from _____ moorings. (3)

10. Several customers mentioned _____ finding flaws in the product. (5)

24.1 The Cases of Pronouns (Possessive Case)
• Practice 2

▷ Exercise 1 **Using Pronouns in the Possessive Case.** Write the correct word from the parentheses to complete each sentence.

EXAMPLE: We must give them ____*theirs*____ . (theirs, their's)

1. I spoke to Ralph about _____ chewing gum in class. (his, him)

2. There is no question that this is _____ . (yours, your's)

3. Our kitten hurt _____ front paw. (it's, its)

4. The president asked for _____ resignation. (his, his's)

5. _____ speeding finally got him into trouble. (His, Him)

6. We told him that this is _____ . (our's, ours)

7. They want _____ cutting to stop immediately. (his, him)

8. _____ winnings will be divided equally. (They're, Their)

9. May I borrow _____ ? (your's, yours)

10. I feel that _____ too expensive. (its, it's)

11. _____ singing leaves much to be desired. (Our, Us)

12. I finally said that it was _____ . (mine's, mine)

13. _____ leaving will cause much embarrassment. (Your, You)

14. Is it really _____ ? (hers, her's)

15. _____ constant smiling cheers us all up. (Him, His)

16. _____ not really prepared to dance. (Your, You're)

17. I thought he would understand _____ joking. (our, us)

18. Mother was worried about _____ growing. (me, my)

19. _____ really none of your business. (Its, It's)

20. The ship veered off _____ course. (its, it's)

▷ Exercise 2 **Using All Three Cases.** Write the correct word from the parentheses to complete each sentence.

1. My neighbor helped _____ with the model. (he, him)

2. _____ policy is very strict. (Their, They're)

3. The professor said that it was _____ . (she, her, her's)

4. _____ girls will decorate the gym. (We, Us)

5. Dr. Stevenson gave _____ and _____ his blessing. (she, her) (he, him)

6. Our puppy wagged _____ tail. (its, it's)

7. I waited for _____ while _____ changed clothes. (they, them) (they, them)

8. Can _____ work on _____ projects now? (we, us) (our, our's)

9. Your costume is the best of all of _____ . (them, their's)

10. Why were _____ and _____ late to class? (he, him) (she, her)

Name _____ Date _____

 24.2 # Special Problems with Pronouns (*Who* and *Whom*, Elliptical Clauses) • Practice 1

Using *Who* and *Whom* Correctly   *Who* is nominative and should be used for a subject or a predicate nominative. *Whom* is objective and should be used for a direct object or the object of a preposition. *Whose*, not *who's*, is possessive.

CASE FORMS OF *WHO*	
Nominative	*Who* told you that story?
	Who will be the winner?
	I wonder *who* will play.
	Jed asked *who* the leader was.
Objective	*Whom* shall we choose?
	Whom have you written to?
	That is the girl *whom* I met at the party.
	Those are the people *whom* we had dinner with.
Possessive	*Whose* jacket is this?
	That is a poet *whose* work I admire.

Using Pronouns Correctly in Elliptical Clauses   In elliptical clauses beginning with *than* or *as*, use the form of the pronoun that you would use if the clauses were fully stated.

PRONOUNS IN ELLIPTICAL CLAUSES	
Elliptical Clauses	**Completed Clauses**
Ellie studies harder than (*I* or *me*).	Ellie studies harder than *I* [do].
The teacher gave Jon a higher mark than (*I* or *me*).	The teacher gave Jon a higher mark than [she gave] *me*.
Mom gives Carl more attention than (*I* or me).	Mom gives Carl more attention than [she gives] *me*.
	Mom gives Carl more attention than *I* [give him].

▶ **Exercise 1**   **Using *Who* and *Whom* Correctly.**   Write *who* or *whom* to complete each sentence.

EXAMPLE: Jake is someone _____*whom*_____ I greatly respect.

1. _____ shall we choose as chairman?

2. Mr. Zimmerman is a teacher _____ inspires his students.

3. The owner offered a reward to anyone _____ finds the dog.

4. _____ is your favorite poet?

5. We must choose someone _____ can do a good job.

▶ **Exercise 2**   **Using Pronouns in Elliptical Clauses.**   Complete each sentence with the correct form of the pronoun in parentheses.

EXAMPLE: Sue has more clothes than _____*I*_____ . (I, me)

1. My parents give my brother more allowance than _____ . (I, me)

2. Surely none of the other guests were as late as _____ . (they, them)

3. Jim is not as busy as _____ . (he, him)

4. The movie upset Mom more than _____ . (I, me)

5. All of a sudden, my younger brother is taller than _____ . (I, me)

24.2 Special Problems with Pronouns (*Who* and *Whom*, Elliptical Clauses) • Practice 2

> **Exercise 1** **Using *Who* and *Whom* in Questions and Clauses.** Complete each sentence with the correct form of the pronoun in parentheses.

EXAMPLE: She is the candidate for ___*whom*___ I voted. (who, whom)

1. I know _____ the culprit is. (who, whom)

2. Can you tell us _____ they really want? (who, whom)

3. Fritz is the only barber _____ I trust. (who, whom)

4. We accept contributions from all _____ will give. (who, whom)

5. The girl _____ you like is a friend of mine. (who, whom)

6. Into _____ classroom have they gone? (whose, who's)

7. I met the man _____, all the polls said, will win. (who, whom)

8. To _____ were you writing? (who, whom)

9. It is he with _____ you should speak. (who, whom)

10. Take these roses to the man _____ lives next door. (who, whom)

11. The lieutenant _____ won was later promoted. (who, whom)

12. My father is the man _____ prepared the schedule for the volunteer fire department. (who, whom)

13. _____ the student with the highest score? (Who's, Whose)

14. Ask all _____ are concerned to aid our cause. (who, whom)

15. With _____ were you visiting? (who, whom)

16. Is she the saleswoman to _____ you spoke? (who, whom)

17. The shortstop _____ you saw at today's game is having a poor season. (who, whom)

18. To _____ will you give the job? (who, whom)

19. _____ is the teacher you want us to meet? (Who, Whom)

20. We are the ones _____ are to blame. (who, whom)

> **Exercise 2** **Identifying the Correct Pronoun in Elliptical Clauses.** Rewrite each sentence by choosing one pronoun in parentheses and correctly completing the elliptical clause.

EXAMPLE: She is as short as ___*I am*___. (I, me)

1. Beth has more experience than _____. (I, me)

2. She writes better than _____. (I, me)

3. He feels that he is as skilled as _____. (she, her)

4. I have better manners than _____. (he, him)

5. He was more seriously injured than _____. (she, her)

6. My brother is as advanced in chemistry as _____. (she, her)

7. Helen can type as fast as _____. (I, me)

8. Mrs. Pratt gave me a higher grade than _____. (he, him)

9. I worked longer last night than _____. (he, him)

10. Find out if he earned more money than _____. (she, her)

25.1 Subject and Verb Agreement (Number, Singular and Plural Subjects) • Practice 1

Number: Singular and Plural Number refers to the two forms of a word: singular and plural. Singular words indicate one; plural words indicate more than one.

NUMBER OF WORDS			
Part of Speech	**Singular**	**Plural**	**Singular or Plural**
Nouns	baby toy child	babies toys children	fish deer moose
Pronouns	I, he, she, it	we, they	you
Verbs	travels has gone am, is, was		(I, you, we, they) travel (I, you, we, they) have gone (you, we, they) are, were

Singular and Plural Subjects A singular subject must have a singular verb. A plural subject must have a plural verb. A phrase or clause that interrupts a subject and its verb does not affect subject-verb agreement.

SUBJECT-VERB AGREEMENT	
Singular	**Plural**
She enjoys reading mysteries. A box of cookies is in the cupboard. That fish has unusual colors.	We have just missed the bus. Two boxes of books are missing. These fish have long whiskers.

▶ **Exercise 1** **Determining the Number of Words.** Label each word below as *sing.* (singular), *plur.* (plural), or *both*.

EXAMPLE: should _____*both*_____

1. potatoes _____
2. are _____
3. reindeer _____
4. defendants _____
5. puts _____

6. like _____
7. women _____
8. digit _____
9. amuses _____
10. were given _____

▶ **Exercise 2** **Making Subjects and Verbs Agree.** Complete each sentence by writing the verb form from parentheses that agrees with the subject. Then label each sentence *S* if the subject is singular or *P* if it is plural.

EXAMPLE: Some players on that team _____*have*_____ been disqualified. (has, have) ___*P*___

1. That song by the Weavers _____ become a classic (has, have) _____
2. The students in Mr. Long's class _____ going to the opera. (is, are) _____
3. Both the trout that Dana caught _____ quite large. (was, were) _____
4. The carton of Christmas decorations _____ in the basement. (is, are) _____
5. The team with the most wins _____ the league. (lead, leads) _____

25.1 Subject and Verb Agreement (Number, Singular and Plural Subjects) • Practice 2

▶ **Exercise 1** **Determining the Number of Nouns, Pronouns, and Verbs.** Identify each item as *singular*, *plural*, or *both*.

EXAMPLE: speaks _____*singular*_____

1. car _____
2. lifeguards _____
3. tomatoes _____
4. woman _____
5. he _____
6. lizard _____
7. demonstrators _____
8. writes _____
9. soldiers _____
10. she _____
11. helps _____
12. is _____
13. was _____
14. was plotting _____
15. grow _____
16. seeks _____
17. loses _____
18. has been watching _____
19. choose _____
20. you _____

▶ **Exercise 2** **Making Subjects Agree With Their Verbs.** Write the verb from parentheses that agrees with the subject of each sentence.

EXAMPLE: He ____*jogs*____ two miles every day. (jog, jogs)

1. A tall tree _____ in our front yard. (stands, stand)
2. The ships _____ passing the island. (was, were)
3. It seems that the baby _____ an inch every day. (grows, grow)
4. Our blackboards _____ all scratched. (was, were)
5. Candles _____ quite expensive. (is, are)
6. Yesterday the newspaper _____ not delivered. (was, were)
7. His pictures _____ in the gallery. (belongs, belong)
8. Mr. Cody _____ reading poems in a dramatic voice. (was were)
9. At sunrise the ships _____ from the harbor. (sails, sail)
10. At the quarry the noises _____ deafening. (is, are)

25.1 Subject and Verb Agreement (Compound Subjects) • Practice 1

Compound Subjects A singular subject after *or* takes a singular verb. A plural subject after *or* takes a plural verb. Compound subjects joined by *and* take a plural verb unless they are thought of as one thing or modified by *every* or *each*.

AGREEMENT WITH COMPOUND SUBJECTS	
Joined by *or* or *nor*	Ed, Sue, or Pam *has* a good chance of winning. Neither the cats nor the dogs *eat* table scraps. Either the servants or the owner *shows* tourists around. Either the owner or the servants *show* tourists around.
Joined by *and*	Hot dogs and hamburgers *are* traditional picnic foods. Ian and Pete *are* on the same team. Bacon, lettuce, and tomato *is* my favorite sandwich. Every man, woman, and child *has* a separate seat.

▶ **Exercise 1** **Compound Subjects Joined by *Or* or *Nor*.** Write the verb form from parentheses that agrees with the subject in each sentence.

EXAMPLE: Louise or her sisters ____*are*____ usually home in the evening. (is, are)

1. Neither Elmer nor his children _____ fried chicken. (like, likes)

2. Pat, Dana, or Tony _____ a good person to ask for directions. (is, are)

3. The twins or their sister _____ for the Harpers. (baby-sit, baby-sits)

4. Either Dad or Mom _____ bought corn for dinner. (has, have)

5. Nelly, Dobbin, or Prince _____ a good name for the horse. (is, are)

6. Erik or the twins _____ always welcome here. (is, are)

7. Neither Dawn nor her mother _____ faddish clothes. (buy, buys)

8. Either the magician himself or his assistants _____ up the audience. (warm, warms)

9. Mom or my brothers _____ sweet rolls on Sunday morning. (get, gets)

10. Kim or Kelly _____ the daily paper. (deliver, delivers)

▶ **Exercise 2** **Compound Subjects Joined by *And*.** Write the verb form from parentheses that agrees with the subject in each sentence.

EXAMPLE: Peanut butter and jelly ____*is*____ a favorite sandwich with children. (is, are)

1. My brother and sister _____ been very cooperative lately. (has, have)

2. Every glass and plate in the house _____ dirty after the party. (was, were)

3. Both the painter and the carpenter _____ coming today. (is, are)

4. The chairs and table _____ made of oak. (is, are)

5. The Stars and Stripes _____ the United States. (represent, represents)

25.1 Subject and Verb Agreement (Compound Subjects) • Practice 2

▶ **Exercise 1** **Making Compound Subjects Agree With Their Verbs.** Write the verb form from parentheses that agrees with the subject in each sentence.

EXAMPLE: Either Kelly or Jim ____*plays*____ the lead role. (play, plays)

1. The door and the window _____ stuck. (is, are)

2. Neither Mother nor Father _____ phoned. (has, have)

3. The dog or the cats _____ always howling. (is, are)

4. Apples and bananas _____ been my favorite fruits for years. (has, have)

5. Mary or Louise _____ to the bridge club. (belongs, belong)

6. Each morning Tom or the children _____ fresh rolls at the bakery. (buys, buy)

7. Both the man with the appliances and the plumber _____ arrived. (has, have)

8. My son and daughter _____ never been so cooperative. (has, have)

9. Mark and David _____ in the office yet. (isn't, aren't)

10. Two large packages and a letter _____ delivered. (was, were)

11. Either the children or I _____ into town for the mail. (walks, walk)

12. Joan and Ellen _____ called in a month. (hasn't, haven't)

13. My car or Ted's _____ always available. (is, are)

14. His messiness and my chattering _____ Mother. (annoys, annoy)

15. Every cup and saucer _____ broken in the move. (was, were)

▶ **Exercise 2** **Making Compound Subjects Agree With Their Verbs in Sentences.** Write a sentence for each compound subject, making sure that the compound subject and verb agree.

EXAMPLE: time and temperature

_____The time and temperature are displayed on the sign in front of the bank._____

1. neither Jason nor Julie

_____

2. radio and television

_____

3. computers and the Internet

_____

4. beets, carrots, or celery

_____

5. an apple or a banana

_____

25.1 Subject and Verb Agreement (Confusing Subjects) • Practice 1

Confusing Subjects   Always check certain kinds of subjects carefully to make sure they agree with their verbs.

AGREEMENT WITH CONFUSING SUBJECTS	
Subject After Verb	In the middle of the second act *appear* two *elves*. Beyond the pasture *lies* a dense *forest*.
Subject Versus Predicate Nominative	These two *socks are* a pair. A *pair is* two objects of the same kind.
Collective Nouns	The *family makes* decisions together. (as a group) The *family share* their feelings. (as individuals)
Plural Form with Singular Meaning	*Mumps was* once a common illness. *Sports is* the only thing I ever watch on television.
Amounts	Two *weeks is* never enough vacation. Three *cups* of sugar *is* a lot for that recipe.
Titles	*A Tale of Two Cities* is a classic novel.
Indefinite Pronouns	*One* of the cups *is* missing. (always singular) *Both* of the cups *are* missing. (always plural) *Some* of the soup *is* still simmering. *Some* of the cookies *have* been eaten.

▶ **Exercise 1**   **Deciding on the Number of Subjects.**   Assume that each item below is to be the subject of a sentence. Label each one *S* if it needs a singular verb or *P* if it needs a plural verb.

EXAMPLE: *All the King's Men* ____S____

1. Some of the students _____
2. Econometrics _____
3. Aesop's *Fables* _____
4. Half of the students _____
5. German measles _____
6. Each of the men _____
7. *Pride and Prejudice* _____
8. Six months _____
9. Both of the cars _____
10. All of the pie _____

▶ **Exercise 2**   **Choosing Verbs to Agree With Difficult Subjects.**   Write the correct verb form from parentheses to complete each sentence.

EXAMPLE: Here ____are____ the books you ordered. (is, are)

1. The news on the front page _____ often distressing. (is, are)
2. The committee sometimes _____ among themselves. (disagree, disagrees)
3. High winds _____ a major threat to coastal property. (is, are)
4. Half of the students _____ chicken pox. (has, have)
5. The whole group _____ the same schedule. (follow, follows)

25.1 Subject and Verb Agreement (Confusing Subjects) • Practice 2

▶ **Exercise 1**   **Making Confusing Subjects Agree With Their Verbs.**   Write the verb form from parentheses that agrees with the subject of each sentence.

EXAMPLE: All of the apples ___are___ rotten. (is, are)

1. Near the top of the closet _____ an old electric fan. (is, are)

2. The committee _____ been unable to reach an agreement. (has, have)

3. Rich foods _____ one cause of oily skin. (is, are)

4. Economics _____ my sister's major in college. (was, were)

5. _____ exotic plants thrive in this climate? (Do, Does)

6. The group of tourists _____ left on the bus. (has, have)

7. The jury _____ left their seats but will soon return. (has, have)

8. He said that civics _____ his favorite subject. (was, were)

9. _____ some of the soup still available? (Is, Are)

10. _____ more volunteers for the clean-up crew. (Here's, Here are)

11. The problem at the picnic _____ bees. (was, were)

12. There _____ two excellent reasons for his choice. (is, are)

13. Politics _____ one of his major interests. (was, were)

14. The entire faculty _____ voiced their opinions. (has, have)

15. _____ the captains of both teams. (There's, There are)

16. *Green Mansions* _____ her favorite novel. (is, are)

17. There _____ only one possible explanation. (is, are)

18. Another example of the area's underdevelopment _____ the narrow dirt roads. (is, are)

19. Mumps _____ a dangerous disease for adults. (is, are)

20. The team _____ has been squabbling with each other again. (has, have)

▶ **Exercise 2**   **More Work With Confusing Subjects.**   Write the verb form from parentheses that agrees with the subject of each sentence.

1. One of the girls _____ hurt on the soccer field. (was, were)

2. Few _____ volunteered for the assignment. (has, have)

3. Somebody in the room above _____ to be quite ill. (seems, seem)

4. Several of the contestants _____ arrived. (has, have)

5. Some of the food _____ not cooked thoroughly. (was, were)

6. Ten dollars _____ an outrageous price for the book. (is, are)

7. Each of the guards _____ sworn allegiance. (has, have)

8. Why _____ everyone so unhappy? (is, are)

9. None of the cakes _____ thrown away. (was, were)

10. Three fourths of the fence _____ installed. (was, were)

25.2 Pronoun and Antecedent Agreement
(Between Personal Pronouns and Antecedents) • Practice 1

Agreement Between Personal Pronouns and Antecedents   A personal pronoun must agree with its antecedent in person, number, and gender. Use a singular personal pronoun with two or more singular antecedents joined by *or* or *nor*. Use a plural personal pronoun with two or more antecedents joined by *and*. When gender is not specified, use the masculine or rewrite the sentence.

PRONOUN-ANTECEDENT AGREEMENT
My uncle likes *his* new job.
The cat has *its* own basket.
Alicia says this is *hers*.
Dawn or Sue will give you *her* notes.
Ed, Jon, and Bob brought *their* gloves.
Each player has *his* own uniform.
All the players have *their* own uniforms.

▶ **Exercise 1**   **Choosing Personal Pronouns to Agree With Antecedents.**   Assume that each item below is an antecedent for a personal pronoun. After each, write *his, her, its,* or *their* to show which pronoun you would use.

EXAMPLE: Eloise or Mary ____*her*____

1. several students _____
2. the toy train _____
3. either Kevin or Bruce _____
4. Lucy, Cindy, or Karen _____
5. only one girl _____
6. Paul and Harry _____
7. each boy _____
8. many inventions _____
9. our neighbor's dog _____
10. the famous actress _____

▶ **Exercise 2**   **Pronoun-Antecedent Agreement in Sentences.**   Write an appropriate personal pronoun to complete each sentence.

EXAMPLE: My sister and I visited ____*our*____ grandparents last weekend.

1. Henry called loudly from the cave, but no one heard _____.
2. The second-hand table has only a few scratches on _____ surface.
3. Neither Linda nor Carol had a pencil with _____.
4. The mayor and the city council announced _____ new proposal.
5. Grandpa likes to have us visit _____.

25.2 Pronoun and Antecedent Agreement
(Between Personal Pronouns and Antecedents) • Practice 2

▶ **Exercise 1** **Making Personal Pronouns Agree With Their Antecedents.** Write an appropriate personal pronoun to complete each sentence.

EXAMPLE: Either Mark or Bill will drive _____*his*_____ car.

1. Mrs. Berger described _____ plans for the new store.

2. Carol will read _____ own report.

3. The goat shook _____ head in confusion.

4. My father gave us _____ secret recipe for muffins.

5. The city officials explained _____ reasons for the curfew.

6. Marie sealed the letter; then _____ tore it open again.

7. Neither Nancy nor Carol explained _____ position.

8. Uncle Roy sent us a package, but _____ never arrived.

9. I told John and Irene that _____ should be here by noon.

10. The nurse asked us about _____ eating habits.

▶ **Exercise 2** **Making Personal Pronouns Agree With Their Antecedents.** Write an appropriate personal pronoun to complete each sentence in the paragraph.

EXAMPLE: Neither Jill nor Suzy wore (1) *her* coat in the mall.

Joel and Henry ran along the path, each one wondering how much longer

(1) _____ could last. It was a cool day, and (2) _____ both were

in good shape. Still, (3) _____ had been running for about forty minutes, and for each

of (4) _____ , this was a sufficient amount of exercise. Joel looked over at

(5) _____ best friend and saw that (6) _____ did not even seem

tired. Henry looked over at Joel and felt that (7) _____ was not even out of breath.

"Say, Joel," said Henry. "Are (8) _____ about ready to stop?"

"Not yet," said Joel. "Why? Is this too much for (9) _____ ?"

"Not at all," said Henry. "My mom just told (10) _____ this morning that she

thought (11) _____ was getting stronger every day. Since you and

(12) _____ started this program, I've been improving. I just thought that

(13) _____ might be getting tired."

"No," said Joel. "(14) _____ stamina has increased during the past few weeks.

Let's keep running."

As the two friends continued (15) _____ run, each one hoped that the other

would stop soon.

25.2 # Pronoun and Antecedent Agreement (With Indefinite Pronouns and With Reflexive Pronouns)

• Practice 1

Agreement with Indefinite Pronouns   Use a singular personal pronoun when the antecedent is a singular indefinite pronoun. Use a plural personal pronoun when the antecedent is a plural indefinite pronoun. With an indefinite pronoun that can be either singular or plural, agreement depends on the antecedent of the indefinite pronoun.

AGREEMENT WITH INDEFINITE PRONOUNS
Each of the girls has *her* own room.
Both of the boys rode *their* bikes.
All of the cake has icing on *it*. (cake = singular antecedent)
All of the boys wore *their* ties. (boys = plural antecedent)

Agreement with Reflexive Pronouns   A reflexive pronoun must agree with an antecedent that is clearly stated.

REFLEXIVE PRONOUN AGREEMENT	
Incorrect	**Correct**
The trouble between Sue and *myself* arose over jealousy.	The trouble between Sue and *me* arose over jealousy.

▷ **Exercise 1**   **Making Personal Pronouns Agree With Indefinite Pronouns.**   Write an appropriate personal pronoun to complete each sentence.

EXAMPLE: Each of the houses must have a street number on ___*it*___ .

1. Some of the wood has insects in _____ .

2. Several of the players have purchased extra uniforms on _____ own.

3. Most of the coins have mold on _____ .

4. Neither of those books has much useful information in _____ .

5. Somebody from the League of Women Voters said _____ would speak to us.

6. Most of my friends get along well with _____ families.

7. Little of the yard has grass growing in _____ .

8. Anybody from that Boy Scout troop will gladly show you _____ catalog.

9. Do all of the brownies have nuts in _____ ?

10. Many of those homes have alarm systems in _____ .

▷ **Exercise 2**   **Using Reflexive Pronouns Correctly.**   Underline the misused reflexive pronoun in each sentence. Write the correct pronoun on the line.

EXAMPLE: Both Jim and yourself should come. ___*you*___

1. Give that to myself when you're finished with it. _____

2. The Palmers invited the Youngs and ourselves for dinner. _____

3. Trudy and herself share a room. _____

4. Luis and myself will take the dog for a walk. _____

5. We hope Alice and yourself can go on the picnic. _____

Pronoun and Antecedent Agreement (With
Indefinite Pronouns and With Reflexive Pronouns)
• **Practice 2**

▶ **Exercise 1**   **Making Personal Pronouns Agree With Indefinite Pronouns.**   Write the correct
pronoun to complete each sentence.

EXAMPLE: All of the boys lost _____*their*_____ money. (his, their)

1. Few at the conference gave _____ approval. (its, their)

2. Every one of the boys has _____ instructions. (his, their)

3. Each of the girls is responsible for _____ own room. (her, their)

4. Neither of the boys agreed to ask _____ parents. (his, their)

5. Every one of the girls agreed to ask _____ opinion. (her, their)

6. One of the fellows will have to volunteer _____ time. (his, their)

7. Both of my aunts sent _____ congratulations. (her, their)

8. Several of the men volunteered _____ service. (his, their)

9. Each of the women was given _____ lieutenant bars. (her, their)

10. Neither of the men could remember _____ number. (his, their)

11. Each of the ballerinas gave us _____ autograph. (her, their)

12. All of the women refused to give _____ consent. (her, their)

13. Several of the ships had _____ sails destroyed. (its, their)

14. Each of the boys must pay _____ dues soon. (his, their)

15. Some of the foods had lost _____ flavor. (its, their)

16. Neither of the girls brought _____ new records. (her, their)

17. Most soldiers in the battalion admired _____ lieutenant. (his, their)

18. Nobody in the boys' group brought _____ radio. (his, their)

19. Each of the sales women announced _____ results. (her, their)

20. Only one of the committees gave _____ consent. (its, their)

▶ **Exercise 2**   **Using Reflexive Pronouns Correctly.**   Rewrite each sentence, correcting the
misused reflexive pronoun.

EXAMPLE: Both Todd and myself are going to the game.

_____*Both Todd and I are going to the game.*_____

1. Bob and I think the best person for this job is yourself.

_____

2. The Parkinsons and ourselves went to the opera together.

_____

3. Neither Francine nor myself knew who left the package.

_____

4. A guard directed the teacher and ourselves to the entrance.

_____

5. Sal was worried that he would hurt himself or myself.

_____

Name _____   Date _____

 25.2 # Pronoun and Antecedent Agreement (Four
Special Problems) • Practice 1

Four Special Problems in Pronoun Agreement   A personal pronoun should have a clear, single, close, and logical antecedent, stated or understood.

Problems	Corrections
They make a lot of mistakes in the paper.	Newspaper stories are not always accurate. That paper has many typographical errors.
Bruce told Danny *his* mother was sick.	Bruce told Danny that Danny's mother was sick. Bruce told Danny that Bruce's mother was sick.
When Joyce invited Anna and her family to come for the weekend, *she* forgot to check the date.	When Joyce invited Anna and her family …, Joyce forgot to check the date when she invited Anna and …
In English literature *you* will read Shakespeare and Milton.	A student of English literature will read Shakespeare and Milton.

▷ **Exercise 1**   **Solving Special Problems in Pronoun Agreement.**   Write the word or words from parentheses that best complete each sentence.

EXAMPLE: I thought ____*the forecasters*____ said it would rain today. (they, the forecasters)

1. The form says _____ must mail the entries by June 1. (you, contestants)

2. Mike spoke to Danny as soon as _____ got home. (he, Mike)

3. Take the dishes out of the cartons and put _____ downstairs. (them, the cartons)

4. It was rude for _____ to boo the opposing pitcher. (them, the fans)

5. The children and their parents agreed that _____ would be home before dark. (they, the children)

6. After dinner _____ can enjoy dessert on the lakeside patio. (you, guests)

7. The winner was stunned when _____ gave her the news. (they, the judges)

8. Aunt Helen told Mom what _____ had been doing. (her children, our cousins)

9. In the last year _____ may choose more electives. (you, students)

10. Why do _____ always demonstrate oxygen masks? (they, flight attendants)

▷ **Exercise 2**   **Correcting Special Problems in Pronoun Agreement.**   Rewrite each sentence below to correct any problems in pronoun agreement.

EXAMPLE: Tasha told Annie that she must not be late for the party.
         Tasha told Annie that Annie must not be late for the party.

1. Why do they always make tests so hard?

2. Sandy left the car in the garage without locking it.

3. In that program, they expect you to do a lot of independent work.

4. Paul told Steve that his bicycle had a flat tire.

5. How do they make that product look so attractive?

© Prentice-Hall, Inc.   Pronoun and Antecedent Agreement (Four Special Problems) • 149

25.2 Pronoun and Antecedent Agreement (Four Special Problems) • Practice 2

▶ **Exercise 1** **Correcting Special Problems in Pronoun Agreement.** Write the word or words from parentheses that more clearly complete each sentence.

EXAMPLE: The defendant was shocked when _____*the judge*_____ read the verdict. (they, the judge)

1. Going to a big city all alone often makes _____ feel more responsible. (you, a young person)

2. Why did _____ show that movie in the middle of the night? (they, the station)

3. William was very angry with Jonathan, but no one knew what _____ had said. (he, William)

4. Take the books from the shelves and dust _____ with a clean cloth. (them, the shelves)

5. In camp they expect _____ to rise early and exercise. (you, everyone)

6. The catalog says that _____ must pay all fees by May. (you, students)

7. He ate everything on his plate but did not even thank us for _____ . (it, the meal)

8. I liked the match, but _____ were rude. (they, the players)

9. Debby gave Rita the news right after _____ arrived. (she, Rita)

10. The phone call frightened her because _____ hung up. (they, the anonymous caller)

▶ **Exercise 2** **More Work With Special Problems in Pronoun Agreement.** Rewrite each sentence, correcting the error in pronoun agreement.

EXAMPLE: The road was dangerous because they had not yet cleared the snow.

_____*The road was dangerous because it had not yet been cleared of snow.*_____

1. When Mother shops for my sister, she is very pleased.

   _____

2. The brochure says that you must be eighteen to enlist.

   _____

3. A student must learn that homework is important to them.

   _____

4. The captain gave orders to the troops. Each man quickly took up his post. An hour later he checked to see that all was well.

   _____

5. After forgetting her lines in the show, my sister did not want to try it again.

   _____

26.1 Degrees of Comparison (Recognizing Degrees of Comparison, Regular Forms) • Practice 1

Recognizing Degrees of Comparison Most adjectives and adverbs have different forms to show degrees of comparison.

DEGREES OF COMPARISON			
	Positive	**Comparative**	**Superlative**
Adjectives	few	fewer	fewest
	recent	more recent	most recent
	bad	worse	worst
Adverbs	soon	sooner	soonest
	recently	more recently	most recently
	badly	worse	worst

Regular Forms Use—*er* or *more* to form the comparative degree and—*est* or *most* to form the superlative degree.

REGULAR FORMS OF COMPARISON			
One- and two-syllable modifiers	large	larger	largest
	pretty	prettier	prettiest
	helpless	more helpless	most helpless
Three or more syllables	beautiful	more beautiful	most beautiful
	comfortable	more comfortable	most comfortable

▷ **Exercise 1** **Recognizing Degrees of Comparison.** Identify the degree of comparison of the underlined word in each sentence by writing *pos.* (positive), *comp.* (comparative), or *sup.* (superlative).

EXAMPLE: Andrew sleeps on the <u>lower</u> bunk.   *comp.*

1. We are hoping for <u>better</u> weather tomorrow. _____
2. Lucy interviewed a <u>famous</u> movie star. _____
3. Jesse is the <u>strongest</u> pitcher in the bull pen. _____
4. This is the <u>juiciest</u> orange I ever ate. _____
5. Garlic is the <u>most strongly</u> flavored monocotyledon. _____
6. Cheetahs run <u>more swiftly</u> than any other animal. _____
7. The dancers moved <u>gracefully</u> across the stage. _____
8. That is the <u>largest</u> pizza I have ever seen. _____
9. The patient seems somewhat <u>better</u> today. _____
10. That singer has a <u>loyal</u> fan club. _____

▷ **Exercise 2** **Comparing Adjectives and Adverbs.** Write the missing forms of each modifier.

EXAMPLE: narrow ___*narrower*___ ___*narrowest*___

1. amazing _____ _____
2. _____ _____ fastest
3. _____ more rapidly _____
4. modern _____ _____
5. oddly _____ _____

26.1 Degrees of Comparison (Recognizing Degrees of Comparison, Regular Forms) • Practice 2

▶ **Exercise 1** **Recognizing Positive, Comparative, and Superlative Degrees.** Identify the degree of comparison of the underlined word in each sentence by writing *pos.* (positive), *comp.* (comparative), or *sup.* (superlative).

EXAMPLE: Today's test was the <u>hardest</u> one of all. _____sup._____

1. This is the <u>largest</u> room in the house. _____
2. Dad's health is <u>more robust</u> than it has been in years. _____
3. Your memory is <u>better</u> than mine. _____
4. The tractor moved <u>slowly</u> across the field. _____
5. Our house is the <u>farthest</u> one from the corner. _____
6. Getting medicine to the victims is <u>more urgent</u> than getting food to them. _____
7. Tim is the <u>shortest</u> player on the team. _____
8. A poet would describe the scene <u>more lyrically</u> than I. _____
9. His mother is <u>stricter</u> with him than mine is with me. _____
10. Greenwald was the <u>best-known</u> painter in the exhibition. _____
11. Marilyn is <u>happiest</u> when she is dancing. _____
12. We reminded him of his <u>important</u> responsibility. _____
13. My sister has been <u>more successful</u> than I. _____
14. The <u>finest</u> piece of jade sold for $25,000. _____
15. I thought the movie was <u>more interesting</u> than the book. _____
16. This behavior is <u>typical</u> of him. _____
17. She is <u>better</u> in biology than she is in math. _____
18. The <u>sunniest</u> day all week was Tuesday. _____
19. Copland's <u>most famous</u> piece is *Fanfare for the Common Man.* _____
20. You will feel <u>warmer</u> by the fire. _____

▶ **Exercise 2** **Forming Regular Comparative and Superlative Degrees.** Write the comparative and the superlative form of each modifier.

EXAMPLE: large _____larger_____ _____largest_____

1. tough _____ _____
2. heavy _____ _____
3. strong _____ _____
4. comfortable _____ _____
5. interesting _____ _____
6. pretty _____ _____
7. popular _____ _____
8. confusing _____ _____
9. frightening _____ _____
10. clearly _____ _____

Degrees of Comparison (Irregular Forms)
• Practice 1

Irregular Forms   The irregular comparative and superlative forms of certain adjectives and adverbs must be memorized.

IRREGULAR MODIFIERS		
Positive	**Comparative**	**Superlative**
bad	worse	worst
badly	worse	worst
far (distance)	farther	farthest
far (extent)	further	furthest
good	better	best
ill	worse	worst
late	later	last *or* latest
little (amount)	less	least
many	more	most
much	more	most
well	better	best

▶ **Exercise 1**   **Forming Irregular Comparative and Superlative Degrees.**   Write the appropriate form of the modifier in parentheses to complete each sentence.

EXAMPLE: Tanya is a ____*better*____ athlete than her twin sister. (good)

1. Soccer is the sport Eddy plays _____ of all. (well)

2. We hiked until we could go no _____. (far)

3. Hillary felt _____ about the unkind remark than about anything else. (bad)

4. Phil ate the _____ amount of food of anyone at the party. (little)

5. Elsa was the _____ guest to leave. (late)

6. Jed needed no _____ explanation. (far)

7. This is the _____ meal I ever ate. (good)

8. Suddenly the patient became _____ than before. (ill)

9. I did _____ of all on Part IV of the test. (badly)

10. This week's winner won the _____ money ever in a sweepstakes. (much)

▶ **Exercise 2**   **Using Adjectives and Adverbs to Make Comparisons.**   Use each modifier in a sentence of your own that shows a clear comparison. Use three comparative forms and two superlatives.

EXAMPLE: (many) ____*Jenny ate more cookies than I did.*____

1. (bad) _____

2. (badly) _____

3. (good) _____

4. (little) _____

5. (well) _____

26.1 # Degrees of Comparison (Irregular Forms)
• Practice 2

▶ **Exercise 1** **Forming Irregular Comparative and Superlative Degrees.** Write the appropriate form of the underlined modifier to complete each sentence.

EXAMPLE: I may have <u>little</u> money, but you have _____*less*_____ than I.

1. Cod is a <u>good</u> fish, but Boston scrod is even _____.

2. Grandmother is <u>well</u> today, but she felt even _____ yesterday.

3. Utica is <u>farther</u> from New York City than Albany, but Ithaca is the _____ from New York City of the three.

4. Trissy did <u>badly</u> on the first three tests of the term, but her performance on the final test was the _____ of all.

5. Terry is still <u>ill</u>, but she was _____ two hours ago.

6. Billy's house is <u>far</u> from the center of town, but Tom's house is even _____ away.

7. Michael danced very <u>well</u> in the contest, but Karyn danced even _____.

8. Although my mother's chocolate cake tastes very <u>good</u>, my grandmother's tastes much _____.

9. Jonathan arrived <u>late</u> for the party, and Tina and Jim arrived even _____.

10. There has been <u>much</u> talk of a tax break, but during the campaign there will be even _____.

11. There were not <u>many</u> visitors this morning, but there will be _____ this evening.

12. I thought *The Empire Strikes Back* was <u>better</u> than *Return of the Jedi*, but *Star Wars* was the _____ of the three movies.

13. Cynthia was <u>late</u> for class; Carol was _____.

14. The singer's first song during the concert was quite <u>good</u>, but his second was much _____.

15. The rehearsal went <u>well</u> today, but it went _____ yesterday.

▶ **Writing Application** **Using Adjectives and Adverbs to Make Comparisons.** Use each item in a sentence of your own.

EXAMPLE: most frightening _____*That was the most frightening movie I've ever seen.*_____

1. hungrier _____

2. proudest _____

3. farther _____

4. more quickly _____

5. fastest _____

6. most foolish _____

7. worst _____

8. good _____

9. well (as adjective) _____

10. well (as adverb) _____

26.2 Clear Comparisons (Using Comparative and Superlative Degrees) • Practice 1

Using Comparative and Superlative Degrees Use the comparative degree to compare two people, places, or things. Use the superlative degree to compare three or more people, places, or things.

Comparative (comparing two)	Superlative (comparing three or more)
I often get *higher* grades than my brother.	Of all the students in my class, Liz usually gets the *highest* grades.
One of these shoes feels *tighter* than the other.	This car can maneuver into even the *tightest* parking spaces.
If you had called *more promptly*, we could have been *more helpful*.	Ali responded the *most promptly* of everyone we invited.

▷ **Exercise 1** **Using the Comparative and Superlative Degrees Correctly.** Write the form from parentheses that correctly completes each sentence.

EXAMPLE: Paul plays the piano _____*better*_____ than Andrew. (better, best)

1. Waldo is often grumpy, but he is _____ agreeable when tired. (less, least)

2. Christine is the _____ of my five cousins. (older, oldest)

3. In this weather, the basement is the _____ place in the house (cooler, coolest)

4. Mickey Mouse is probably the _____ famous of all cartoon characters. (more, most)

5. Which of Shakespeare's plays is _____ ? (longer, longest)

6. I have never seen anyone move_____ gracefully than Margot. (more, most)

7. That fan cools the room _____ effectively than we thought it would. (more, most)

8. Which has _____ calories, the cheesecake or the chocolate mousse? (fewer, fewest)

9. At present, the _____ trains in the world are in Japan. (faster, fastest)

10. Of the three candidates, Elkins answered the questions _____ honestly. (more, most)

▷ **Exercise 2** **Recognizing Inappropriate Comparisons.** In the sentences below, underline any problems that exist in comparisons. On the line below, rewrite each sentence correctly. If a sentence contains no problem, write *correct* on the line.

EXAMPLE: Portia is one of Shakespeare's <u>famousest</u> heroines.

_____*Portia is one of Shakespeare's most famous heroines.*_____

1. Lenore studies more harder than the rest of us.

_____

2. The oldest of my two sisters is a doctor.

_____

3. Tom's problem sounds worser than it really is.

_____

4. Parents usually want what seems best for their children.

_____

5. That restaurant has the more carefully prepared food in town.

_____

26.2 Clear Comparisons (Using Comparative and Superlative Degrees) • Practice 2

▶ **Exercise 1** **Using the Comparative and Superlative Degrees Correctly.** Write the correct comparative or superlative form from parentheses to complete each sentence.

EXAMPLE: He is ____more____ patient than his sister. (more, most)

1. Which of the twins swims _____? (better, best)
2. She is the _____ talented actress in The Thespians. (more, most)
3. My sister is _____ than I. (hungrier, hungriest)
4. Are you the _____ in your family? (stronger, strongest)
5. He is _____ responsible than his older brother. (less, least)
6. She was the _____ beautiful child I've ever seen. (more, most)
7. My health is _____ today than it was yesterday. (worse, worst)
8. Of the two, Copenhagen is the _____ city. (cleaner, cleanest)
9. That actor is _____ than he appears on television. (smaller, smallest)
10. Tim is _____ willing to cooperate than his friend. (less, least)

▶ **Exercise 2** **Supplying the Comparative and Superlative Degrees.** Write the appropriate comparative or superlative degree of the modifier in parentheses.

EXAMPLE: Of the two plays, *Macbeth* is ____shorter____. (short)

1. This year, June 21 will be the _____ day of the year. (long)
2. The weather is _____ today than it was yesterday. (bad)
3. Ted is the _____ of Uncle John's three sons. (old)
4. This is the _____ train I've ever been on. (fast)
5. Today is the _____ day of my life. (happy)
6. Louise is _____ than the other dentist in town. (capable)
7. Bill is the _____ person I know. (kind)
8. Aunt Sarah is _____ this morning than she was last night. (ill)
9. Edward speaks French _____ than I do. (fluently)
10. Arthur's essay is the _____ in the class. (good)
11. St. Louis is _____ from New Orleans than Memphis is. (far)
12. Alan does _____ on English tests than I do. (well)
13. Kim is the _____ of the three children. (young)
14. This is the _____ meal I've ever eaten. (delicious)
15. Your computer is _____ than mine. (versatile)
16. Faulkner is a _____ novelist than Hemingway is. (difficult)
17. Jill arrived _____ than Joan. (late)
18. The living room is the _____ room in the house. (warm)
19. I'm feeling _____ than I did yesterday. (well)
20. This chair is _____ than that one. (comfortable)

26.2 # Clear Comparisons (Balanced Comparisons, *Other* and *Else* in Comparisons) • Practice 1

Balanced Comparisons   Make sure that your sentences compare only items of a similar kind.

Unbalanced Comparisons	Correct
Jon's score was better than *Tom*. *My record collection* is bigger than *my brother*.	*Jon's score* was better than *Tom's*. *My record collection* is bigger than *my brother's*.

***Other* and *Else* in Comparisons**   When comparing one of a group with the rest of the group, use the word *other* or the word *else*.

Illogical	Correct
John Kennedy was *younger than any* American president. Michael bats *better than anyone* on the team.	John Kennedy was *younger than any other* American president. Michael bats *better than anyone else* on the team.

▶ **Exercise 1**   **Making Balanced Comparisons.**   Rewrite each sentence, correcting the comparison.

EXAMPLE: My room is even messier than my brother.

　　　　　My room is even messier than my brother's.

1. Carol's clothes are much more elegant than Angie.

   _____

2. My brownies are richer than Aunt Polly.

   _____

3. Judson's essay was harder to understand than Len.

   _____

4. Clare's version of the story sounds even stranger than Pete.

   _____

5. The fish that I caught was even bigger than Dad.

   _____

▶ **Exercise 2**   **Using *Other* and *Else* in Comparisons.**   Rewrite each sentence, correcting the comparison.

EXAMPLE: Dave has a lower ERA than any pitcher in the league.

　　　　　Dave has a lower ERA than any other pitcher in the league.

1. Mr. Talbert is a better teacher than anyone on the faculty.

   _____

2. My brother Jason is more trustworthy than anyone in the family.

   _____

3. That chef is better than any cook in town.

   _____

4. I like Emily Dickinson's work better than any poet's.

   _____

5. Our street curves more dangerously than any road in town.

   _____

26.2 Clear Comparisons (Balanced Comparisons, *Other* and *Else* in Comparisons) • Practice 2

▶ **Exercise 1**   **Making Balanced Comparisons.**   Rewrite each sentence, correcting the unbalanced comparison.

EXAMPLE: Valerie's eyes are bluer than Annie.

_____*Valerie's eyes are bluer than Annie's.*_____

1. His swimming record is better than his chief rival.

   _____

2. Dad's cooking is better than Mom.

   _____

3. The rooms in my dorm are bigger than this hotel.

   _____

4. My gloves are in poorer condition than Sandra.

   _____

5. I like Cynthia's costume better than her twin.

   _____

6. Isn't my haircut more stylish than Joan?

   _____

7. My old bike's tires are bigger than my new bike.

   _____

8. Her coin collection is more valuable than her brother.

   _____

9. Jennifer's grades are higher than Keith.

   _____

10. My brother's wardrobe is more varied than my sister.

   _____

▶ **Exercise 2**   **Using *Other* and *Else* in Comparisons.**   Rewrite each sentence, correcting the illogical comparison.

EXAMPLE: Beth is nicer than anyone in class.

_____*Beth is nicer than anyone else in class.*_____

1. This ice cream is better than any I've ever tasted.

   _____

2. The guitarist plays better than anyone in the band.

   _____

3. Senator Hammer's record is better than any senator's.

   _____

4. Ty Cobb hit better than any baseball player.

   _____

5. He spends more money on clothing than anyone I know.

   _____

27.1 # Negative Sentences • **Practice 1**

Recognizing Double Negatives   Do not write sentences with double negatives.

Double Negatives	Correct Negative Sentences
I *can't* wait *no* longer.	I *can't* wait any longer.
	I can wait *no* longer.
Jack *isn't no* friend of mine.	Jack *isn't* a friend of mine.
	Jack is *no* friend of mine.
Why doesn't *nobody* help me?	Why *doesn't* somebody help me?
	Why does *nobody* help me?

Forming Negative Sentences Correctly   Do not use two negative words in the same clause. Do not use *but* in its negative sense with another negative. Do not use *barely, hardly,* or *scarcely* with another negative.

More Double Negatives	Correct Negative Sentences
There was*n't nothing* to do.	There was*n't* anything to do.
	There was *nothing* to do.
There is*n't but* one cookie left.	There is *but* one cookie left.
	There is *only* one cookie left.
We could*n't hardly* wait.	We could*n't wait.*
	We could hardly *wait.*

▶ **Exercise 1**   **Avoiding Problems With Negatives.**   Write the word from parentheses that makes each sentence negative without creating a double negative.

EXAMPLE: The stranded explorers had not had ___*any*___ food for days. (any, no)

1. You shouldn't have said _____ about our plans. (anything, nothing)

2. Toward the end of the movie, we _____ hardly stand the suspense. (could, couldn't)

3. Are you sure I _____ bring but one suitcase? (can, can't)

4. The missing dog _____ nowhere in sight. (was, wasn't)

5. You can be sure Tim won't eat _____ of those fish eggs. (any, none)

6. Ms. Lawson didn't say _____ about a test. (nothing, anything)

7. We don't need _____ two other players. (but, more than)

8. They can't _____ hope to win that way. (ever, never)

9. By morning, there _____ barely a trace of snow. (was, wasn't)

10. I have hardly _____ seen a more beautiful ballet. (ever, never)

▶ **Exercise 2**   **Using Negatives Correctly.**   Write a sentence of your own, correctly using each negative word given.

EXAMPLE: (barely) ____*I got barely any sleep last night.*____

1. (nowhere) _____

2. (but) _____

3. (shouldn't) _____

4. (hardly _____

5. (never) _____

Negative Sentences • Practice 2

▶ **Exercise 1** **Avoiding Double Negatives.** Write the word from parentheses that makes each sentence negative without forming a double negative.

EXAMPLE: She couldn't find ____*any*____ of the lost coins. (none, any)

1. He has never done _____ to help us. (anything, nothing)

2. I don't want _____ more spinach. (no, any)

3. We couldn't read _____ of the writing in the letter. (none, any)

4. Don't strike a match _____ near the gasoline. (anywhere, nowhere)

5. I did _____ of the things they accused me of. (none, any)

6. The children didn't eat _____ of their dinner. (any, none)

7. No one at the party ate _____ of the cake. (any, none)

8. Nobody said _____ to me about a meeting. (nothing, anything)

9. We could get _____ out of the burning house. (nothing, anything)

10. I haven't _____ more sentences to write. (no, any)

▶ **Exercise 2** **Avoiding Problems With Negatives.** Underline the word in parentheses that makes each sentence negative without creating a double negative.

EXAMPLE: John (could, couldn't) hardly believe he'd won.

1. I don't want (anything, nothing).

2. Remember that I have done (anything, nothing) wrong.

3. Lila (could, couldn't) scarcely catch her breath.

4. We haven't (any, no) strong feelings about it.

5. I couldn't have (anything, nothing) for dessert.

6. There (were, weren't) but three choices.

7. I (can, can't) hardly believe my eyes.

8. Don't you have (anything, nothing) more exciting to read?

9. She doesn't write to me (any, no) more.

10. Luke (had, hadn't) but two days of provisions left when he was found.

▶ **Exercise 3** **Correcting Double Negatives.** Rewrite each sentence, correcting the double negative.

EXAMPLE: Dad would never accept no charity.
_____*Dad would never accept any charity.*_____

1. I promise that I won't tell nobody.

_____

2. Mary can't hardly read the small print.

_____

3. My father hadn't never been to Athens.

_____

4. I haven't but a few minutes left to work.

_____

5. She didn't have no lunch.

_____

27.2 # Fifty Common Usage Problems • **Practice 1**

Solving Usage Problems   Study the items in the usage glossary in your textbook, paying particular attention to similar spellings, words that should never be used, pairs that are often misused, and problems with verb forms.

TYPES OF PROBLEMS	
Similar Spellings	*accept* and *except; than* and *then*
Wrong Words	*ain't alright somewheres*
Misused Pairs	*among* and *between; bring* and *take*
Verb Forms	*has done should have*

▶ **Exercise 1**   Avoiding Some Common Usage Problems.   Write the word from parentheses that correctly completes each sentence.

EXAMPLE: Free ____*advice*____ is often worth what it costs. (advice, advise)

1. This lawn mower _____ work as well as it used to. (don't, doesn't)

2. Mom told Paul he had _____ in bed long enough. (laid, lain)

3. I should _____ known he couldn't keep a secret. (have, of)

4. Air pollution _____ elderly people most of all. (affects, effects)

5. The twins and I had only two dollars _____ us. (among, between)

6. Will you _____ this book back to the library when you go? (bring, take)

7. My answer to the last problem is different _____ yours. (from, than)

8. Carrot and celery sticks make a good and _____ snack. (healthful, healthy)

9. Customers with _____ than six items can use the express line. (fewer, less)

10. Who says you can't _____ an old dog new tricks. (learn, teach)

▶ **Exercise 2**   Avoiding Other Common Usage Problems.   Write the word from parentheses that correctly completes each sentence.

EXAMPLE: What are your ideas ____*about*____ the best solution? (about, as to)

1. When are they going to _____ the flag? (rise, raise)

2. I was _____ disappointed in the result. (kind of, somewhat)

3. Let's go _____ the lobby to wait for them. (in, into)

4. A few fans _____ in the bleachers in spite of the rain. (sat, set)

5. This short cut seems _____ than the regular way. (farther, further)

6. _____ the chips fall where they may. (Leave, Let)

7. The player _____ pinch hit for the pitcher struck out. (that, which)

8. The hikers still had a long _____ to go before nightfall. (way, ways)

9. The _____ of the new drug are not fully known. (affects, effects)

10. The prisoner returned to jail that night _____ he said he would. (as, like)

Fifty Common Usage Problems • Practice 2

▶ **Exercise 1** **Avoiding Usage Problems.** Write the correct expression from the parentheses to complete each sentence.

EXAMPLE: The ___effects___ of the experiment startled us. (affects, effects)

1. I can't find my classes _____. (anywhere, anywheres)

2. I hope you can _____ him properly. (advice, advise)

3. Everyone visited the museum _____ my father. (accept, except)

4. There _____ a dry eye in the auditorium. (ain't, isn't)

5. Is everything _____ at home? (all right, alright)

6. The horses were huddled _____. (all together, altogether)

7. Are you _____ to go? (all ready, already)

8. What is the _____ of the new law? (affect, effect)

9. Pete _____ the machine for a particular job. (adapted, adopted)

10. Your _____ was very helpful. (advice, advise)

▶ **Exercise 2** **Avoiding Usage Problems.** Write the correct expression from the parentheses to complete each sentence.

1. The old man stood _____ the tree. (beside, besides)

2. _____ you asked, I will tell you the story. (Being that, Since)

3. _____ your empty tray over here. (Bring, Take)

4. The sergeant _____ into the room. (burst, busted)

5. This new pen is much different _____ my old one. (from, than)

6. I can't help _____ to go with you. (but want, wanting)

7. I don't know where _____. (I'm at, I am)

8. They had no suggestions _____ what to do next on our vacation. (as to, about)

9. Practice is canceled _____ the coach is sick. (being as, because)

10. The reason I am not going is _____ I am exhausted from my trip yesterday. (because, that)

▶ **Exercise 3** **Avoiding Usage Problems.** Write the correct expression from the parentheses to complete each sentence.

1. My brother _____ care much for rock music. (doesn't, don't)

2. We _____ our French homework already. (done, have done)

3. I have _____ classical records in my collection than my sister does. (fewer, less)

4. My parents _____ to a movie. (gone, have gone)

5. There was _____ damage after the tornado than we had expected at first. (fewer, less)

6. _____ his poor record, he was dropped from the team. (Due to, Because of)

7. _____ your friend care whether you borrow his new bicycle? (Doesn't, Don't)

8. I _____ all that I can for you. (done, have done)

9. His explanation led her to seek _____ answers from other experts in the field. (farther, further)

10. The diver jumped _____ the water from the cliff. (in, into)

Capitalization (Sentences) • **Practice 1**

Capitals for Sentences   To capitalize means to begin a word with a capital letter. Capitalize the first word in a sentence. Capitalize the first word in a quotation if the quotation is a complete sentence. Capitalize the first word after a colon if the word begins a complete sentence.

SENTENCES THAT STAND ALONE
Declarative: The trail leads to the river bank. *Interrogative:* What is the name of your favorite novel? *Imperative:* Take a taxi to the airport terminal. *Exclamatory:* What a pleasant surprise!
SENTENCES IN QUOTATIONS
Mother replied, "You'll have to work harder." "You'll have to work harder, " Mother replied.
SENTENCES AFTER COLONS
Everyone asked the same question: How will we raise funds?

▶ **Exercise 1**   **Using Capitals to Begin Sentences.**   Underline the word or words that should be capitalized in each sentence.

EXAMPLE: sally asked, "can I help pack?"

1. after school, I often work on my coin collection.

2. this is the problem: we can't afford a new car.

3. we joined the volleyball team last year.

4. the doctor said, "exercise and get enough rest."

5. how will we get to the ballpark from the station?

6. the treasurer explained our goal: we must raise five hundred dollars.

7. how happy we were to see our cousins!

8. my teacher asked, "who has completed the report?"

9. mark includes radishes and scallions in his salads.

10. have you read a good biography this year?

▶ **Exercise 2**   **Using Capitalized Words.**   Complete each sentence by adding an appropriate capitalized word.

EXAMPLE: Billy replied, " _____Peaches_____ are my favorite fruit."

1. _____ are a good source of protein.

2. Father said, "_____ phoned last night."

3. _____ , would you reply to that question?

4. Here is the problem: _____ is too expensive.

5. _____ laughed, "I can't remember her name."

6. _____ the letter in the morning.

7. _____ would make the best treasurer?

8. This is important: _____ follow the directions exactly.

9. _____ teacher said, "Please write the paper over."

10. We agreed, "_____ can't start again."

Capitalization (Sentences) • Practice 2

Exercise 1 **Using Capitalization Correctly in Sentences.** Underline the word or words that should be capitalized in each sentence.

EXAMPLE: what a difficult mountain that was to climb!

1. show me what you are holding in your hand, young man.
2. getting my school schedule worked out for next year is causing problems.
3. "every hero becomes a bore at last, " observed Emerson.
4. when will dinner be ready?
5. my grandmother taught me one important lesson: giving more than 100 percent is the surest way to get ahead.
6. we found a twenty-dollar bill on the sidewalk!
7. at one time Confucius warned, "the cautious seldom err."
8. the store down the street is holding a big sale today.
9. will you go on many weekend ski trips this winter?
10. sit still while the barber finishes cutting your hair.
11. "if you would wish another to keep your secret, " advised Seneca, "first keep it yourself."
12. where did you take the camera to be repaired?
13. we saw quite a feat at the circus: a young man did a high-wire act without any safety nets below him.
14. the company gave us a substantial salary increase today!
15. many people put more salt on their food than is healthful.
16. they spent yesterday buying gifts: a stuffed panda, an electric razor, and a giant rubber plant.
17. "we can stay as long as we want, " she said. "they have given us permission."
18. what in the world were you thinking of?
19. "why not try, " she asked, "to climb a mountain?"
20. he was afraid: he had never climbed a mountain.

Exercise 2 **Using Capitalization Correctly in Paragraphs.** Underline the words that should be capitalized in the following paragraphs.

karly said, "yesterday i was walking through the woods, and a porcupine crossed my path."

phil answered, "the porcupine is such a strange animal. did you know," he continued, "that people who live in the mountains often call the porcupine a quill-pig?"

"yes, i did know that," answered Karly. "the animal is certainly as clumsy and slow-moving as any pig, but it is not a pig at all. it is actually a rodent, with sharp teeth somewhat like those of a rabbit or a squirrel. even though it is a mere rodent, nearly every other wild creature in the forest is afraid to attack it. do you know why?"

"well, yes, i do," said Phil. "the reason is this: the porcupine's body is thickly sprinkled with stiff, needle-sharp quills. these quills are from half an inch to four inches long. a porcupine might have as many as 20, 000 or 25, 000 of these peculiar weapons. interestingly, when one is lost, a new one grows quickly to replace it. if you were a forest creature, you'd probably be afraid of porcupines, too!"

28 # Capitalization (Proper Nouns, Proper Adjectives)
• Practice 1

Capitals for Proper Nouns   Capitalize all proper nouns.

PROPER NOUNS	
Names of people: Jane Eyre	*Geographic names:* Pikes Peak
Specific events: World Series	*Organizations:* Rotary Club
Religious references: God	*Special items:* Pulitzer Prize

Capitals for Proper Adjectives   Capitalize most proper adjectives.

With Capitals	Without Capitals
a Broadway play	Common terms: french fries
a Mexican treaty	Most prefixes: pro-American event
a Franklin stove	Parts of compounds: French-speaking tourists

▶ **Exercise 1**   **Recognizing Proper Nouns and Proper Adjectives.**   Underline the proper nouns
and proper adjectives that should be capitalized.

EXAMPLE: I visit <u>canada</u> each summer.

1. In europe she visited france and belgium.

2. I know that william faulkner received a nobel prize.

3. Will ted develop into an all-american?

4. Ask judy whether she wants some french fries.

5. My family always buys the same brand of televisions and radios, electrosonic.

6. The chamber of commerce sponsored the contest.

7. The cuban exiles chanted pro-american slogans.

8. Many people pray to god and read the bible.

9. The fortress of louisbourg is in nova scotia.

10. Have you met any french-speaking canadians?

▶ **Exercise 2**   **Using Proper Nouns and Proper Adjectives.**   Fill in each blank with a proper noun
or proper adjective.

EXAMPLE: My favorite two cities are ____*Boston*____ and ____*Chicago*____

1. Frank wants a _____ camera for his birthday.

2. Last summer she traveled to _____ and _____.

3. Nancy is an all- _____ field hockey player.

4. _____ is the writer I like the best.

5. The professional football season ends with the _____.

6. I live in _____.

7. After the meeting, I spoke to _____ and _____.

8. The _____ River passes through several states.

9. Sudan and Nigeria are on the _____ continent.

10. In my religion we study the _____.

Capitalization (Proper Nouns, Proper Adjectives)
• Practice 2

▶ **Exercise 1** **Capitalizing Proper Nouns.** Underline the words that should be capitalized.

EXAMPLE: After the sun sets, <u>venus</u> will be visible in the west.

1. To see a play that has been running for twenty-five years, you should go to st. martin's theater in london.

2. One well-known suspension bridge is the golden gate, which spans san francisco bay.

3. Both the shoshone and the arapaho make up a part of the population of wyoming.

4. By checking a perpetual calendar, I found that benjamin franklin was born on sunday, january 17, 1706.

5. In the northeast winters are quite harsh and long.

6. Astronauts will probably visit jupiter some day.

7. The lowest point in all north america is in death valley.

8. thomas mckean, a lawyer from pennsylvania, signed the declaration of independence.

9. Some of the major airline companies that went bankrupt were eastern, national, and people's express.

10. In october 1976, congress repealed the homestead act of 1862 since there was no longer any land available for homesteading.

11. In ancient mythology the goddess athena dispensed wisdom.

12. The kentucky derby is held annually in the spring at churchill downs.

13. A well-known race horse, secretariat, won many races.

14. The torah, the talmud, and the midrash are the sacred writings of judaism.

15. You can find out about the great smoky mountains by writing to the chamber of commerce, 505 fesslers lane, nashville, tennessee 37210.

16. I think arabic is a difficult language to master.

17. The nebula award is presented for outstanding works of science fiction.

18. The nuclear regulatory commission regulates all civilian uses of atomic energy.

19. The white house uses the blue room as its official reception room.

20. About one half of our national leaders have been republicans and the other half have been democrats.

▶ **Exercise 2** **Capitalizing Proper Adjectives.** Underline the words that should be capitalized.

EXAMPLE: I am taking a <u>chinese</u> cooking course.

1. Open-air theaters are often used for the performance of elizabethan plays.

2. Many african american groups have held several conferences during the past few years to discuss their heritage.

3. Large crowds at an american political rally gave the police some crowd-control problems.

4. The anglo-saxon invasion of Britain took place in the fifth and sixth centuries.

5. Some early buddhist monasteries were caves that were elegantly carved and decorated.

6. Her old pictureperfect camera accompanied her on all her travels.

7. A sino-russian pact could have a significant effect on foreign policy.

8. Those who own pre-columbian sculptures have valuable art pieces in their possession.

9. A lovely indian woman in a sari came into the store asking for the manager.

10. The franklin d. roosevelt years were marred by World War II.

Capitalization (for Titles, in Letters) • Practice 1

Capitals for Titles   Capitalize titles of people and titles of works.

People	Works
Doctor Vance	*Great Expectations*
Colonel Andrews	*News Review Magazine*
the President	"Gunga Din"
Grandfather Wilkins	"The Cask of Amontillado"
Mr., Ms., Dr., Jr.	*Portrait of a Man with a Red Cap*

Capitals in Letters   Capitalize the first word and all nouns in letter salutations and the first word in letter closings.

Salutations	Closings
Dear Cousin Beth,	Yours truly,
Dear Dr. Stanton:	Sincerely yours,
My dear Friends,	Very truly yours,

▶ **Exercise 1**   **Using Capitals in Titles.**   Underline the words that should be capitalized.

EXAMPLE: I just read Frost's "at woodward's gardens."

1. I lunched with captain perez yesterday.
2. Susan just finished reading "the most dangerous game."
3. The chief justice of the United States just resigned.
4. What are the symptoms of this disease, doctor gilbert?
5. We saw *portrait of a lady* at the National Gallery.
6. Can I borrow your copy of *the member of the wedding*?
7. Have you been introduced to bishop wilson?
8. I know that ms. greer and mr. kelly will volunteer.
9. Does *nature's beauty magazine* still have great photos?
10. I bought a copy of Grant Wood's *american gothic.*

▶ **Exercise 2**   **Using Capitals for Salutations and Closings.**   Rewrite each of the following letter parts, adding the missing capitals.

EXAMPLE: dear aunt maria, _____*Dear Aunt Maria,*_____

1. dear mr. stevenson, _____
2. respectfully yours, _____
3. my dear uncle, _____
4. very truly yours, _____
5. dear senator brock: _____
6. sincerely yours, _____
7. affectionately, _____
8. dear colonel cobb: _____
9. dear ms. brody: _____
10. with deepest regret, _____

Capitalization (for Titles, in Letters) • **Practice 2**

▶ **Exercise 1**   **Capitalizing Titles of People.**   Underline the words and abbreviations that should be capitalized.

EXAMPLE: The recruits saluted <u>major general caruthers</u>.

1. Could you direct me, sir, to this address?

2. We invited dr. and mrs. strutner to the play.

3. One of the greatest mystery writers of all time was dame agatha christie.

4. It is my great pleasure to present the president of the United States.

5. The ex-secretary of state is writing his memoirs.

6. Lieutenant governor taylor ran our state last week while governor hull was away on a business trip.

7. We expect colonel green to inspect the troops today.

8. We visited grandmother, who teaches in a small country school.

9. Please tell us, senator, how you expect to vote.

10. The reverend john hyder and father madison met to discuss some of the concerns facing their parishes.

▶ **Exercise 2**   **Capitalizing Titles of Things.**   Underline the words that should be capitalized.

EXAMPLE: Have you read the novel *the red pony* by Steinbeck?

1. *the financial journal* is a respected newspaper that presents news from the point of view of business people.

2. The only classes they are offering that I want to take are psychology, german, and art.

3. The story "the lottery" by Shirley Jackson makes the reader contemplate some of humanity's baser instincts.

4. When registration opened, english 1A, biology 45, and all the calculus courses filled up immediately.

5. *the making of the past: the egyptian kingdoms* contains some excellent pictures of ancient tomb treasures.

6. Robert Graves based much of his novel *i, claudius* on the Roman historian Suetonius's *the lives of the caesars*.

7. Loren Eisley's *the man who saw through time* is a collection of essays about the Elizabethan scientist Francis Bacon.

8. Edgar Allan Poe once wrote a very fine poem entitled "a dream within a dream."

9. One of Phyllis McGinley's best books for children is *the horse who lived upstairs*.

10. *measure for measure* is one of Shakespeare's lesser-known plays.

29.1 # End Marks • **Practice 1**

Uses of the Period   Use a period to end a declarative or imperative sentence, an indirect question, and most abbreviations.

PERIODS
Declarative Sentence: The stone is large and smooth. *Interrogative Sentence:* Open the window about six inches. *Indirect Question:* I asked him what he wanted. *Abbreviations:* Conn. (Connecticut) Rd. (Road)

Uses of the Question Mark   Use a question mark to end an interrogative sentence.

QUESTION MARKS
Interrogative Sentence: What is your telephone number?

Uses of the Exclamation Mark   Use an exclamation mark to end an exclamatory sentence, an urgent imperative sentence, and most interjections.

EXCLAMATION MARKS
Exclamatory Sentence: What a remarkable pass! *Imperative Sentence:* Don't let go of the wheel! *Interjection:* Good grief ! She won.

▶ **Exercise 1**   **Using End Marks Correctly.**   Write the proper end mark at the end of each item.

EXAMPLE: What a wonderful achievement ___!___

1. How many pairs of shoes do you have _____
2. Beethoven wrote nine symphonies _____
3. I have an interview with Rinaldo and Son, Inc _____
4. June won the first prize. Hurray _____
5. We asked them when they wanted to leave _____
6. Some batteries contain sulfuric acid _____
7. Where is Ethiopia _____
8. What an astounding performance _____
9. Have you read *A Day No Pigs Would Die* _____
10. Choose another uniform _____

▶ **Exercise 2**   **Supplying End Marks.**   Write a sentence using each of the following end marks.

EXAMPLE: Period ___*She wrote a report on proper manners.*___

1. Question Mark _____
2. Exclamation Mark _____
3. Period _____
4. Question Mark _____
5. Exclamation Mark _____

29.1 End Marks • Practice 2

▶ **Exercise 1**   **Using the Period Correctly.**   Add the necessary periods to the following sentences.

EXAMPLE: John R Carlson asked you to return his call
  John R. Carlson asked you to return his call.

1. The American humorist S J Perelman was once a scriptwriter for the Marx Brothers
2. My parents wondered what grade I received on the test
3. Address the package to Mr Arthur Grover, Jr
4. I think Elizabeth Bishop is a fine modern American poet
5. She prefers the title Mrs to the title Ms
6. I asked Mrs Ramos to go with us
7. Schedule a certain amount of time for studying every day
8. Elizabeth P Peabody started the first kindergarten in the United States in 1860
9. The son of Efrem Zimbalist, Sr, a violinist, is an actor
10. Dr Elvira M Thackery spoke at the seminar

▶ **Exercise 2**   **Using the Question Mark Correctly.**   Some of the following sentences are direct questions and require question marks. Others are indirect questions and require periods. Add the necessary punctuation.

EXAMPLE: What was comedian Milton Berle's nickname
  What was comedian Milton Berle's nickname?____?____

1. How much money did Lucille Ball make from her television series _____
2. Many have wondered whether more people watched Lucille Ball or President Eisenhower's inauguration _____
3. How did Dinah Shore customarily end her shows _____
4. Who was known as Mr. Television _____
5. What were two of the popular TV shows that children of the 1950's liked to watch _____
6. Before 1951, what percentage of the American public was asleep by midnight _____
7. Some wondered whether shows like the Steve Allen and Jack Paar talk shows were responsible for people staying up later _____
8. In what TV show did Mary Martin fly through the air on wires _____
9. In what show did audiences see Joe Friday _____
10. During the 1953–1954 season, which show was rated first _____

▶ **Exercise 3**   **Using the Exclamation Mark Correctly.**   Add the necessary exclamation marks to the following items. Then identify each use as *exclamatory, imperative,* or *interjection.*

EXAMPLE: What a terrifying movie that was
  What a terrifying movie that was! ____*exclamatory*____

1. Our dog had four puppies last night _____
2. There goes the thief _____
3. Quick hide Mother's birthday present _____
4. Help me _____
5. We have just three minutes before the plane takes off _____

29.2

Commas That Separate Basic Elements
(Compound Sentences, Items in a Series, Adjectives)
• Practice 1

Commas With Compound Sentences   Use a comma before the coordinating conjunction in a compound sentence.

COMPOUND SENTENCES
Jose wanted to attend the game, but he decided to do his report instead.
Either we will win tonight, or we will have to face a sad crowd afterward.

Commas Between Items in a Series   Use commas to separate three or more words, phrases, or clauses in a series.

SERIES
Ellen bought new jeans, a plaid skirt, and a pair of gloves.
They drove to the post office, parked the car, and unloaded the boxes.

Commas Between Adjectives   Use commas to separate adjectives of equal rank. (Do not use commas to separate adjectives that must stay in a specific order.)

With Commas	Without Commas
A narrow, rough road led to the country market.	Many new books on sports are on display in the library.

> **Exercise 1**   **Using Commas Correctly.**   Add commas where they are required. One sentence needs no commas.

EXAMPLE: During the night it rained but the day was brilliant.
　　　　　　During the night it rained, but the day was brilliant.

1. Mary Grace lives in a dark wooded area.

2. The crash awoke Father and he jumped out of bed.

3. Buy tomatoes cucumbers scallions and lettuce.

4. An exhausted discouraged team limped into the locker room.

5. Betty must have reached home safely or she would have phoned.

6. I found many old stamps in Grandfather's collection.

7. The rain has stopped but it is still very humid.

8. An angry determined speaker addressed the mayor.

9. Frank planned to read his speech but he lost his notes.

10. I prepared a salad cooked a roast and baked some cookies.

> **Exercise 2**   **Understanding the Use of Commas.**   The sentences below are correctly punctuated. Identify the use of commas by writing the words *compound, series,* or *adjectives.*

EXAMPLE: She stared at the horizon lined with old, withered trees. ____*adjectives*____

1. I will take the train, or I will drive to work. _____

2. Steve bought an umbrella, boots, and a rain hat. _____

3. A happy, smiling crowd greeted the contestants. _____

4. You must go, but I will stay. _____

5. She wanted to go swimming, get some sun, and just relax. _____.

Name _____ Date _____

 # Commas That Separate Basic Elements
(Compound Sentences, Items in a Series, Adjectives)
• Practice 2

▶ **Exercise 1** **Using Commas With Compound Sentences.** Add the necessary commas.

EXAMPLE: I have been sending funny Valentine cards to many of my friends every year but I never place my name on them.

I have been sending funny Valentine cards to many of my friends every year, but I never place my name on them.

(1) Valentine's Day is celebrated by most Americans yet few people know the story of how the holiday first began. (2) The holiday originated in ancient Rome but the actual date of its origin is about A.D. 270. (3) According to legend Emperor Claudius II would not allow the troops of the Roman army to marry for he felt that married men made poor soldiers. (4) A priest called Valentinus took pity on two young lovers and he secretly married them against Emperor Claudius's orders. (5) Valentinus was arrested and thrown in jail and Claudius had him beheaded several months later. (6) It was from this Roman jail that the first Valentine card was sent for Valentinus supposedly cured the jailer's daughter of blindness and sent her a note signed "From Your Valentine." (7) You may want to believe this legend or you may feel that this is just a romantic tale that was concocted to explain the origin of Valentine's Day. (8) The first Valentines in America were not covered with sweet verses nor were they elaborate and lacy works of art. (9) Boys and girls of the late 1850's loved to send "Penny Dreadfuls" on Valentine's Day and they looked forward to receiving them from their friends in turn. (10) A typical Penny Dreadful might contain a message such as this one: 'Tis all in vain your fluttering lids, your curly hair, your tinted cheeks, for finding you a Valentine will take at least a HUNDRED weeks!

▶ **Exercise 2** **Using Commas Between Items in a Series.** Add commas to each sentence that needs them. If a sentence does not need commas, write *correct.*

EXAMPLE: The speaker was intelligent talented and poised.

The speaker was intelligent, talented, and poised.

1. The student driver nervously pressed down the accelerator turned the key and put the car in gear. _____

2. The flash flood raced through the narrow canyon over the flatlands and into the town's main street. _____

3. Mrs. Robertson offered the children peanut butter and jelly bacon and avocado or cheese and bologna sandwiches. _____

4. The children bowled the parents kept score and the grandparents watched. _____

5. He ate breakfast she read the newspaper and then they both left for work. _____

6. The sheepdog pushed and coaxed and prodded his stubborn charges into their pens. _____

7. Skiing skating and dancing burn up many calories. _____

8. The physician said he wanted to take some X-rays check the results and call us later in the day. _____

9. Did you pack a bathing suit pajamas a sweatshirt and a toothbrush? _____

10. The ball flew over the pitcher's head above the center fielder's glove and into a spectator's waiting hands. _____

29.2 Commas That Set Off Added Elements
(Introductory Material, Parenthetical Expressions)
• Practice 1

Commas After Introductory Material   Use a comma after an introductory word, phrase, or clause.

INTRODUCTORY MATERIAL
Introductory Word: No, I don't think I can go.
Introductory Phrase: Reaching the lake, she searched for her canoe.
Introductory Clause: When she entered the building, she was confused and frightened.

Commas With Parenthetical Expressions   Use commas to set off parenthetical expressions.

PARENTHETICAL EXPRESSIONS
Names of People Being Addressed: I know, *Susan,* that you will do well.
Certain Adverbs: I decided, *therefore,* to wait.
Common Expressions: Mr. Wong agreed, *I believe,* to go.
Contrasting Expressions: The room is narrow, *not wide.*

▶ **Exercise 1**   **Recognizing Introductory Material.**   Write the introductory word, phrase, or clause in each sentence, and add the needed comma.

EXAMPLE: Yes I will attend. _____*Yes,*_____

1. No I'm afraid his excuse was not acceptable. _____
2. To grow corn you need fertile soil. _____
3. Determined she stalked into the office. _____
4. If she sings I'm sure she will win. _____
5. Waiting patiently she saw the bear emerge. _____
6. When I try I can write very well. _____
7. Since you wrote the situation has changed entirely. _____
8. Cary why don't you use my typewriter? _____
9. To improve our game we practiced every night. _____
10. Really I'm not sure about this new plan of yours. _____

▶ **Exercise 2**   **Using Commas Correctly.**   Add commas where they are needed in each sentence.

EXAMPLE: His ability not his personality is the issue.
　　　　　His ability, not his personality, is the issue.

1. Her room unfortunately is right over the garage.
2. Mrs. Eriksen will you explain that answer again.
3. Our vacation is near the end of July not in August.
4. Although she is excellent at ballet she prefers modern dance.
5. His refusal I am certain can easily be explained.
6. Smiling happily she raced to the front door.
7. You know of course that the President will speak.
8. Yes I certainly would like to visit Walden Pond.
9. To stop the retreat the army landed paratroopers.
10. The decision consequently was reversed by the court.

29.2

Commas That Set Off Added Elements
(Introductory Material, Parenthetical Expressions)
• Practice 2

▶ **Exercise 1** **Using Commas After Introductory Material.** Underline the introductory word, phrase, or clause in each sentence, adding any necessary commas.

EXAMPLE: Boys and girls welcome to the Winchester House.
<u>Boys and girls,</u> welcome to the Winchester House.

(1) After you hear about Sarah Winchester you will probably agree that she was an eccentric woman. (2) Following a short and romantic courtship Sarah Pardee married William Winchester of Winchester rifles. (3) Upon her husband's death Sarah inherited twenty million dollars from his estate. (4) Fearing the ghosts of people killed by Winchester guns she felt she must build continuously to keep them from haunting her. (5) With a great deal of determination she bought an eighteen-room house and hired sixteen workmen to add rooms to it. (6) To keep the ghosts confused she had doors open into brick walls and stairs lead up into the ceiling. (7) Oh the workmen must have thought her strange, but good wages kept them building for thirty-eight years. (8) Testing their loyalty to her Mrs. Winchester occasionally had the gardeners plant her orange trees upside down. (9) When she died it took six moving vans and six weeks to empty the house. (10) Within her 160-room mansion carpenters had installed 2,000 doors and 10,000 windows.

▶ **Exercise 2** **Using Commas With Parenthetical Expressions.** Add the necessary commas to set off the parenthetical expressions in each sentence.

EXAMPLE: It is warm enough I think to plant the tomatoes.
It is warm enough, I think, to plant the tomatoes.

1. The new plants however did not survive the frost.
2. I will vacuum Hazel if you will wash the windows.
3. He went to Harvard Law School I believe.
4. The young rascal furthermore put salt in my sugar bowl.
5. Spread lime in the garden not near the evergreens.
6. Typing your paper you know will make it easier to read.
7. The plane therefore did not arrive on time.
8. Tennis not golf is my favorite sport.
9. May I help you carry that package Mr. Goodman?
10. If it rains the picnic will be postponed until next week I suppose.
11. Did you know Cynthia that tomorrow is Dan's birthday?
12. Aunt Marie similarly enjoys wearing large hats.
13. The twins in any case will be here by noon.
14. Dr. Sanchez not Dr. Monroe is my dentist.
15. Did you have an appointment Ms. Martinez?
16. The backyard on the other hand is well tended.
17. The newspapers and paperbacks however should be recycled.
18. She is friendly enough in my opinion to be a good social coordinator.
19. Dina likes apple not pecan pie.
20. The leaves of course should be raked.

Commas That Set Off Added Elements
(Nonessential Expressions) • Practice 1

Commas With Nonessential Expressions A nonessential expression, short or long, gives additional information about someone or something in a sentence. Because it can be left out without changing the basic meaning of the sentence, it is set off with commas.

ESSENTIAL AND NONESSENTIAL EXPRESSIONS
Essential: My cousin *the computer expert* is growing rich.
Nonessential: Cathy, *a computer expert*, knows BASIC and COBOL.
Essential: The man *standing in the corridor* is the principal.
Nonessential: Dr. Rogers, *now standing in the corridor*, is the principal.
Essential: The boy *who lives in the next house* plays the French horn.
Nonessential: My cousin Phil, *who lives in the next house*, plays the French horn.

▶ **Exercise 1** **Using Commas With Nonessential Expressions.** Add commas to set off nonessential expressions. Not every sentence contains a nonessential expression.

EXAMPLE: Our new car a used Ford has radial tires.
            Our new car, a used Ford, has radial tires.

1. Jackie Robinson a fine hitter was a daring base runner.

2. The girl who leads the chorus speaks three languages.

3. Mendelssohn who was born in 1809 gave his first performance at the age of nine.

4. Alex who works after school makes the Honor Roll each year.

5. The flowers growing in the window box were purchased in a nursery.

6. Ottawa the capital of Canada is a beautiful, clean city.

7. The tape recorder that he wants is very expensive.

8. The story "The Scarlet Ibis" is about the relationship of two brothers.

9. This is Sagamore Hill the home of Theodore Roosevelt.

10. Nashville which is near the center of Tennessee is the home of country music.

▶ **Exercise 2** **Writing Essential and Nonessential Expressions.** Complete each sentence. Set off the nonessential expressions with commas.

EXAMPLE: Her shoes _____, a pair of sandals,_____ were surprisingly uncomfortable.

1. The woman _____ will tell you where his office is.

2. We visited San Francisco and Los Angeles _____ .

3. March _____ was rapidly approaching

4. Stop by and see Mrs. Harding _____ .

5. The program _____ was very boring.

6. The car _____ is my brother's.

7. His grandfather _____ tutors students in math.

8. Snacks _____ will be served at intermission.

9. We saw slides of my two favorite cities _____ .

10. The dog _____ was barking loudly.

29.2 Commas That Set Off Added Elements
(Nonessential Expressions) • Practice 2

▶ **Exercise 1**   **Using Commas With Nonessential Expressions.**   Add commas to set off all nonessential expressions in the following sentences.

EXAMPLE: Esmeralda our curious and friendly dog likes to explore the neighborhood.
Esmeralda, our curious and friendly dog, likes to explore the neighborhood.

 1. My orthodontist who just came back from a trip to Hawaii tightened my braces.

 2. The woman who was hired as a company consultant made some fine suggestions to the management.

 3. The President's wife is the one boarding the plane right now.

 4. Calligraphy the art of beautiful writing takes practice and skill in order for one to become proficient at it.

 5. The suit worn by the model on the left probably costs a fortune.

 6. The museum held the saddle of John Wayne one of the most famous Hollywood cowboys.

 7. Have you ever visited the Alamo a fascinating building in Texas?

 8. Yosemite Falls which drops 2,425 feet to the river below almost dries up after a hot summer.

 9. Joanne Lewis who happens to be my cousin writes news articles for local television.

10. Pélé a famous soccer player from Brazil played in the United States several years ago.

11. This strange locust which spends seventeen years developing in the earth lives only six weeks as an adult.

12. Dinosaurs the animals that dominated the earth for over 140 million years became extinct 65 million years ago.

13. The newborn guppy called a fry must swim to the surface and take a gulp of air before it can swim well.

14. Mark Twain the author of *The Adventures of Huckleberry Finn* used a riverboat term as his pen name.

15. Patricia's last vacation a bicycle trip across China did not cost as much as she had anticipated.

▶ **Exercise 2**   **Writing Sentences With Nonessential Expressions.**   Write a sentence for each nonessential expression. Be sure to set off the nonessential expression with a comma or commas.

EXAMPLE: the capital of our state

_____ *Sacramento, the capital of our state, has a diverse population.* _____

 1. Alex's best friend

    _____

 2. my neighbor's cat

    _____

 3. the first one to taste the soup

    _____

 4. Tim's favorite program

    _____

 5. who means a great deal to me

    _____

29.2

Commas That Set Off Added Elements
(Places, Dates, Titles, Other Uses) • Practice 1

Commas With Places, Dates, and Titles When a geographical name or a date is made up of two or more parts, use a comma after each item except in the case of a month followed by a day. Use commas to set off a title following a name.

Geographical Name	Houston, Texas, is a rapidly growing city.
Date	On September 19, 1939, German panzers invaded Poland.
Name With Title	Jim Thon, M.D., discussed safe ways to lose weight.

Other Uses of the Comma Use commas in the situations shown in the chart below.

Address	Send the package to J. Brown, 10 Elk Lane, Glen Cove, New York 11542.
Salutation and Closing	Dear Peter, Very truly yours,
Numbers	31,654 envelopes
Elliptical Sentence	Lorraine plays the guitar; her brother Sam, the flute.
Direct Quotation	"In a few minutes," laughed Julio, "you'll know the surprise."
To Prevent Confusion	For Carla, Jonas had designed a unique costume.

▶ **Exercise 1** **Adding Commas to Sentences.** Insert commas where they are needed.

EXAMPLE: Sean Miles D.D.S. lectured on dental hygiene.
　　　　　　Sean Miles, D.D.S., lectured on dental hygiene.

1. Write to Real-Trucks 72 Wall Avenue Norwalk Connecticut 06850.

2. The math assignment took forty-five minutes; the science an hour.

3. The population of the next county is 42375.

4. The band director remarked "We'll have our next rehearsal on January 10."

5. John Briggs Jr. inherited his father's business.

6. After the storm clouds were white and fleecy.

7. On June 20 1793 Eli Whitney applied for a patent for his cotton gin.

8. In 1957 the United States had 1558691 hospital beds in 6818 hospitals.

9. "For the last time" exclaimed Sue "will you be quiet!"

10. In spring planting begins.

▶ **Exercise 2** **Punctuating a Letter.** Add commas wherever necessary in the following letter.

　　　　　　　　　　　　　　154 Morris Drive
　　　　　　　　　　　　　　Los Angeles California 90039
　　　　　　　　　　　　　　October 12 1985

Dear Pam

　　I am researching the Lindbergh kidnapping case. On March 1 1932 Lindbergh's eighteen-month-old son was taken from the Lindbergh home in Hopewell New Jersey. A ransom note demanding $50000 was found. Bruno Hautpmann was arrested for the crime on September 15 1934. Police found $14000 of the ransom money in his home. Found guilty, Hautpmann was executed on April 3 1936.

　　　　　　　　　　　　　　Your friend

　　　　　　　　　　　　　　Gina

29.2 Commas That Set Off Added Elements
(Places, Dates, Titles, Other Uses) • Practice 2

▶ **Exercise 1** **Using Commas With Places, Dates, and Titles.** Add the necessary commas in the following sentences.

EXAMPLE: On June 9 1987 we moved to Houston Texas.
On June 9, 1987, we moved to Houston, Texas.

1. Microtec Inc. opened on the New York Stock Exchange at $14 per share.

2. The bus stopped in Texarkana on its way to Little Rock Arkansas.

3. The nurse signed her letter of resignation "Allison Evans R.N."

4. On July 4 1884 the Statue of Liberty was officially presented to the United States.

5. Is it true that your ancestors traveled from St. Louis Missouri to San Francisco California by wagon train?

6. Professor John H. Coleman Ph.D. accepted a position at another university.

7. Please cancel delivery of our newspaper from Tuesday August 8 to Sunday August 19.

8. Are Randall Knudtsen Sr. and Randall Knudtsen Jr. working for the same electronics company now?

9. The boy was an exchange student from Stuttgart Germany.

10. The boat will stop in Bridgetown Barbados on January 11.

▶ **Exercise 2** **Using Commas in Other Situations.** Add the necessary commas in the following sentences.

EXAMPLE: Ann guessed that the jar contained 3864 jelly beans.
Ann guessed that the jar contained 3,864 jelly beans.

1. The last-known address of the Parker family was 1318 View Ridge Drive Missoula Montana.

2. Chicago is 2189 miles from Los Angeles.

3. The parents headed off to work; the children to school.

4. Regina was born on September 15 1972 in Honolulu Hawaii.

5. Outside the house looked as new as the day we bought it.

6. Someone once said "A grandparent is a child's best press agent."

7. The school's address is P.O. Box 900 Cupertino California 95014.

8. When reading the boy hears nothing around him.

9. "It is much easier to be critical than to be correct" Benjamin Disraeli once observed.

10. The first horse shown was an Arabian; the second a quarter horse; the third a thoroughbred.

29.3 The Semicolon • Practice 1

Semicolons and Independent Clauses   Use a semicolon to join independent clauses not already joined by a comma and a coordinating conjunction. A semicolon can also be used to join two independent clauses joined by a conjunctive adverb or a transitional expression.

Two Independent Clauses	Alan reached the mouth of the cave first; he peered inside and decided to wait for his friends.
Independent Clauses With a Conjunctive Adverb	Karen wants a new car; however, she will wait until she has saved $2,000 for a down payment.
Independent Clauses With a Transitional Expression	My sister is an outstanding student; as a result, she won a four-year college scholarship.

Semicolons Used to Avoid Confusion   Use a semicolon to avoid confusion when independent clauses or items in a series already contain commas.

EXAMPLE:
My aunt traveled to Lisbon, Madrid, and Seville; and, next year, she hopes to visit England and France.

▶ **Exercise 1**   **Using Semicolons Correctly.**   In each sentence a comma is used instead of a semicolon. Circle the comma to show that a semicolon is needed.

EXAMPLE: Ben arrived later (,) consequently, he missed the meeting.

1. My sister likes to save money, in fact, she already has saved a thousand dollars.
2. We bought peaches, plums, and nectarines, but the peaches were not ripe.
3. The dog, whose tail wagged continuously, barked, but its owner, a nice man, reassured us.
4. Billy, wait for little Joey, he can't walk that fast.
5. Selling ice cream, Beth earned almost $100, that was the most for any one day.
6. We sang, danced, and went for a moonlit swim, and a good time was had by all.
7. It's time to mow the lawn, also, the garden needs to be weeded.
8. You can't start writing now, first, you must do some research.
9. Paris, Florence, and Venice are all beautiful cities, but my favorite is Florence.
10. I had been there before, as a result, I didn't pay attention to the directions.

▶ **Exercise 2**   **Writing Compound Sentences With Semicolons.**   Complete the sentences below.

EXAMPLE: ____I love exotic food____ ; however, ____that meal was too much for me.____

1. _____ ;
   however, _____
2. _____ ;
   for instance, _____
3. _____ ;
   otherwise, _____
4. _____ ; _____
5. _____ ;
   on the other hand, _____

29.3 The Semicolon • Practice 2

> **Exercise 1** **Using Semicolons to Join Independent Clauses.** For each sentence write the word that goes before the semicolon, the semicolon, and the word that goes after it.

EXAMPLE: A raccoon has claws its name means "scratcher." _____claws; its_____

(1) Raccoons sometimes live in hollow trees they have also been found living in burrows made by other animals. (2) These creatures seem to be quite intelligent they can learn how to open small packages and to turn on appliances. (3) When raccoons are young, their mother provides food when they are older, they must find their own. (4) Some raccoons love fish others prefer bird and turtle eggs. (5) Raccoons can distinguish between different sounds one raccoon appears to like listening to Beethoven. (6) Raccoon litters may include only two babies they sometimes include as many as seven. (7) Some people think baby raccoons make good pets usually, however, they do not. (8) Raccoons are sometimes pests to farmers they get into the garbage cans and the poultry house. (9) Raccoons also raid garbage cans in suburban neighborhoods they sometimes make nuisances of themselves at camp sites and garbage dumps. (10) Raccoon hats were popular during frontier days raccoon coats were popular during the 1920's.

1. _____   6. _____
2. _____   7. _____
3. _____   8. _____
4. _____   9. _____
5. _____   10. _____

> **Exercise 2** **Using Semicolons and Commas to Join Clauses.** Some of the following sentences are missing semicolons; some are also missing commas. Make the necessary corrections.

EXAMPLE: Stocks were soaring to an all-time high in 1929 consequently people were buying more stocks.
Stocks were soaring to an all-time high in 1929; consequently, people were buying more stocks.

(1) Stockholders hoped to get rich when their stocks rose in price therefore many borrowed money to buy stocks. (2) On Black Thursday in October 1929, stocks tumbled to forty percent of their original value as a result many people lost almost everything they owned. (3) Pandemonium broke out on the stock exchange floor fist fights for instance were common. (4) Frantic orders to sell came into the exchange many orders to sell however could not be completed because there were no buyers. (5) Some stockholders were forced to sell their homes, businesses, and other possessions to pay back money they had borrowed others could not pay their debts at all. (6) There were several short rallies in stock prices nevertheless prices generally spiraled down. (7) Some tragedies were caused by the stock market crash in fact the president of Union Cigar jumped to his death when his stock dropped over $100 in one day. (8) The President assured the public that business was good many business leaders continued to buy stocks. (9) Some of the richest people did manage to survive the stock market crash most people however had barely enough left to survive. (10) The collapse of the stock market almost destroyed the business world it is a tragic lesson to people today.

29.3 The Colon • Practice 1

The Colon as an Introductory Device   Use a colon before a list of items following an independent clause, to introduce a quotation that is formal or lengthy or not preceded by a verb that shows speech, to introduce a sentence that summarizes or explains the sentence before it, and to introduce a formal appositive.

List	Grandfather always grew a variety of vegetables: tomatoes, beans, cucumbers, carrots, and squash.
Quotation	The judge nodded slowly: "Case dismissed."
Explanatory Sentence	In conclusion, the speaker emphasized her main point: Leash laws protect dogs as well as people.
Formal Appositive	She showed slides of the most isolated spot on Earth: Antarctica.

Special Uses of the Colon   Use a colon in a number of special writing situations.

Numerals Giving Time	9:10 A.M. 10:15 P.M.
References to Periodicals	*Cornell Law Review* XIV: 76 (volume: page)
Biblical References	Ecclesiastes 1:5 (chapter: verse)
Subtitles for Books and Magazines	"Emotion: Learning to Control Feelings"
Salutations in Business Letters	Dear Ms. Green: Gentlemen:
Labels Used to Signal Important Ideas	Warning: This product is for external use only.

▶ **Exercise 1**   **Using the Colon as an Introductory Device.**   Add colons where they are needed.

EXAMPLE: I examined the parts of the book preface, text, and index.
          I examined the parts of the book: preface, text, and index.

1. The salad contains three ingredients lettuce, tomatoes, and mushrooms.
2. She glanced at herself in the mirror "I could certainly use a haircut."
3. We're pleased to have with us tonight Elmwood's most widely traveled citizen Bess Simca.
4. On our trip we took three forms of transportation train, bus, and airplane.
5. There is only one lesson to be learned from this experience Think before you speak.
6. The day brought all sorts of weather sun, showers, haze.
7. The master of ceremonies announced "Please rise for the national anthem."
8. It's been a pleasure to work with a thoroughly professional actress Meryl Streep.
9. She listed her three favorite sports baseball, football, and hockey.
10. I read four magazines every month *National News, Stereo Listening, Popular Collectibles,* and *World Review.*

▶ **Exercise 2**   **Using Colons in Special Writing Situations.**   Add colons where they are needed.

EXAMPLE: My favorite childhood book was *Lad A Dog.*
          My favorite childhood book was *Lad: A Dog.*

1. The text of the sermon was Psalms 23 1.
2. Did she take the 6 05 or the 6 37 from Penn Station?
3. The book was called *Gourmet Cooking Recipes for the Beginner.*
4. The quotation comes from *The Ohio State Quarterly* X 132.
5. Note The cover of this bottle is not childproof.

29.3 The Colon • Practice 2

▷ **Exercise 1**   **Using Colons as Introductory Devices.**   Read each sentence and decide where colons are required. Write the word that goes before the colon, the colon, and the word that goes after it, adding any necessary capitals. One of the sentences is already correct. For this sentence, write *correct.*

EXAMPLE: The huge metal eagle on the roof of the high school sparked my interest in a new hobby collecting weather vanes.

_____ *hobby: collecting* _____

(1) Weather vanes were first used two thousand years ago in a mighty, noble city Athens. (2) Years later, the Pope sent out an important order a statue, or weather vane, of a rooster was to be placed on top of every Christian church. (3) The rooster-shaped weather vanes had a significant purpose it was to remind church members to attend church regularly. (4) The symbol of the rooster was chosen because of Christ's prediction "I tell you, Peter, the cock will not crow this day, until you three times deny that you know me." (5) As weather vanes began to be made in other shapes, those made in the shape of a banner were given a special name bannerets. (6) Only one group was entitled to use bannerets in medieval times this was the nobility. (7) In later centuries, countries in which weather vanes could be found included England, France, and the United States. (8) In the United States, many different shapes of weather vanes could be seen barnyard animals, carriages, fire engines, ships, and lions, among others. (9) In the nineteenth century, weather vanes often took the shape of the following patriotic symbols flags, liberty bells, and eagles. (10) These weather vanes could be seen on the tops of a variety of buildings barns, houses, churches, schools, and government offices.

1. _____   6. _____
2. _____   7. _____
3. _____   8. _____
4. _____   9. _____
5. _____   10. _____

▷ **Exercise 2**   **Using Colons in Special Writing Situations.**   Add the necessary colons in each of the following items.

EXAMPLE: Warning The contents of this bottle are poisonous.
           Warning: The contents of this bottle are poisonous.

1. One of my favorite stories in the Bible is Mark 4 3.

2. Dear Mr. Harrison

3. The schedule indicated that the train from Chicago should arrive at 5 38 P.M.

4. Note The following information has not yet been verified by the main office.

5. Our coach suggested that we read *Playing Team Soccer A Study in Offense and Defense Skills.*

6. My teacher suggested I check in *Business News* 61 12 for further information for my report.

7. Dear Mrs. Phillips

8. I took out a reference book called *Rules for Writing A Guide to Better Compositions.*

9. The minister asked the congregation to turn to Exodus 6 2.

10. Are we supposed to leave at 6 15 A.M. or 6 45 A.M.?

Quotation Marks With Direct Quotations
(Introductory, Concluding, Interrupting Expressions)
• Practice 1

Direct Quotations   Use quotation marks before and after an uninterrupted direct quotation.

One Sentence	"The sea lies all around us."—Rachel Carson
Two Sentences	"Nonviolence is the first article of my faith. It is also the last article of my creed."—Mohandas Gandhi
Phrase	In the words of Theodore Roosevelt, we must have our "eyes on the stars" and our "feet on the ground."

Introductory, Concluding, and Interrupting Expressions   Expressions such as *she said* or *they replied* are often used to identify the speaker in a direct quotation. These expressions can occur at the beginning, at the end, or in the middle of the quote.

Rules for Punctuation	Examples
Use a comma after an introductory expression.	My father confided, "I expect to get a promotion today."
Use a comma, question mark, or exclamation mark after a quote followed by a concluding expression.	"I am very pleased," said Mother. "When will you leave?" I asked. "That's absurd!" she exclaimed.
Use a comma before and after an interrupting expression.	"I know," she smiled, "what you really want for your birthday."

► **Exercise 1**   **Punctuating Direct Quotations.**   Place quotation marks, commas, and other punctuation marks where they are required.

EXAMPLE: I agree said the teacher that the grade is low.
    "I agree," said the teacher, "that the grade is low."

1. This is the first time I've heard of that process he said.

2. In spite of everything I still believe that people are really good at heart—Anne Frank

3. This report Mr Gray said does not contain footnotes.

4. Mother asked me Don't you hear the telephone

5. What wonderful news Ted exclaimed.

6. Which bus asked the visitor should I take

7. What can that letter mean asked Alice

8. Coach Willis said We need this game to make the finals

9. I like basketball she said much more than baseball

10. Anne Morrow Lindbergh called mothers and housewives the great vacationless class.

► **Exercise 2**   **Writing Direct Quotations.**   Complete the sentences below.

EXAMPLE: "_____It was in the year 1960_____," she answered.

1. "_____?" he asked.

2. Father explained, "_____."

3. "_____," I said. "_____."

4. "_____!" Pam exclaimed.

5. "_____," she agreed, "_____."

29.4 Quotation Marks With Direct Quotations
(Introductory, Concluding, Interrupting Expressions)
• Practice 2

▶ **Exercise 1** **Recognizing Direct Quotations.** Decide whether the underlined material in each of the following items is a direct or indirect quotation. Add the necessary quotation marks and capitals to each direct quotation.

EXAMPLE: He often thought, <u>someday I will know enough to become a poet.</u>

He often thought, "Someday I will know enough to become a poet."

1. Christine said that <u>she would like to play badminton tomorrow afternoon.</u>

2. Each fact that a person learns is, in the words of E.L. Youman, <u>a key to other facts.</u>

3. Eleanor Roosevelt once said, <u>no one can make you feel inferior without your consent.</u>

4. Carlyle once defined endurance in two precise words: <u>patience concentrated.</u>

5. After listening to a weather forecast, our coach announced that <u>there would be no practice today.</u>

6. You must know which song contains the words <u>in the dawn's early light.</u>

7. During the first lap, Andrea decided, <u>I must win today since my parents are watching.</u>

8. Later in the race, she decided that <u>they would have to be satisfied with second place this time.</u>

9. <u>A book with an unhappy ending</u> were the words he used to describe his checkbook.

10. Emerson once wrote, <u>the creation of a thousand forests is in one acorn.</u>

▶ **Exercise 2** **Writing Direct Quotations With Introductory, Concluding and Interrupting Expressions.** Rewrite the following quotations, correctly punctuating and capitalizing them.

EXAMPLE: my mother cautioned you better be home on time this evening

My mother cautioned, "You better be home on time this evening."

1. persuasively, the sales clerk added this particular radio won't be on sale much longer

_____

2. the park will be closed the ranger said so that we can repair the picnic area

_____

3. that jacket looks nice on you my father said as he walked in the door

_____

4. with growing irritation, the taxi driver asked have you decided where we are going yet

_____

5. Henry Ward Beecher once made this important distinction between work and worry it is not work that kills me; it is worry

_____

6. he who has imagination without learning warns Joubert has wings but no feet

_____

7. when you get to the rodeo my cousin warned watch out for wild horses and bulls

_____

8. don't forget june 15 his wife reminded him that's our anniversary

_____

9. you've got to keep your eye on the ball every second instructed my coach

_____

10. when the dance is over my date informed me we are going to go out for some pizza

_____

29.4 # Quotation Marks With Direct Quotations
(With Other Punctuation Marks, Special Situations)
• Practice 1

Quotation Marks With Other Punctuation Marks   Place commas and periods inside the quotation marks. Place semicolons and colons outside. Use the meaning of the whole sentence to determine the placement of question marks and exclamation marks.

PLACING OTHER PUNCTUATION MARKS	
Commas and Periods	"I think," she said, "this will be enough."
Colons and Semicolons	Bob remarked, "We need help"; he was right.
Question Marks and Exclamation Marks	Dolores asked, "Where is the key?" Did Dolores say, "I lost the key"?

Quotation Marks in Special Situations   For dialogue, use a new paragraph for each new speaker. For long quotations, use quotation marks at the beginning of each paragraph and at the end of the final paragraph. For a quotation within a quotation, use single quotation marks.

SPECIAL SITUATIONS	
Dialogue	"Do it now," my friend said. "I'm much too busy," I replied.
Quotation Within a Quotation	The policeman testified, "When we asked her, she said, 'I've never been there before.'"

▶ **Exercise 1**   **Punctuating Direct Quotations.**   In each sentence one or two punctuation marks are missing. Add them correctly to the sentences.

EXAMPLE: Dr. Wang said "You are in perfect health"

<u>Dr. Wang said, "You are in perfect health."</u>

1. "I will meet your train at the station" she replied.

2. "His explanation" I thought "is difficult to accept."

3. Marion stormed "What an outrage!"

4. Bill reported, "Ted said, See you soon, as he departed."

5. "I agree" Jean said "to follow your suggestions."

6. "Let's pay all our bills now" Father said.

7. The teacher smiled and said "I think you need an up-to-date atlas"

8. Judy nodded, "I heard Sid say, Good luck, to the gymnast."

9. How amazing it was when she said, "It's OK"

10. "My efforts" said the captain "were in vain."

▶ **Exercise 2**   **Paragraphing Dialogue.**   Circle the first word in each sentence that requires indentation for a new paragraph.

"I really would like to go shopping with you, Mother," said Joan, "but I want to finish my report." "How much more do you have?" asked Mother. "I have another five pages to write and revise," said Joan, "and I also have to put together a table of contents and an index." Mother asked, "Can't you do that tomorrow? After all, it's only Saturday." "All right," said Joan, "you win."

29.4 Quotation Marks With Direct Quotations
(With Other Punctuation Marks, Special Situations)
• Practice 2

▶ **Exercise 1** **Using Punctuation With Direct Quotations.** One or two punctuation marks are missing in each of the following sentences. Add the punctuation marks to the sentences.

EXAMPLE: "Please hand in your papers" Miss Smithson said.

_____"Please hand in your papers," Miss Smithson said._____

1. The boys shouted, "We won the championship"

2. "When the film comes back" Jim announced, "we will set up a slide show"

3. The teacher said, "You will need to study hard for this test" he also said we should get plenty of rest the night before the test.

4. The salesperson in the shoe department asked, "Do those boots pinch your toes"

5. Carlos shouted frantically, "The man in the gray parka stole my wallet"

6. The clerk asked, "Are you certain you want just a one-way ticket"

7. My mother felt my forehead and said, "You get into bed right this minute"

8. She constantly reminded us of "the keys to success" hard work, a goal, and a little luck.

9. Did the coach say, "Be at the field at eight in the morning or at eight in the evening"

10. The garage attendant said, "Your exhaust pipe has a hole in it" however, he didn't offer to fix it.

▶ **Exercise 2** **More Work With Punctuation.** Follow the instructions given in Exercise 1.

1. I got the lead in this year's one-act play: "Roses and Wine"

2. My friend asked, "Why don't you go jogging with me in the morning before school"

3. "The plane will take off" the flight attendant stated, "as soon as the fog clears a bit more"

4. The new father proudly announced, "We have a beautiful baby girl"

5. Are you certain the doctor specifically said, "Take two pills fifteen minutes before eating"

6. She gave us her list of "absolute travel necessities" makeup, hair dryer, and bathing suit.

7. Did Emerson say, "If a man owns land, the land owns him"

8. Angela confessed, "I should read the newspaper more"

9. "We must try harder" he said, "if we truly want to win this debate"

10. I heard him ask, "Can you tell me where a drinking fountain is"

Underlining and Other Uses of Quotation Marks • Practice 1

Underlining   Underline the titles of books, plays, long poems, magazines, newspapers, movies, radio and TV series, long musical compositions, albums, and art

WORKS THAT ARE UNDERLINED
Book: The Wizard of Oz   *Movie:* The Yellow Submarine
Magazine: City Life   *Paper:* The New York Herald Tribune
Musical Composition: Vivaldi's The Four Seasons

Quotation Marks   Use quotation marks around the titles of short written works and songs.

WORKS WITH QUOTATION MARKS
Short Story: "The Ransom of Red Chief"
Poem: "When I Was Young and Twenty"
Chapter of Book: "Recalled to Life" from A Tale of Two Cities

Titles Without Underlining or Quotation Marks   Do not underline or place in quotation marks mentions of the Bible or other holy scriptures or the titles of government charters, alliances, treaties, acts, statutes, or reports.

EXAMPLES: the Bible, the Koran (religious works) the Constitution, the Magna Carta (government documents)

▶ **Exercise 1**   **Punctuating Different Types of Works.**   Use underlining or quotation marks with the works in each sentence. A few items require no punctuation.

EXAMPLE: I read Robert Frost's A Young Birch to the class.

> *I read Robert Frost's "A Young Birch" to the class.*

1. The Saturday Evening Post was an excellent magazine.
2. Do you still study the Bible regularly?
3. I have just read Anne Tyler's book If Morning Ever Comes.
4. Everyone should read Steinbeck's The Grapes of Wrath.
5. I think Malamud's best short story is The Magic Barrel.
6. I borrowed Anne Roger's album Keep It Real.
7. The Bridge Over the River Kwai won many Academy Awards.
8. Did you buy Pat Stanton's new album Awareness?
9. James Baldwin has a beautiful short story called The Rock Pile.
10. The Constitution of the United States is must reading.

▶ **Exercise 2**   **Choosing the Correct Form.**   Circle the correct form below.

EXAMPLE: DeMaupassant's short story "The Necklace" or The Necklace

1. The Christian Review or "The Christian Review"
2. O. Henry's short story "The Last Leaf" or The Last Leaf
3. George Orwell's essay "Why I Write" or Why I Write
4. Shakespeare's play "Romeo and Juliet" or Romeo and Juliet
5. The Old Testament or the Old Testament

29.4 # Underlining and Other Uses of Quotation Marks • Practice 2

▶ **Exercise 1**   **Underlining Titles, Names, and Words.**   Underline each title, name, and word that requires underlining in each of the following sentences. If there are no such items in a sentence, write *correct.*

EXAMPLE: <u>Ben Hur</u>, starring Charlton Heston, is my all-time favorite movie.

1. The book David Copperfield by Charles Dickens is considered a classic.
2. The Concert by Jan Vermeer is one of only thirty-six existing paintings by this Dutch artist.
3. Gemini 5 played an important role in the U.S. space program.
4. I always have trouble spelling the word occasion.
5. The works of Picasso make a valuable addition to any individual's art collection.
6. The first two sections of Lord Byron's Childe Harold, published in 1812, shocked English society and established the young poet's reputation.
7. When I walked into the room, I had a strong sense of déjàvu.
8. I like to read the newspaper The New York Mirror and watch the TV series Direct Line on Sunday mornings.
9. Our high school is putting on the operetta The Mikado by Gilbert and Sullivan.
10. The Empire State Building is no longer the tallest building in the world.

▶ **Exercise 2**   **Using Quotation Marks With Titles.**   Either enclose in quotation marks or underline the titles from the following sentences.

EXAMPLE: We listened to Solveig's Song from Grieg's Peer Gynt Suite.

      "Solveig's Song"   <u>Peer Gynt Suite</u>

1. We were studying the chapter called The Character Sketch.
2. Trifles by Susan Glaspell can be found in a collection called Plays.
3. We listened to the Surprise Symphony from The Complete Symphonies of Haydn.
4. Almost everybody in California knows the song California Here I Come.
5. I read an article in Science World entitled Frog Talk: Chirp, Chuckle, and Thump.
6. Edgar Allan Poe wrote a good horror story when he wrote The Masque of the Red Death.
7. Emily Dickinson wrote an interesting poem on death called I Heard a Fly Buzz—When I Died.
8. Public Broadcasting Television showed The Prince and the Pauper on Once Upon a Classic.
9. Once More to the Lake by E. B. White is an essay that looks back to the childhood of the writer.
10. Eleanor Clark's short story Hurry, Hurry begins and ends with the activities of a poodle named de Maupassant.

29.5 # Dashes • **Practice 1**

Uses of the Dash   Use dashes to indicate an abrupt change of thought, a dramatic interrupting idea, or a summary statement. Dashes are also used to set off certain nonessential modifiers.

FOUR USES OF THE DASH	
To show an abrupt change of thought	I found this information in an old reference book—you know, I found it only by accident.
To set off interrupting ideas dramatically	The musical star—I've never seen a better dancer—gave an interview to student editors.
To set off a summary statement	Good grades, school service, some sports activities, and decent SATs—all of them help in getting into a good college.
To set off certain nonessential appositives and modifiers	Some acronyms—NATO, UNESCO, CARE—are now recognized by most readers. The report—which included a table of contents, footnotes, bibliography, and index—took days to type.

▶ **Exercise 1**   **Using the Dash.**   Add one or two dashes to each sentence.

EXAMPLE: I had three good reasons oh, forget it.

_____ *I had three good reasons—oh, forget it.* _____

1. Basketball, baseball, hockey, football, and tennis all these sports are popular at our school.

2. I went to the library it was a rainy, dismal day and did all the research for my report.

3. Four of Steinbeck's novels *The Pearl, Cannery Row, Tortilla Flat,* and *The Grapes of Wrath* portray the lives of poor, humble people.

4. The house was built you may find this somewhat amazing in fewer than six weeks.

5. I spent most of the period trying to do my homework in class oh, here comes our teacher now.

▶ **Exercise 2**   **More Work With Dashes.**   Follow the instructions for Exercise 1.

1. A clean windshield, good tires, good brakes, and the use of seat belts all of these contribute to safe driving.

2. Some parents unfortunately, my father and mother are included are opposed to long trips by teenagers on their own.

3. Many American presidents I'm thinking of Harry Truman, Richard Nixon, Gerald Ford, and John Kennedy have served in Congress.

4. Shall we open some of the presents now I really can't wait for everyone to arrive.

5. The concert, which was held in of all places the Municipal Stadium, attracted a huge crowd.

29.5 ## Dashes • Practice 2

▷ **Exercise 1** **Using the Dash.** Add the necessary dashes to the following sentences.

EXAMPLE: Shall we pack a lunch it's such a beautiful day and go on a picnic?

Shall we pack a lunch—it's such a beautiful day—and go on a picnic?

1. Food, housing, and clothing all of these are getting more expensive.
2. Tobogganing sounds like something oh, here comes Mario.
3. We will play tennis or at least attempt to play tennis at school today.
4. The man underwent an emergency appendectomy the surgical removal of an appendix and is now recovering.
5. Our guest speaker who had a flat tire as he was coming here was a little late.
6. I'd like to introduce you to what did you say your name was?
7. That the plane burned huge amounts of fuel this was the concern voiced by the conservationists.
8. The Crusades there were four major ones, weren't there? were not an overwhelming success.
9. Some of the instruments the drums, guitars, and piano still need to be loaded onto the truck.
10. The parents say that their talented they use this term loosely daughter will perform in a piano recital.
11. Pencils, paper, book covers, and pens these will all be required in this course.
12. That old table which is on its last legs, to say the least was the first item sold at the flea market.
13. Feeding, exercising, and providing the necessary medical care all of these constitute important aspects of pet ownership.
14. I got Danielle a bracelet for her why, Dani, what a surprise to see you!
15. Our club raised fifty dollars more or less for the U.S. Olympic team.
16. Some horror writers for instance, Stephen King have wonderful imaginations.
17. It bothers me when you continually oh, never mind.
18. Eating, watching fireworks, and being with friends there is no better way to celebrate the Fourth of July.
19. They sent me four identical forms why, I'll never understand for the insurance claim I'm submitting.
20. Some bad habits biting your nails, grinding your teeth, and drumming your fingers seem almost impossible to break.

▷ **Exercise 2** **Using the Dash in Paragraphs.** Add necessary dashes to the following paragraph.

EXAMPLE: The mayor's greatest achievement finding shelter for the homeless was not easy to accomplish.

The mayor's greatest achievement—finding shelter for the homeless—was not easy to accomplish.

Fishing Don's favorite sport is something that he can do any time of the year. His favorite time if he had to choose one is in the winter. During this time I'm sure you already know this many lakes in the eastern and midwestern United States are frozen solid. Don likes to chop a hole in the ice and fish through it a fishing method that was developed long ago by the Native Americans. Ice fishermen like Don build small sheds and put them on sled runners can you just imagine doing this? The shed is pulled out onto the lake and a hole is chopped in the ice with an axe or a heavy iron rod this rod is called a _spud_. The ice is then chipped away what a tedious task! to make an opening about twelve inches square. The shed is then pulled over the hole and the fisherman sits in a comfortable chair if you can believe this to do the fishing. Because it is dark inside the shed, the fisherman can see the fish swimming in the water below it hardly seems fair to the poor little fish. Just give Don a fishing shed, a frozen lake, and fishing gear that's all he needs to be happy.

29.5 # Parentheses • **Practice 1**

Uses of Parentheses   Parentheses are used to enclose phrases and sentences that offer nonessential explanations. They also enclose letters, numbers, and dates.

Phrases	For a while I slept in the basement (near the door).
Sentences	This is a new school policy. (The old one just seemed to fade away.)
Letters, Numbers, and Dates	Our teacher suggested three types of book reports: (a) oral, (b) written, and (c) a combination of both. Tom Paine wrote *Common Sense* (1776).

Capitalization and Punctuation with Parentheses   Follow the examples in the chart below to punctuate and capitalize material in parentheses.

Declarative Sentence in Parentheses	The lead guitar player (it was a woman) was terrific.
Interrogative or Exclamatory Sentence in Parentheses	The party last night (Why did I go?) was horrible.
Parenthetical Sentence Between Two Sentences	He relaxed. (In fact, he almost fell asleep.) Then he perked up.
Punctuation in Main Sentence	When you arrive (I hope it's early), you can help with preparations.

> **Exercise 1**   **Using Parentheses.**   Add parentheses wherever they are appropriate.

EXAMPLE: Three ingredients are needed: 1 bananas, 2 cream, and 3 sugar.

Three ingredients are needed: (1) bananas, (2) cream, and (3) sugar.

1. Joseph C. Brown opened and mapped the Santa Fe Trail 1825–27.

2. We have had this policy for some time. In fact, I can no longer remember the old one.

3. The tree the one across the road was struck by an auto.

4. That dog Can you believe he's ten years old? is always ready for action.

5. We can improve extracurricular activities by a developing new clubs, b getting more advisers, c adding a ninth period to the day, and d getting more student support.

> **Exercise 2**   **More Work With Parentheses.**   Rewrite each item, adding parentheses and capitalization where necessary.

EXAMPLE: She laughed it was a hearty chuckle at her mother's remark.

She laughed (it was a hearty chuckle) at her mother's remark.

1. The most important point we hope you agree is to do this as cheaply as possible.

_____

2. If I understand you correctly I think I do, the work was satisfying.

_____

3. Paul did a report on Mozart 1756–1791, who began composing at the age of five.

_____

4. The high point of the concert what a concert it was! came just before intermission.

_____

5. Jane Lawson called you do you know her?; however, your line was busy.

_____

29.5 Parentheses • Practice 2

> **Exercise 1** **Using Parentheses.** Add the necessary parentheses to the following sentences.

EXAMPLE: We sang the songs of Woody Guthrie 1912–1967.

_____We sang the songs of Woody Guthrie (1912–1967)._____

1. The lamp sale held only twice a year at Bueners usually offers some outstanding bargains.

2. The first place winner was Ronald Carmassi Italy with a world-record-breaking time.

3. We will study character development Chapter 6 in the text as it relates to this novel.

4. My grandmother 1900–1980 saw many changes occur during her lifetime.

5. Don't forget the four cans 16-ounce size of canned tomatoes.

6. The kit calls for the following tools: 1 screwdriver, 2 hammer, and 3 wrench.

7. The ice cream machine more often than not, broken took my quarter and dime but didn't give me any ice cream again today.

8. The angler a fisher who uses a hook and line pulled in a 25-pound northern pike to win the competition.

9. We listened to the last song "The Night They Drove Old Dixie Down" and then left.

10. The Dachshund Races a favorite event on Picnic Day were fun to watch.

11. The bill said she owed sixty-four dollars and ten cents $64.10.

12. Steve stifled a yawn having been up thirty-six hours straight and tried to look interested.

13. I must get some items at the store: a cleansing powder, b paper towels, and c window cleaner.

14. My paper route brings in a steady income though getting up so early is a strain.

15. She made a lot of mistakes seventeen, to be exact during rehearsal today.

> **Exercise 2** **Capitalizing and Punctuating With Parentheses.** In the following sentences, add any necessary punctuation and underline any word that should be capitalized.

EXAMPLE: The flight we are taking (how I love to fly) leaves at noon.

_____The flight we are taking (_How_ I love to fly!) leaves at noon._____

1. I have an appointment today (right after the game)

2. Will you meet me at 716 Elm Street (the building right across from the library)

3. The dress (it was the most beautiful shade of blue) fit perfectly.

4. When we go to Seacliff Beach (a resort just south of Santa Cruz) we will have a picnic on the beach or possibly a clambake.

5. Something in the refrigerator smelled (some meat had gone bad) so I cleaned it out.

6. I watched the ants. (there was an ant hole within three feet of me) They were busy gathering crumbs from the sandwich I was trying to eat for lunch.

7. She has honey-blonde hair (do you think it is natural) and blue eyes.

8. Using the flowers (dahlias, I think) I created a lovely centerpiece.

9. The road appears to be lined with oaks. (do you think that is the right type of tree)

10. I slowly savored the pistachio ice cream (my favorite flavor) until it was gone.

29.5 # Hyphens • Practice 1

When to Use the Hyphen   A hyphen is used to form numbers from twenty-one to ninety-nine and with fractions that are used as modifiers. Hyphens are also used with certain prefixes and suffixes, with compound words, and for clarity.

USES OF THE HYPHEN	
With Numbers	thirty-two colors, four-fifths majority
With Prefixes and Suffixes	ex-president, anti-American, self-contained, commissioner-elect
With Compound Nouns	carry-all, secretary-treasurer, sister-in-law
With Compound Modifiers	never-to-be-forgotten concert, well-attended lecture
For Clarity	doll-like, three quart-bottles

Rules for Dividing Words at the End of a Line   Divide words only between syllables. Do not leave a single letter or -*ed* alone on a line. Do not divide proper nouns and adjectives. Divide a hyphenated word only after the hyphen.

Correct	Incorrect
cen-ter	a-part
hea-then	walk-ed
dis-tance	Mar-y
self-sufficiency	self-suf-ficiency

▶ **Exercise 1**   **Using Hyphens.**   Place hyphens where they are needed.

EXAMPLE: My brother is an ex lieutenant.

$\underline{\textit{My brother is an ex-lieutenant.}}$

1. My father owns a three fourths share of this business.
2. I was able to reach my sister in law and my father in law.
3. The sergeant said, "Round up all able bodied men."
4. There were anti French demonstrations in the capital.
5. I wrote immediately to the governor elect.
6. The old man of war sat in the harbor.
7. What a beautiful bright eyed young lady!
8. My grandmother was a well educated woman even then.
9. My father loves old fashioned dresses.
10. She bought twenty two greeting cards and thirty five small gifts for children.

▶ **Exercise 2**   **Hyphenating Words.**   Draw vertical lines between syllables that can be divided at the end of a line. Circle words that should not be divided at the end of a line.

EXAMPLE: below   be | low   jumped

1. athlete
2. drudge
3. custom
4. study
5. partridge

6. mountain
7. compound
8. tennis
9. incite
10. remark

29.5 Hyphens • Practice 2

▶ **Exercise 1** **Using Hyphens With Compound Numbers, Word Parts, and Words.** Add necessary hyphens to the following paragraph.

EXAMPLE: Chocolate is my all time favorite kind of candy.

___Chocolate is my all-time favorite kind of candy.___

(1) The able bodied explorer Columbus introduced the well loved treat chocolate to Western Europe. (2) When Columbus returned from the Central American terrain with some chocolate beans, the Spanish king did not recognize their potential. (3) Hernando Cortes, however, did see the potential of the dark, bitter drink he was served by Montezuma, and he dreamed up a far fetched plan to cultivate chocolate beans in Spain. (4) This quick witted explorer had his sailors learn to cultivate the bean. (5) For over ninety nine years, Spain was the sole European producer of a thickly sweet drink they had made from the beans. (6) But other Western European nations were not left out for long. (7) They discovered the sought after secret and were soon enjoying chocolate. (8) During the post Renaissance period, chocolate was expensive, and less than one fourth of the population could afford it. (9) However, mass produced chocolate was soon available to the general public. (10) Today, chocolate is greatly loved in the United States and around the world.

▶ **Exercise 2** **Dividing Words.** If a word has been divided correctly, write *correct*. If not, rewrite the word, dividing it correctly or writing it as one word if it cannot be divided.

EXAMPLE: The teacher told me that my essay was too word-

y. ___wordy___

1. When I read the directions, I saw they were self-expla-

   natory. _____

2. Yesterday, we drove past countless fields of grazing ca-

   ttle. _____

3. With Marion helping, it didn't take long to clean the ta-

   ble. _____

4. The high altitude in the mountains gave me a very head-

   y feeling. _____

5. After crossing the rickety bridge, we slowly walked do-

   wn to the water's edge. _____

6. The three of us had an early morning meeting with Super-

   intendent Glaros. _____

7. As we watched from afar, the horse and her colt gallop-

   ed across the pasture. _____

8. Do you suppose that your invitation to Maryann Ellins-

   worth will arrive in time? _____

9. The building was so badly burnt that it was unrecogniza-

   ble. _____

10. The man ahead of me bought a first-class ticket to New Zea-

    land. _____

29.6 The Apostrophe (With Possessive Nouns, Joint and Individual Ownership) • Practice 1

Apostrophes With Possessive Nouns   Use the following rules to form the possessives of nouns.

FORMING POSSESSIVE NOUNS	
Add an apostrophe and -s to show the possessive of most singular nouns.	a girl's notebook the inventor's sketch
Add an apostrophe to show the possessive case of plural nouns ending in -s or -es.	three girls' notebooks the nurses' passes
Add an apostrophe and -s to show the possessive case of plural nouns that do not end in -s or -es.	the children's toys three men's watches
Make the last word in a compound noun possessive.	Red Cross's volunteers station wagons' drivers
Treat time and amount like other possessives.	a month's vacation two months' vacation

Joint and Individual Ownership   To show joint ownership, add an apostrophe and -s to the last noun of a series. To show individual ownership, add an apostrophe and -s at the end of each noun in a series.

Joint Ownership	Keller and Schmidt's two-family house
Individual Ownership	Karen's, Sue's, and Pam's reports

▷**Exercise 1**   **Writing Possessive Forms.**   Write the possessive form in the space provided.

EXAMPLE: the radio of my cousin _____*my cousin's radio*_____

1. the books of the women _____
2. a vacation for a week _____
3. the campus of City College _____
4. the career of an actress _____
5. the children of Ken and Pam _____
6. the worth of two dollars _____
7. the coats of Jim and Susan _____
8. the absences of pupils _____
9. the textbook of my sister _____
10. the pizza of my father-in-law _____

▷**Exercise 2**   **Using Possessives.**   Add an appropriate possessive noun to each sentence.

EXAMPLE: _____*Mrs. Johnson's*_____ car wouldn't start Monday morning.

1. The next meeting of the photography club will be at _____ house.
2. _____ speech was by far the best we heard today.
3. His _____ response was not what he had hoped for.
4. Three _____ names were mentioned in the article.
5. She put the saddle on the _____ back.

29.6 The Apostrophe (With Possessive Nouns, Joint and Individual Ownership) • Practice 2

▶ **Exercise 1** **Using Apostrophes to Make Singular Nouns Possessive.** Write the underlined nouns, putting them in the possessive form.

EXAMPLE: The door of the bird cage was open. _____bird's_____

1. The student paper discussed the book in great detail. _____
2. Phyllis hair looked good styled that way. _____
3. The dog water bowl needs to be refilled. _____
4. Andrew pet turtle wandered from his bowl sometime last night. _____
5. The new representative performance on the floor of the House of Representatives was quite impressive. _____
6. New courses were listed in the college fall catalog. _____
7. Jim coat shrank in the wash. _____
8. The cat claws need to be trimmed. _____
9. We read three of Robert Graves books. _____
10. A part of each month wages was added to our small but growing savings account. _____

▶ **Exercise 2** **Using Apostrophes to Make Plural Nouns Possessive.** Write the underlined nouns, putting them into the possessive form.

EXAMPLE: The members dues should be paid this week. _____members'_____

1. The ladies desserts came with their coffee. _____
2. The children toys were scattered all over the floor. _____
3. The twins presents were to be kept hidden until their birthday. _____
4. Many important issues were discussed at the governors conference. _____
5. The critics reviews helped boost the confidence of the actors. _____
6. The presidential candidate promised to uphold the people interests. _____
7. The relatives invitations must be mailed immediately. _____
8. Neat and well-written was the best way to describe the women tests. _____
9. The visitors suitcases had not yet been unpacked. _____
10. The report said that the cities problems continue to grow worse each year. _____

▶ **Exercise 3** **Using Apostrophes with Compound Nouns.** In each blank, write the possessive form of the compound noun in each sentence.

EXAMPLE: The Red Cross lifesaving class starts next week. _____Red Cross's_____

1. The Secretary of State home was the scene of a recent reception for foreign dignitaries. _____
2. Colbert and Nelson store is having a three-day sale on sandals. _____
3. My father-in-law hair has a streak of gray in it. _____
4. The police chief wife is a police officer, too. _____
5. The Camp Fire Girls summer program teaches children a great deal about nature. _____

The Apostrophe (With Pronouns) • **Practice 1**

Apostrophes With Pronouns Use an apostrophe and an *-s* with indefinite pronouns to show possession. Do not use an apostrophe with possessive forms of personal pronouns. Personal pronouns are already possessive.

POSSESSIVE FORMS OF PRONOUNS		
Indefinite		**Personal**
someone's	one another's	my, mine, our, ours
everybody's	one's	your, yours
anyone's	each other's	his, her, hers, its, their, theirs

▶ **Exercise 1** **Using Apostrophes Correctly With Pronouns.** Write the correct pronoun from parentheses to complete each sentence.

EXAMPLE: The tree has lost two of ____*its*____ lower branches. (it's, its)

1. I lost my camera, but I borrowed _____. (theirs, their's)

2. Our teacher was pleased with _____ success. (everyones', everyone's)

3. Did you try to get _____ opinion? (somebody elses', somebody else's)

4. I don't know too much about _____ new schedule. (their, they're)

5. It is important to respect _____ country. (one's, ones')

6. _____ record collection was taken, not mine. (Someone else's, Someone elses')

7. This set of notes probably belongs to _____. (her, her's)

8. The grizzly bear carefully protected _____ lair. (its, it's)

9. You received Steve's birthday card, but did you get _____ ? (ours, our's)

10. We looked at _____ photograph albums. (one another's, one anothers')

▶ **Exercise 2** **Writing Sentences With Pronouns.** Use each set of words to write an original sentence showing possession with pronouns.

EXAMPLE: Someone-game ____*Someone's game was found yesterday.*____

1. everybody-favorite _____

2. its-kittens _____

3. anyone-CD player _____

4. his-answer _____

5. someone else-house _____

6. theirs-jackets _____

7. one-success _____

8. our-request _____

9. another-jewelry _____

10. hers-skates _____

29.6 # The Apostrophe (With Pronouns) • Practice 2

▶ **Exercise 1** **Using Apostrophes with Pronouns.** If a sentence uses apostrophes correctly, write *correct*. If not, rewrite the sentence correcting all of the errors.

EXAMPLE: Someone's else's package was delivered to them.
_____ *Someone else's package was delivered to them.* _____

1. Robin gave his' coconut cake to her.
_____

2. When the coat didn't fit, he decided he had picked up another's by mistake.
_____

3. It's my duty to fight crime whenever and wherever I find it.
_____

4. Her's was the first car to be pulled over for routine inspection.
_____

5. Someone's car keys have been left behind on the kitchen table.
_____

6. Everybodys' presents were so thoughtful and generous.
_____

7. When he was cooking the steaks, he cooked their's a little longer since they liked them well-done.
_____

8. According to the job description, emptying trash cans is nobodys' responsibility.
_____

9. Is that your umbrella that is making that huge puddle on the floor?
_____

10. Anybody elses' actions would have been suspect, but nobody doubts his word.
_____

▶ **Exercise 2** **Using Possessive Forms of Pronouns.** Complete each sentence by writing in the blank the possessive form of the type of pronoun indicated in parentheses.

EXAMPLE: Did you find ____*your*____ keys? (personal)

1. That afternoon, the peach sherbet was _____ favorite dessert. (indefinite)
2. Where did you get _____ new bicycle? (personal)
3. _____ keys were found under the couch. (indefinite)
4. This definitely falls under the heading of _____ problem, not mine. (personal)
5. The two cats ate from _____ plate. (indefinite)

29.6

The Apostrophe (With Contractions, Special Uses)
• Practice 1

Apostrophes With Contractions   Use an apostrophe in a contraction to indicate the position of the missing letter or letters. The most common contractions are those formed with verbs.

CONTRACTIONS WITH VERBS		
Verbs + not	aren't (are not) don't (do not)	isn't (is not) wasn't (was not)
Pronouns + the verb *will*	I'll (I will) she'll (she will)	we'll (we will) who'll (who will)
Pronouns and nouns + the verb *be*	I'm (I am) it's (it is)	we're (we are) Bob's (Bob is)
Pronouns + the verb *would*	I'd (I would) he'd (he would)	we'd (we would) who'd (who would)

Special Uses of the Apostrophe   Use an apostrophe and *-s* to write the plurals of numbers, symbols, letters, and words used to name themselves.

EXAMPLES: two 7's   too many *!*'s   his *p*'s and *q*'s
Why do you keep using so many *like*'s?

▶ **Exercise 1**   **Using Contractions Correctly.**   Make contractions from the words in the parentheses and fill them in where they belong.

EXAMPLE: going to the beach later. (We are)

_____*We're*_____ going to the beach later.

1. _____ Mary's turn to walk the dog. (It is)

2. I wonder whether _____ coming tonight. (they are)

3. _____ willing to build the sets for the play. (George is)

4. You use far too many _____ in your writing papers. (*and*)

5. Do you think _____ like the bracelet I bought? (she will)

6. _____ bring the ice cream and soda? (Who will)

7. I _____ want to hear your excuses again. (do not)

8. You write your _____ very much like your _____. (*m, w*)

9. _____ you ready yet? (Are not)

10. _____ lend you her stereo if you pick it up. (Sue will)

▶ **Exercise 2**   **Supplying Contractions.**   Add an appropriate contraction in each sentence.

EXAMPLE: _____*They'd*_____ be much happier if they had quieter neighbors.

1. Do you expect _____ arrive in time for the concert?

2. _____ be right with you.

3. _____ they at the depot when you arrived?

4. _____ baby-sit for you if she had the time.

5. I know that _____ qualified for this job.

29.6

The Apostrophe (With Contractions, Special Uses)
• Practice 2

▶ **Exercise 1** **Using Apostrophes With Contractions.** If a contraction is underlined in the following sentences, write the two words that make it up. If two words are underlined, write the contraction they would form.

EXAMPLE: I've always been an Alfred Hitchcock fan.

_____ I have _____

Alfred Hitchcock was a filmmaker of whom many people said, "This (1) man's a legend in his own time." The legend of Alfred Hitchcock began in England, when he produced his first film, *Pleasure Garden*. However, we (2) don't see the now-famous Hitchcock style until his third film, *The Lodger*. Hitchcock moved to the United States early in his career, but he (3) did not plan to remain here. However, he and his wife (4) could not return to England, considering his growing popularity here. Instead, they decided (5) they'd become residents of California. (6) It has been the movies of Alfred Hitchcock that have brought a new dimension to the horror film. His films (7) aren't just shock; (8) they're stories that explore artistically the irrational aspects of life. In these films, (9) we've got the quality (10) we'd like to find in all films. Among the films (11) he has made in the most creative periods in his life—the (12) '30's, '40's, and '50's — (13) you'll find such thrillers as *Notorious* and *Psycho*. You (14) should not ignore these films; (15) they're classics (16) that will entertain movie fans for years to come. We (17) shouldn't forget the contributions this man has made. One (18) thing's certain: (19) We'll never forget the thrills his (20) work's brought us.

1. _____ 11. _____
2. _____ 12. _____
3. _____ 13. _____
4. _____ 14. _____
5. _____ 15. _____
6. _____ 16. _____
7. _____ 17. _____
8. _____ 18. _____
9. _____ 19. _____
10. _____ 20. _____

▶ **Exercise 2** **Recognizing Special Uses of the Apostrophe.** Write each sentence, adding an apostrophe and an -s wherever necessary. Underline any items that appear in italics.

EXAMPLE: Please dot all your *i* carefully.

_____ Please dot all your *i*'s carefully. _____

1. I cut out six *8* for my bulletin board.

_____

2. Do you spell this word with one *c* and two *s* or two *c* and one *s* ?

_____

3. Should I put two *?* in this sentence, Miss Mellgren?

_____

4. I had to write twenty *f* in my calligraphy class before I was able to master that letter.

_____

5. Now that we have a new house number, we will need to buy two more *4*.

_____

Diagraming Basic Sentence Parts (Subjects, Verbs, and Modifiers: Adding Conjunctions) • Practice 1

Subjects, Verbs, and Modifiers

In diagrams of sentences, words that make up the basic sentence pattern are written on a horizontal line. A vertical line separates the subject from the predicate. Articles, adjectives, and adverbs are written on slanted lines below the words they modify.

SUBJECT AND VERB	QUESTION	ORDER	EXPLETIVE *THERE* (OR INTERJECTION)
The jumbo jet landed safely.	Has the last guest arrived yet?	Come here.	There was no sun today.

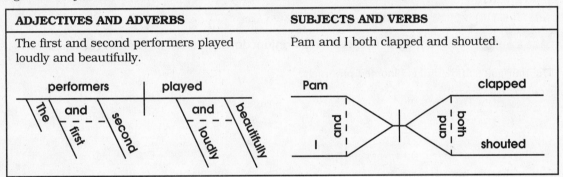

Adding Conjunctions

In diagrams, conjunctions are written on dotted lines between the words they connect.

ADJECTIVES AND ADVERBS	SUBJECTS AND VERBS
The first and second performers played loudly and beautifully.	Pam and I both clapped and shouted.

▶ **Exercise 1** **Diagraming Subjects, Verbs, and Modifiers.** Correctly diagram each sentence. Refer to the examples above if necessary.

1. Several colorful floats passed by.   2. A graceful seagull soared overhead.

▶ **Exercise 2** **Diagraming Sentences with Conjunctions.** Diagram this sentence correctly. Refer to the examples above if necessary.

The excited and eager fans whistled and shouted loudly.

Diagraming Subjects, Verbs, and Modifiers
• Practice 2

▶ **Exercise 1** Diagraming Subjects, Verbs, and Modifiers. Correctly diagram each sentence

1. Come here.

2. The huge crowed cheered very loudly.

3. The long freight train crawled slowly forward.

▶ **Exercise 2** Diagraming Sentences with Conjunctions. Correctly diagram each sentence.

1. The marigolds and zinnias bloomed profusely.

2. Bob walks fast but runs slowly.

3. The sparrow and the finch flew upward and quickly disappeared.

Diagraming Basic Sentence Parts (Complements)

• Practice 1

Complements

In diagrams, most kinds of complements are placed on the base line after the verb. A straight line that meets the base line separates a direct object from the verb. A slanted line that meets the base line comes before an objective complement or a subject complement. An indirect object is joined to the rest of the sentence below the verb. Compound complements are joined as other compound parts.

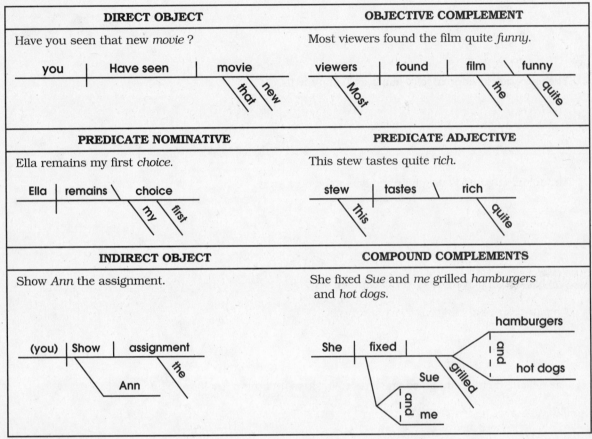

| DIRECT OBJECT | OBJECTIVE COMPLEMENT |

Have you seen that new *movie*?

Most viewers found the film quite *funny*.

| PREDICATE NOMINATIVE | PREDICATE ADJECTIVE |

Ella remains my first *choice*.

This stew tastes quite *rich*.

| INDIRECT OBJECT | COMPOUND COMPLEMENTS |

Show *Ann* the assignment.

She fixed *Sue* and *me* grilled *hamburgers* and *hot dogs*.

▶ **Exercise 1** **Diagraming Complements.** Correctly diagram this sentence.

1. The prospective buyer found the old house attractive and sound.

▶ **Exercise 2** **More Work with Complements.** Correctly diagram this sentence.

1. The music sounded harsh and too loud.

Diagraming Basic Sentence Parts (Complements)
• Practice 2

▷**Exercise 1** **Diagraming Complements.** Correctly diagram each sentence.

1. Many pesky mosquitoes annoyed the campers.

2. The carpenter used a large hammer and shiny nails.

3. Mr. Johnson gave his daughter and son some new toys.

4. The basketball players elected Bill captain.

5. The delighted children named one kitten Whiskers and the other kitten Fluffy.

6. This is the one.

Diagraming Phrases (Prepositional Phrases, Appositives and Appositive Phrases) • Practice 1

Prepositional Phrases

A prepositional phrase is diagramed to show how it relates the object of the preposition to another word in the sentence. The preposition is written on a slanted line joined to the word the phrase modifies. The object is written on a horizontal line. Modifiers are diagramed in the usual way. The model on the right below shows prepositional phrases that do not modify words on the base line.

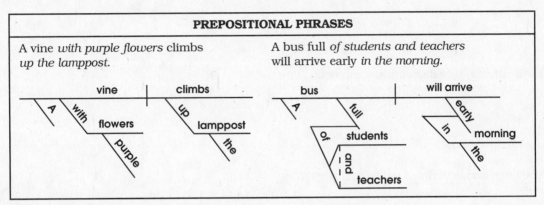

PREPOSITIONAL PHRASES

A vine *with purple flowers* climbs *up the lamppost*.

A bus full *of students and teachers* will arrive early *in the morning*.

Appositives and Appositive Phrases

An appositive is diagramed in parentheses next to the noun or pronoun it renames. Any modifiers in an appositive phrase are diagramed as usual.

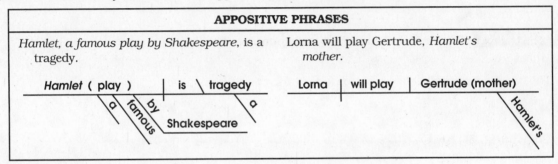

APPOSITIVE PHRASES

Hamlet, a famous play by Shakespeare, is a tragedy.

Lorna will play Gertrude, *Hamlet's mother*.

▶ **Exercise 1**   **Diagraming Prepositional Phrases.**   Correctly diagram this sentence.

1. A row of rose bushes twines around the fence in the yard.

▶ **Exercise 2**   **Diagraming Appositives and Appositive Phrases.**   Correctly diagram each sentence.

1. My brother Tony has taken a job in Minneapolis.

2. Our speaker, the director of the science museum, talked about dinosaurs.

Diagraming Prepositional Phrases (Prepositional Phrases, Appositives and Appositive Phrases) • Practice 2

▶ **Exercise 1**　**Diagraming Prepositional Phrases.**　Correctly diagram each sentence.

1. The corporation is moving to another city.

2. I will put the clean dishes in the cabinet.

3. The large tree in the yard sways in the wind.

▶ **Exercise 2**　**Diagraming Appositives and Appositive Phrases.**　Correctly diagram each sentence.

1. The newscaster, a radio announcer for forty years, will retire soon.

2. This is our new mayor, Ms. Peterson.

3. The giant vehicle, an oversized dump truck, has a flat tire.

Diagraming Phrases (Participles and Participial Phrases, Gerunds and Gerund Phrases) • Practice 1

Participles and Participial Phrases

The diagram for a participle or a participial phrase looks much like the diagram for a prepositional phrase, below the noun or pronoun it modifies. Notice, though, that the participle is written beginning on the slanted line and continuing onto the horizontal line.

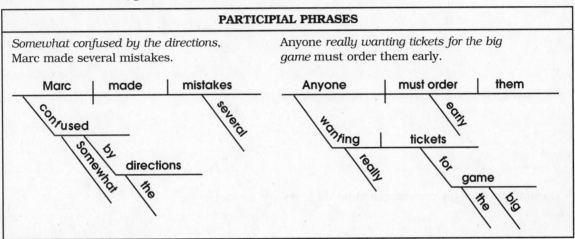

PARTICIPIAL PHRASES

Somewhat confused by the directions, Marc made several mistakes.

Anyone *really wanting tickets for the big game* must order them early.

Gerunds and Gerund Phrases   When a gerund is used as a basic sentence part, its pedestal is placed on the base line where that sentence part would normally be. The gerund itself is written on the stepped line, and modifiers and complements, if any, are written in their usual positions. A gerund or gerund phrase used as an indirect object or object of a preposition is written on a stepped line attached to the slanted line down from the base line.

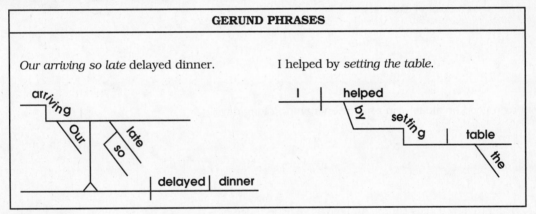

GERUND PHRASES

Our arriving so late delayed dinner.

I helped by *setting the table.*

▶ **Exercise 1**   **Diagraming Participles and Participial Phrases.**   Correctly diagram the sentence.

1. The cat sitting in the tree looked at the barking dog.

▶ **Exercise 2**   **Diagraming Gerunds and Gerund Phrases.**   Correctly diagram the sentence.

1. Ms. Nelson appreciated our helping with the decorations.

Diagraming Phrases (Participles and Participial Phrases Gerunds and Gerund Phrases) • Practice 2

▷ **Exercise 1** Diagraming Participles and Participial Phrases. Correctly diagram each sentence.

1. Frowning at me, Ned shook the broken radio.

2. My brother, laughing with each word, repeated the joke.

3. Opening the lid of the container, I found the chocolate cookies.

▷ **Exercise 2** Diagraming Gerunds and Gerund Phrases. Correctly diagram each sentence.

1. Swimming is a form of exercise.

2. Eating a good breakfast can provide energy for a long day.

3. Traveling to new places can be an enjoyable experience.

Diagraming Phrases (Infinitives and Infinitive Phrases)
• Practice 1

Infinitives and Infinitive Phrases

An infinitive or infinitive phrase used as a noun is diagramed on a pedestal in any of the positions a noun or pronoun would occupy. Subjects, complements, or modifiers of the infinitive—if any—occupy normal positions. Notice how an omitted *to* is handled. An infinitive or infinitive phrase used as an adjective or an adverb is diagramed in much the same way as a prepositional phrase.

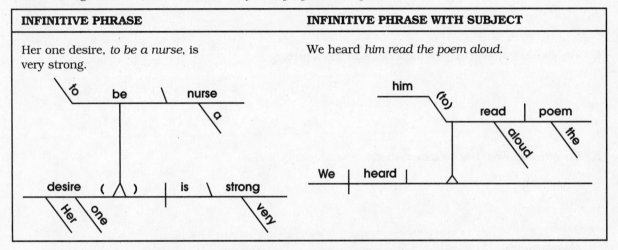

INFINITIVE PHRASE	INFINITIVE PHRASE WITH SUBJECT
Her one desire, *to be a nurse,* is very strong.	We heard *him read the poem aloud.*

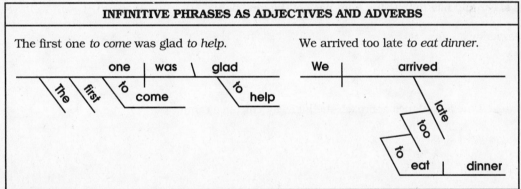

INFINITIVE PHRASES AS ADJECTIVES AND ADVERBS

The first one *to come* was glad *to help.*

We arrived too late *to eat dinner.*

▶ **Exercise 1**　Diagraming Infinitives and Infinitive Phrases Used as Nouns.　Correctly diagram the sentence.

1.　We offered to prepare a very special meal.

▶ **Exercise 2**　Diagraming Infinitives and Infinitive Phrases Used as Adjectives and Adverbs.　Correctly diagram the sentence.

1.　The man to see about that job will call you tomorrow.

Diagraming Phrases (Infinitives and Infinitive Phrases)
• Practice 2

▶ **Exercise 1**   Correctly diagram each sentence.

1. This is the brand to buy.

2. His greatest wish is to grow more crops in the future.

3. To clean your room is your next chore.

4. His sister told him to read the front page of the newspaper.

5. I watched the ambulance approach the highway entrance ramp.

6. She wants to pass her driving test.

Diagraming Clauses (Compound Sentences) • Practice 1

Compound Sentences.   Diagram each independent clause of a compound sentence separately. Then join the verbs with a dotted, stepped line, writing the conjunction or semicolon on the dotted line.

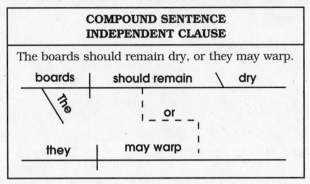

COMPOUND SENTENCE INDEPENDENT CLAUSE

The boards should remain dry, or they may warp.

▶ **Exercise 1**   **Diagraming Compound Sentences.**   Diagram each sentence correctly.

1. Reporters wanted an interview, but the ex-champ refused.

2. Bowser was an ugly mutt, but the family loved him.

▶ **Exercise 2**   **More Work with Compound Sentences.**   Correctly diagram each sentence.

1. King Midas had plenty of gold, but he wanted still more.

2. The liquid must be added slowly, or the sauce will curdle.

3. Cans belong in this bin; bottles go in that one.

Diagraming Clauses (Compound Sentences) • Practice 2

▶ **Exercise 1** Correctly diagram each sentence..

1. He finished his history project, and he studied the math problems.

2. We can go to the movies today, or we can wait for a better picture.

3. Spring begins soon, but we are still shoveling snow.

4. Television can be fun, but reading is more enjoyable.

5. I found the video, and I returned it to Adam.

6. The baby shook her rattle, and then she dropped it on the floor.

Diagraming Clauses (Complex Sentences) • Practice 1

Complex Sentences   Both adjective and adverb clauses are diagramed on a line beneath the independent clause and connected to the independent clause by a dotted line. With an adjective clause, the dotted line extends from the noun or pronoun the clause modifies to the relative pronoun or relative adverb in the clause. With an adverb clause, the dotted line extends from the word modified to the verb in the adverb clause. The subordinating conjunction is written along the dotted line.

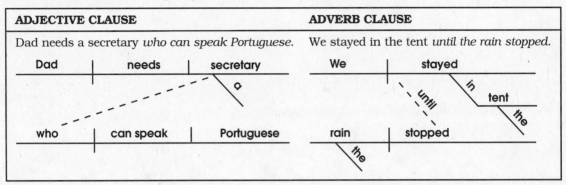

A noun clause is placed on a pedestal extending upward from the position it fills in the independent clause. If the introductory word has no function in the noun clause, it is written along the pedestal.

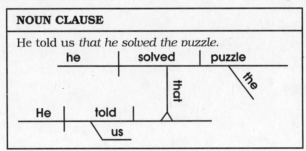

▷ **Exercise 1**   **Diagraming Adjective and Adverb Clauses.**   Correctly diagram the sentence.

1.   Since it was a pleasant day, Natalie went to the beach.

▷ **Exercise 2**   **Diagraming Noun Clauses.**   Correctly diagram the sentence.

1.   The boy soon forgot what he had been told.

Diagraming Clauses (Complex Sentences) • Practice 2

1. The shirt that I chose is blue with a white collar.

2. When Jack visited Florida, he toured a horse farm.

3. The book that you ordered has arrived.

4. The actor was excited because he received good reviews.

5. The lake that we will visit has a beautiful beach.

6. We visited the laboratory where Thomas Edison worked.

Diagnostic Tests

A.
1. Because <u>insects</u> are so small, they must have creative ways to protect themselves, (Sunday) through (Saturday), 365 days a year.

2. A <u>saddleback</u> catepillar has sharp hairs that will break and release posion when they prick your skin.

3. An <u>inchworm</u> and a walkingstick use ~~camoflage~~ <u>camouflage</u>.

4. ~~One~~ Often insects like <u>syrphus flies</u>, which cannot defend <u>themselves</u>, mimic other insects that ~~do~~ have better defenses.

5. One <u>species</u>, found in (North America), looks like a type that tastes bad to birds.

B.
6. Insects do not learn their behavior from their parents.

7. In fact, an adult usually dies before her young are born.

8. Consequently, an insect must rely on its instincts to survive.

9. The behavioral patterns are built deep in the nervous system, and <u>they</u> are apparent when stimulated.

10. Every insect reacts to <u>its</u> surrondings.

11.

12.

13.

14.

15.

16.

Diagraming Phrases (Compound-Complex Sentences)
• Practice 1

Compound-Complex Sentences   When diagraming a compound-complex sentence, begin by diagraming each of the independent clauses. Then diagram the subordinate clause(s).

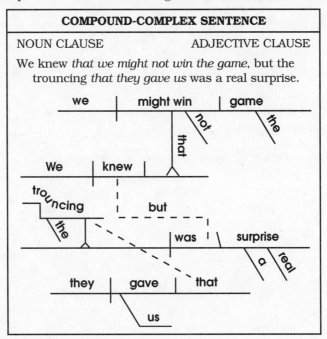

┌───┐
│   **COMPOUND-COMPLEX SENTENCE**   │
│ NOUN CLAUSE   ADJECTIVE CLAUSE   │
│ We knew *that we might not win the game*, but the│
│   trouncing *that they gave us* was a real surprise. │

▶ **Exercise 1**   **Diagraming Compound-Complex Sentences.**   Correctly diagram each sentence.

1. Joan said that she would never forget me, and I believe her.

2. While Beth cleaned the fish, Paula collected firewood, and Nancy unpacked the supplies.

▶ **Exercise 2**   **Diagraming Sentences of Varying Structures.**   Identify the structure of each sentence and diagram it correctly. The sentences may be compound, complex, or compound-complex.

1. We visited the house where Washington had his headquarters.

2. My sister, who lives in Houston, is planning a visit; but we do not know when she will come.

Diagraming Phrases (Compound-Complex Sentences)
• Practice 2

▶ **Exercise 1**   Correctly diagram each sentence.

1. When Jeremy left, Mike hid the presents and Susan phoned the guests.

2. The news that he read was good, but he wore a serious expression.

3. They wished that they could stay, but they could not.

4. When the rescuers reached the trapped miners, some rescuers held flashlights, and others carefully dug.

5. The students looked with disbelief as they approached the library, for the building was closed.

6. Before the game began, the fans were excited and the players were nervous.

HISTORY & GEOGRAPHY 1203

THE AMERICAN PARTY SYSTEM

W9-AOC-023

LIFEPAC Test is located in the center of the booklet. Please remove before starting the unit.

Author:
Brad Zockoll

Editor:
Brian Ring

Revision Editor:
Alan Christopherson, M.S.

Media Credits:
Page 12: © GeorgiosArt, iStock, Thinkstock; **13:** © BackyardProduction, iStock, Thinkstock; **16:** © rodjulian, iStock, Thinkstock; **26:** © CaptureLight, iStock, Thinkstock; **27:** © Purestock, Thinkstock; **30:** © Fredex8, iStock, Thinkstock; **45:** © Digital Vision, Photodisc, Thinkstock; **47:** © bizoo_n, iStock, Thinkstock.

Alpha Omega
PUBLICATIONS

804 N. 2nd Ave. E.
Rock Rapids, IA 51246-1759

The American Party System

Introduction

Where did they come up with the Republican and Democratic party symbols? The donkey and elephant symbols have a long heritage and a humorous history! In 1828 the Democratic hopeful Andrew Jackson was mocked by his political rivals as being stubborn and as stupid as a donkey. The political cartoonists began portraying Jackson as a donkey, and the symbol stuck on him. However, after Jackson won the election, the once-mocking donkey now became a symbol of strength in the political cartoons. It grew more and more popular until it eventually became the symbol of the Democratic Party.

Objectives

Read these objectives. The objectives tell you what you will be able to do when you have successfully completed this LIFEPAC®. When you have finished this LIFEPAC, you should be able to:

1. Understand the importance and goals of the American political party system.

2. Understand the history and development of the Democratic party.

3. Understand the history and development of the Republican party and the significance of third parties in America.

4. Understand how a political party is formed; from selecting candidates to financing a campaign.

5. Understand the organization of a party, from national conventions to local organizations.

6. Demonstrate knowledge of the nomination process and the strengths and weaknesses of closed vs. open primaries.

7. Explore the possibilities and ideas for making voting more effective and efficient.

8. Understand the process and variations of voting worldwide.

Survey the LIFEPAC. Ask yourself some questions about this study and write your questions here.

_____

_____

_____

_____

_____

_____

_____

_____

_____

_____

_____

_____

_____

1. POLITICAL PARTIES

> **"We must all hang together, or assuredly we shall all hang separately."**
> — *Benjamin Franklin at the signing of the Declaration of Independence, July 4, 1776.*

Section Objectives

Review these objectives. When you have completed this section, you should be able to:

1. Understand the importance and goals of the American political party system.
2. Understand the history and development of the Democratic party.
3. Understand the history and development of the Republican party and the significance of third parties in America.

Vocabulary

Study these words to enhance your learning success in this section.

administration . . . . Executive branch of the American government; as in "the Clinton administration".

ballot box . . . . The container into which votes are put.

candidate . . . . A person who desires a position in a political office.

constituency . . . . People of a region who elected a representative; the representative is answerable to these people.

dictatorship . . . . A country with a one-party leader who is in complete control; usually one who is unfair.

partisan . . . . A type of person who will staunchly campaign or vote for only one political party.

political parties . . . . A group of people organized with a governmental agenda in mind.

program . . . . A political plan of action.

provincial . . . . Pertaining to Canada; regional or territorial.

representative democracies . . . . Democracies where the people elect representatives to act as their agents in making laws.

Note: *All vocabulary words in this LIFEPAC appear in* **boldface** *print the first time they are used. If you are not sure of the meaning when you are reading, study the definitions given.*

THE AMERICAN PARTY SYSTEM

The Republican's symbol of the elephant first appeared in 1874, drawn into political cartoons by artist Thomas Nast of the magazine *Harpers Weekly*. The elephant was meant to symbolize the huge Republican vote throughout the country. It, too, was accepted eagerly, and by 1904 the Republican elephant was the party's symbol. Why do they call themselves the G.O.P.? That term first came along during the election of 1896—when the Republican party captured both houses of Congress in addition to the presidency with William McKinley! That was indeed a "large" victory and a boisterous atmosphere of optimism permeated Washington, D.C. A dramatic economic upturn accompanied the Republican sweep, and a grateful American nation nicknamed the Republicans the "Grand Old Party."

Practically every day you read or hear of news about the Democratic Party and the Republican Party. But you may have never heard of the Prohibition Party, the Libertarian party, or even the Bull Moose Party. These were all part of the political scene at some time in American history. **Political parties** have played, and will continue to play, a vital role in the American political drama. For as long as the Constitution has been in existence, the United States has rarely gone without a competitive national two-party system. During the eight-year **administration** of George Washington the United States was without an organized, competitive two-party system. Also, in the early 1800s, the Democratic Republican Party's opposition was too weak to be significant. Since that time we have seen a healthy and vigorous "battle" between at least two parties throughout the lifetime of the United States.

Political parties are more than televised gatherings. We see a lot of balloons, banners, and excitement whenever we watch a political party's convention, but there is much more to the party than just a rousing atmosphere. Serious strategy, long hours of labor, and much sacrifice goes into the formation and growth of a political party. A political party is an organized group of people who control or seek to control a government. In democratic countries, like the United States and Canada, political parties are extremely active on the national, state or **provincial**, and local levels.

Political parties are absolutely necessary to democratic governments such as ours. Most modern democracies are called **representative democracies**. A representative democracy is a democracy where the people elect representatives to act as their agents in making and enforcing laws. In a representative democracy, some process is needed for nominating **candidates** for public office and for selecting issues for public debate. Political parties perform these functions for a representative democracy. At election time, the people go to the polls and vote into office the candidates of their choice. Political parties are totally voluntary organizations and want to obtain as many members as possible. Some of these parties have rules to be obeyed and membership dues. Others have practically no rules and require no dues of their members.

Some countries have only one political party. This type of political system is known as a dictatorship. Under a dictatorship form of government, the party controls the government. For example, in communist nations the Communist Party is always in power. It controls very tightly who may or may not run for election. Therefore, the people have only one choice, the choice of the party.

In this unit you will examine the political party structure in the United States. You will look at the two major political parties and also the minority parties. You will examine the rules for who is eligible to vote and the voting process. You will also examine the different groups who control various aspects of the government regardless of the level.

In the United States political parties are voluntary organizations of voters seeking to gain or keep control of the government, whether on a national, state or local level, in order to achieve the goals of the party. The party members name their candidates, draw up party **programs**, and encourage people to vote for their candidates so that their goals may be reached. The political parties in our country use the **ballot box** instead of revolt and guns to achieve the changes desired for our country.

WHY ARE POLITICAL PARTIES SO IMPORTANT?

For as long as you, your parents, or their parents can remember, we have had political parties. Our two-party system of government assures us of representation in the government and of a continued free nation. If you had been born in a country that had a one-party system, you would face the dangers of a government that could severely limit the freedoms of its citizens. Having a multi-party system helps assure that no particular party can abuse the politics and welfare of the people.

Our American political system is a two-party system. Political parties are the instruments for expressing the wishes of the people. Our political experience in the United States has led to the development of a two-party system. Our two-party system is perhaps the strongest in the world. In addition to the two main political parties, the United States has a history full of minority or third parties which have helped shape American politics. The third parties have played a significant role in the strengthening of our two major parties. After these third parties have served their purpose of protest or proposal, they have often seen their issues and their members taken over by one or the other of the major parties. This type of give-and-take helps keep either of the major parties from becoming too narrow-minded in their agendas.

With very few exceptions   Americans think of *them*selves as either Democrats or Republicans. Even independents, who pride themselves on remaining outside the party organizations and using the attitude of "voting for the best regardless of the party," are forced to choose candidates that are already chosen for them in party conventions or primaries. Two-party systems are most common in the English-speaking countries of the world. Two-party countries include Great Britain, with its Conservative and Labor parties; Canada; and the United States, with both its Democrat and Republican parties. Although these countries may have other parties, one of the two major parties in each country usually controls the government.

The voting patterns are similar in most two-party countries. Generally, the industrial areas of a nation will support the more liberal party; but the rural areas will normally vote for the more conservative party.

Although a nation may have a strong two-party system, one party may control politics in certain areas of the country. For example, Canada has a number of parties from which the voters can choose, but the Liberal Party had almost 40% of the vote, nearly double of the runner-up party, the Reform Party. There are other parties in Canadian politics, such as the Tories, Bloc Quebecois, and the New Democratic Party, but the Liberal party has been dominant in recent elections, holding the most seats in Canadian Parliament. One party can continuously hold a strong power in elections for years and years on end. The party has gained this control because the voters in those particular areas have continually voted for its candidates. In Great Britain, for example, certain constituencies have always supported the Conservative Party, but in certain other areas the Labor Party receives all the support. Therefore, in national elections each party considers certain areas safe for their candidates. If a party leader wants to be sure a certain candidate wins a seat in Parliament, they have him run in a safe constituency. In Great Britain a candidate for national office does not have to live in the **constituency** he hopes to represent. In America, a candidate must live in the constituency for a specified amount of time.

In many states in our country, both the Democratic and the Republican parties have considerable strength. In other states, however, only one of these two parties has traditionally controlled the politics of that state. For example, from the Civil War (1861-1865) until the mid-1960s, the Democrats strongly controlled most of the southern states. During that time span, the Republicans, though not as strong, controlled some New England and Midwestern states. Since the 1960s the Republicans have won increasing support in the South and the Democrats have been making gains in New England and the Midwest. Several of the large industrial and commercial cities in the United States, such as Chicago and New York City, usually vote for the Democratic Party. The rural areas, however, usually support the Republican Party.

Both the Republican and Democratic parties have a spirited and colorful rivalry for the office of president, and in almost every political race. Because of a healthy two-party system, representative government is alive and responsible in the United States. It avoids the extreme of the single party **dictatorship** that is so common in both communist and fascist countries. It also prevents the endless succession of stalemates and weak coalition governments that are common to countries with numerous political parties. France, for example, has suffered from this condition for many years. Weak coalitions do not tend to allow a country to grow properly because of the excessive compromising necessary and because of the behind-the-scenes maneuvering against the party in power.

Because we have active political competition and frequent elections, we are not plagued with the bloody revolutions as other countries have experienced. Sometimes a shift in party control in the government, as occurred in 1932 with the Democrats and in the early 1990s with the Republicans, keeps the political balance and stability that is so important for our government to function properly. State and national elections show hard-fought contests for political party-control of seats in the Senate, House of Representatives, and State legislatures. Even the campaigning for offices in thousands of counties, cities, towns, and lower districts throughout the United States serve as a constant reminder of the importance of political parties in our political system.

People who staunchly campaign or vote for only one political party are known as partisans. Many times a political party is accused of partisan politics if it appears to put their party's agenda ahead of the good of the people. However, although there is the possibility of showing overbearing loyalty to one political party rather than working alongside all elected leaders, there are advantages to becoming an active member of a political party. From learning the political process to seeing an important piece of legislation gain power, an active role in a political party can be quite beneficial to a citizen. You become a member of a political party merely by registering with the party of your choice. In some states registering is not required, nor is it necessary to pay dues or to carry membership cards. With the exception of special officers and active workers in the political machine, no regular party meetings are held.

Political parties play an important role in shaping the future of our nation, so it seems surprising that most people know very little about the activities of party organizations. Many voters are content to confine their political activities to the few minutes required at the voting booths once or twice a year. Because of the lack of interest, the major parties are reaching out to enlist the interests and energies of young people of the nation. Young people can do many things to help like distributing handbills, putting up posters and removing them after the election, addressing and filling envelopes, making phone calls, sending emails, running errands and doing other useful activities. Each individual can do many things to aid the party of his choice.

One of the primary goals for an American political party is to put their candidate in the office of the presidency. Political parties have helped forty-five men achieve that honored post. The political party's victorious candidate can then take the following oath of office: "I do solemnly swear (or affirm) that I will faithfully execute the office of president of the United States, and will to the best to of my ability, preserve, protect, and defend the Constitution of the United States." The following is a list of the presidents of the United States, along with their party affiliation.

PRESIDENTS OF THE UNITED STATES

Time in office	President	Party
1789–1797	George Washington	(Federalist)
1797–1801	John Adams	(Federalist)
1801–1809	Thomas Jefferson	(Democrat-Republican)
1809–1817	James Madison	(Democrat-Republican)
1817–1825	James Monroe	(Democrat-Republican)
1825–1829	John Quincy Adams	(Democrat-Republican)
1829–1837	Andrew Jackson	(Democrat)
1837–1841	Martin Van Buren	(Democrat)
1841 (March–April)	William Henry Harrison	(Whig)
1841–1845	John Tyler	(Democrat)

Time in office	President	Party
1845–1849	James Polk	(Democrat)
1849–1850	Zachary Taylor	(Whig)
1850–1853	Millard Fillmore	(Whig)
1853–1857	Franklin Pierce	(Democrat)
1857–1861	James Buchanan	(Democrat)
1861–1865	Abraham Lincoln	(Republican)
1865–1869	Andrew Johnson	(Republican)
1869–1877	Ulysses S. Grant	(Republican)
1877–1881	Rutherford B. Hayes	(Republican)
1881 (Mar–Sept)	James Garfield	(Republican)
1881–1885	Chester A. Arthur	(Republican)
1885–1889	Grover Cleveland	(Democrat)
1889–1893	Benjamin Harrison	(Republican)
1893–1897	Grover Cleveland	(Democrat)
1897–1901	William McKinley	(Republican)
1901–1909	Theodore Roosevelt	(Republican)
1909–1913	William Howard Taft	(Republican)
1913–1921	Woodrow Wilson	(Democrat)
1921–1923	Warren G. Harding	(Republican)
1923–1929	Calvin Coolidge	(Republican)
1929–1933	Herbert Hoover	(Republican)
1933–1945	Franklin D. Roosevelt	(Democrat)
1945–1953	Harry S. Truman	(Democrat)
1953–1961	Dwight D. Eisenhower	(Republican)
1961–1963	John Fitzgerald Kennedy	(Democrat)
1963–1969	Lyndon Baines Johnson	(Democrat)
1969–1974	Richard M. Nixon	(Republican)
1974–1977	Gerald R. Ford	(Republican)
1977–1981	Jimmy Carter	(Democrat)
1981–1989	Ronald Reagan	(Republican)
1989–1993	George H. W. Bush	(Republican)
1993–2001	Bill Clinton	(Democrat)
2001–2009	George W. Bush	(Republican)
2009–2017	Barack Obama	(Democrat)
2017–present	Donald J. Trump	(Republican)

Matching.

1.1	_____	partisan		**a.**	people of a certain region who elected a representative to whom the representative is answerable

1.1 _____ partisan

1.2 _____ program

1.3 _____ representative democracy

1.4 _____ constituency

1.5 _____ convention

1.6 _____ administration

a. people of a certain region who elected a representative to whom the representative is answerable

b. a type of person who will staunchly campaign or vote for only one political party

c. a political plan of action

d. the executive branch of the American government; particularly used in relation to the office-holder

e. a political party's assembly, usually for the purpose of presenting a candidate

f. a democracy where the people elect representatives to act as their agents

Fill in the blanks.

1.7 Political parties are _____ to express the wishes of the people.

1.8 The two major American political parties are the _____ and the

_____ parties.

1.9 Three countries with two-party systems include _____ , _____ ,

and _____ .

1.10 The two major parties in Great Britain are the _____ and

_____ parties.

1.11 People who will staunchly campaign or vote for only one political party are known as

_____ .

1.12 What is a constituency? _____ .

1.13 Where have dictatorships been most common? _____ and _____
countries.

1.14 Name six Democratic presidents. _____

_____

_____

1.15 Many times a political party is accused of _____ if it appears they put
their party's agenda ahead of the good of the people.

1.16 The third U.S. president was _____ .

Choose one.

1.17 Third parties play a highly important role in

_____ strengthening the two major parties.

_____ weakening the two major parties.

1.18   What party do the large cities tend to support?

_____   Democrat

_____   Republican

1.19   What is a coalition?

_____   a temporary alliance of political parties

_____   a temporary military alliance

_____   a labor alliance

1.20   Which political party controlled the South from 1861 to the early 1960s?

_____   Democrat

_____   Republican

Answer *true* **or** *false*.

1.21   _____   President John F. Kennedy was a Democrat.

1.22   _____   Ronald Reagan was a Democratic president.

> **"In politics, again, it is almost a commonplace, that a party of order or stability, and a party of progress or reform, are both necessary elements of a healthy state of political life ...."**
> — *John Stuart Mill, 1869*

Vocabulary

Study these words to enhance your learning success in this section.

Alien and Sedition Acts	Legislation which gave the president power to deport any alien he deemed dangerous.
Anti-Federalist Party	One of the first two American political parties; it wanted a weak central government.
central government	The federal power of the country.
Constitutional Convention	Gathering for the purpose of creating a Constitution which would frame the laws for running the U.S.
Era of Good Feelings	A period from 1816–1824 where there was only one political party: the Democrat-Republicans.
faction	Group that may not be in agreement with the general direction of the larger population.
Federalist Party	One of the first two American political parties; it wanted a strong central government.
loose construction	Interpretation of the Constitution allowing the federal government powers not specifically denied it.
provision	Arrangement or groundwork laid to establish a program.
strict construction	Interpretation of the Constitution limiting the federal government to the powers in the document.

DEVELOPMENT OF AMERICAN POLITICAL PARTIES

Political parties are special groupings. As powerful as the Democratic and Republican parties seem these days, it is almost incredible to us that there was a day when American politics was not ruled by one of these two organizations. Before the American Revolution, no truly organized political parties existed in America. Voting was so restricted and the power of the elected officials was so limited that there were few issues which would divide the people. There did not seem to be a real need to organize any special groups. With the crisis of the Revolutionary War, however, things changed. The first political groupings developed in the United States, and after the Constitution was written, true and permanent parties began to develop.

With the writing and adopting of the Constitution came the development of the party system in the United States. Two parties came into the political forefront in America: the **Federalist party** and the **Anti-Federalist party**. The Federalists wanted a strong **central government**; the Anti-Federalists (or Democratic-Republicans, as they were also called) wanted a weak central government. These two parties had a healthy political battle for a time and both parties appeared fairly strong. However, within the Democratic-Republican party there was a split during the "Era of Good Feelings" (1816-24) after the decline of the Federalist Party with the Democratic-Republicans becoming the Democratic Party. Other parties such as the Whigs and some of the Democrats unified around 1854 forming the Republican party.

The Republican Party emerged and stayed in power from 1860–1932, with only two Democrats being elected president during this time. Even though the two major powers seemed to be in control through the years, the minority parties played a very important role in the political party system. They influenced several presidential elections, from Theodore Roosevelt's Bull Moose Party of the early century to Ross Perot's United We Stand Party of the early 1990s. Let's go back and look at the beginning of the party system:

Federalists versus Anti-Federalists. The men who would write the Constitution met in Philadelphia in 1787 and, quite frankly, political parties were one of the furthest things from their minds. It was never written in the Constitution, and today as you read it, the Constitution makes no **provision** or mention whatever of political parties. In fact, George Washington, the president of the **Constitutional Convention**, and many other early political leaders opposed the development of political organizations. Despite the initial disinterest, organizations began to develop before George Washington became president in 1789. Shortly after that, two political organizations, the Federalist Party and the Democratic-Republican Party, began to actively oppose each other.

The Federalists were led by such men as John Adams and Alexander Hamilton. They favored the extension of the powers of the Federal government beyond the specific provisions of the Constitution. In other words, they wanted to make the government strong and wide-reaching. The Federalists also favored a **loose construction** of the Constitution, believing that the Federal Government should possess all powers not specifically denied to it.

The Anti-Federalists, later renamed the Democratic-Republicans, were led by Thomas Jefferson, and favored **strict construction**. The Anti-Federalists wanted to limit the Federal government strictly to the powers which the Constitution specifically delegated to it. In other words, they wanted to shackle the powers of the government and keep a tight control on it.

| Thomas Jefferson

Although the Federalist party did not survive as long as the Democratic-Republican party did, it did serve the nation well. The Federalists, under the leadership of Alexander Hamilton, who was the Secretary of the Treasury, set our financial affairs in order, encouraged manufacturing and trade, maintained the country's honor and laid the foundation for a sound constitutional government. In their desire to stay in power, the Federalists passed the **Alien and Sedition Acts** in 1798. These acts gave President John Adams the power to deport any aliens he deemed dangerous, and to fine or imprison editors who criticized him for his actions. These laws angered so many people that the Federalists became very unpopular and lost too much support. As a result, Thomas Jefferson won the presidency in 1800. Because of their opposition to the War of 1812, the Federalists finally lost all their support and eventually disappeared from the political scene.

AMERICA HAD A BRIEF TIME WHERE THERE WAS ONLY ONE POLITICAL PARTY!

"Era of Good Feelings." From 1816 to 1824, the Democratic-Republican party under the direction of James Monroe, was the only party on a national scale in the United States. This period was not totally an "Era of Good Feelings," as it was also a time of trouble within the Democratic-Republican Party. Each of the leaders, John Quincy Adams, Henry Clay, and Andrew Jackson, controlled a **faction** representing a different section of the nation. Through the history of the United States, political conflict and new ideas constantly added new parties, large and small, to the American scene.

Democratic Party. The Democratic Party of today grew out of this struggle between the factions within the Democratic-Republican Party. During the election of 1824, Jackson won the most electoral votes but not the majority needed to win the presidency. The election went to the House of Representatives, where Henry Clay swung his support to John Quincy Adams. Although nothing was illegal about it, the followers of Jackson called the election a "steal." They decided to organize their forces under the new name Democrats and started their campaign to put Jackson in the White House in 1828.

EARLY DEMOCRATIC PARTY: POWERFUL BUT NOT PEACEFUL.

The Democratic Party is the oldest existing political party in the United States. From 1828 to 1860, the Democratic Party won all but two of the presidential elections, those of 1840 and 1848, though its members often disagreed on several issues during those thirty-two years. The Democrats fought, almost literally at times, over banking policies, the slavery issues, and tariff rates. They also met bitter opposition outside the party. In 1832 several groups that opposed Jackson combined to form the Whig Party. The Whigs, however, never sufficiently united to propose a program with as much popular appeal as that of the Democrats.

During the 1850s the Democrats split over whether to oppose or support the extension of slavery in the states of Kansas and Nebraska. As strange as it seems, in 1860 the party even had two candidates for President: John C. Breckinridge and Stephen A. Douglas. Both candidates lost to the Republican candidate, Abraham Lincoln.

From 1850 to 1932, only two Democrats won the presidency, Grover Cleveland in 1884 and 1892 and Woodrow Wilson in 1912 and 1916. The Republican Party had gained so much strength during the Civil War that the Democrats had great difficulty winning

| Statue of Franklin Roosevelt

control of the government, not only on a national level, but also on the state and local level. In addition to this situation, the Republicans accused the Democrats with having started the Civil War and having been disloyal to the Union.

FOUR STRAIGHT TERMS AS PRESIDENT!

The situation changed after 1929. The Democrats blamed the Republicans for the Stock Market Crash of 1929 and for the Great Depression of the 1930s. The Democrats held the presidency from 1933 to 1953. This included a time when Democrat Franklin D. Roosevelt won four consecutive terms as U.S. president. During most of that period, they also controlled both houses of Congress and the majority of the state governments. From 1955 to the early 1990s the Democrats kept control of the Congress, but they had difficulty winning the presidency. They lost the presidency to the Republicans in 1952, 1956, 1968, and 1972, but regained it in 1976 with the election of President Jimmy Carter. They again lost control of the presidency in 1980 and did not regain until the 1992 elections with the election of William Jefferson Clinton. Conversely, when the Republicans lost control of the White House, they gained control of the Congress. The balance of power has shown a pattern of shifting back and forth so that no party has had total Democratic or Republican control for any period of time.

Fill in the blanks.

1.23   The Federalists believed in a(n) _____ of the Constitution.

1.24   The Federalists believed that the _____ should possess all powers not specifically denied to it.

1.25   The Anti-Federalists believed in a(n) _____ of the Constitution.

1.26   The Democrats won all the elections from 1828-1860 except in _____ .

1.27   In the 1860 presidential election the Democratic Party ran two candidates,

_____ and _____ .

1.28   The only Democrats to serve as president from 1860 to 1916 were _____

and _____ .

1.29   Name six Republican presidents. _____

_____

_____

Matching.

1.30   _____ Alexander Hamilton

1.31   _____ John Adams

1.32   _____ George Washington

1.33   _____ Thomas Jefferson

a. secretary of the treasury

b. first president

c. second president

d. third president

Matching.

1.34	_____	loose construction	
1.35	_____	Alien and Sedition Act	
1.36	_____	strict construction	
1.37	_____	faction	
1.38	_____	central government	
1.39	_____	Anti-Federalist party	

a. a group that may not be in agreement with the general direction of the larger population

b. gave the president power to deport any alien he deemed dangerous

c. limit the Federal government strictly to the powers which the Constitution specifically delegated to it

d. allowing the federal government powers not denied it within the Constitution

e. the federal power of the country

f. one of the first two American political parties; they wanted a weak central government

Do these activities.

1.40 The Anti-Federalist would limit the Federal government strictly to: (choose one)

_____ managing of foreign affairs.

_____ coining of money.

_____ the powers the constitution delegated to it.

1.41 Check the statements that are true about the Democratic Party.

_____ It is the oldest political party in the United States.

_____ The Democrats won the presidency in the 1990s but lost control of the Congress.

_____ The Democratic party won considerable political strength during the Civil War.

_____ Abraham Lincoln was a Democrat.

_____ In the 1850s Democrats agreed on supporting slavery in Nebraska.

1.42 The Democrats fought bitterly at times over: (choose one)

_____ banking policies.

_____ slavery issues.

_____ tariff rates.

_____ all of the above.

Answer _true_ **or** _false_.

1.43 _____ The Democrats blamed the Republicans for the Stock Market Crash of 1929.

> "The essence of a republic is representative government.
> Our Congress represents the people and the States."
> — *President Calvin Coolidge, 1925*

Vocabulary

Study these words to enhance your learning success in this section.

carried	Having won the majority of the votes in a particular state; referring to a candidate in a national election.
challenger	A person who does not hold an office but who is trying to unseat an incumbent.
economic unrest	An uneasiness due to the lack of stability in the financial market.
incumbent	A person who currently holds an office.
landslide defeat	A loss by a large margin in an election.
majority	Having the larger number in a house of Congress, assuring strong voting power.
scandal	A public shame or disgrace brought about by illegal or unethical actions.
Stock Market Crash of 1929	Financial panic where the market lost so much power that many of the 1929 people lost their fortunes in days.
Whig party	A party formed mainly to fight the Democratic party and Andrew Jackson; formed in the 1830s.

REPUBLICAN AND THIRD PARTIES

Republican Party. The Republican Party began as a series of anti-slavery political meetings throughout the Midwest in 1854. The **Whig Party** was collapsing, and many Whigs, as well as northern Democrats, opposed the extension of slavery. The Republican Party represented this anti-slavery view and thus gained followers rapidly. The party's first presidential candidate was John C. Fremont, who ran unsuccessfully in 1856 although he **carried** eleven northern states.

From 1860, when Abraham Lincoln was elected president, through 1928, the Republican Party won fourteen of the eighteen presidential elections. Its policies appealed to many groups, including farmers, industrialists, and merchants, but the party did have problems. Financial **scandals** during the presidency of Republican Ulysses S. Grant in the 1870s, as well as general **economic unrest** nearly cost the party the presidential election in 1876. In 1912, President William Howard Taft was the leader of a divided Republican Party. The Progressive

Republicans wanted Theodore Roosevelt, who had served as president from 1901 to 1909, to run for the presidency again. However, the conservative Republicans renominated Taft at the party's 1912

| The Republican Party began as a series of anti-slavery political meetings throughout the Midwest in 1854.

national convention. Roosevelt then withdrew from the Republican Party and formed the Progressive, or "Bull Moose" party. This split helped the Democratic candidate, Woodrow Wilson, win the election. The Republicans lost to Wilson again in 1916, but, they regained the presidency in 1920 and won easy victories in 1924 and 1928. The party's popularity declined after the **Stock Market Crash of 1929**. A Republican did not win the presidency again until 1952.

During World War II (1939–1945), the Republicans began to show signs of recovery. In 1946, they won majorities in both houses of Congress for the first time since 1928. Then, in 1952, Dwight D. Eisenhower brought the Republicans their first presidential victory in twenty-four years. Eisenhower, a popular war hero, won again in 1956, but he had a Republican **majority** in both houses of Congress for only the first two years of his eight years in office.

The Republicans lost a close race to the Democrats in 1960 when John F. Kennedy was elected. In 1964, the Republicans suffered a **landslide defeat** to Lyndon B. Johnson. They regained the presidency in 1968, under Richard M. Nixon and held it in 1972, but the Democrats continued to control Congress. In 1976 Democrat Jimmy Carter won the presidential election, but lost to Republican Ronald Reagan in 1980. The Republicans kept control of the presidency until the 1992 elections when Bill Clinton won two successive terms, the first over the **incumbent** George H. W. Bush and the second over the **challenger** Bob Dole.

Third parties. There have been many third parties in the United States and probably will continue to be. None of these third parties have ever won the presidency, but many of their proposals have gained such widespread support from the public that the two major parties were forced to adopt them. Some of these proposals included the convention system of nominating presidential candidates, the direct election of United States senators and the levying of a Federal income tax.

FROM OPEN SOCIALIST PROTEST TO ASSISTING SPECIFIC PEOPLE, THIRD PARTIES ARE FORMED FOR DIVERSE REASONS.

The third parties in the United States can be divided into five types, according to their origins and goals. The first type consists of groups that broke away from the two major political parties. This may be caused by dissatisfaction with a current candidate or a break in relations over the agenda of the party. The Roosevelt Progressives of 1912 broke from the Republican party when there was a dispute over the selection of William Taft as the choice of the party. The Liberal Republicans of 1872 were another group who left the Republican Party to form a separate party. The Gold Democrats in 1896 and the Dixiecrats in 1948 also split from the Democratic party.

The second type of third party consists of organizations formed chiefly to help a specific group of people. For example, debt-ridden farmers established the Greenback Party in the 1870s and the Populist Party in the 1890s.

The third type is made up of left-wing protest groups. The dominance of the common man— the working class laborer—is the chief goal of these parties. These groups include the Socialist Labor Party, formed in 1877; the Socialist Party, founded in 1901; the American Communist Party, organized in 1919; and the Socialist Worker's Party

formed in 1938. The philosophical statement of the Communist Party U.S.A helps us understand their direction: "We are a Marxist-Leninist working-class party that unites Black, Brown, and white, men and women, youth and seniors. We are a Party that speaks out from a working-class point of view on every vital issue. The People's Weekly World is our voice and the voice of labor, of all militant movements for social progress. We are a party of unity in action. We are an integral part of every struggle and movement for change to eliminate poverty and joblessness, against racism and for full equality. We are participants, initiators, and leaders of every movement to make life better now and much better in a socialist future." Likewise, the Democratic Socialists of America (DSA) tell us their philosophy in their web page statement: "We are socialists because we reject an international economic order sustained by private profit, alienated labor, race and gender discrimination, environmental destruction, and brutality and violence in defense of the status quo."

The fourth type consists of parties that have only one goal. These single-issue parties include the nation's oldest existing third party, the Prohibition Party. Founded in 1869, it seeks to prevent the manufacture and sale of alcoholic beverages in the United States. Though very small, it is still in existence as a party.

The fifth type of third party consists of groups that have broad programs and attempt to gain national favor. Examples include the Progressive parties of 1924, 1948, and 1952 and the American Independent Party, established in 1968. In the early 1990s, billionaire Ross Perot formed the party originally called United We Stand, but it was later renamed the Reform Party. The Reform Party's goals of free trade and financial power place it in this category. The U.S. Taxpayers Party would also fall into this category. The U.S. Taxpayers Party tells of their agenda in a philosophical statement found on their web page: "The U.S. Taxpayers Party stands firmly on the principles of government laid down by our Founding Fathers in the Declaration of Independence and the U.S. Constitution. Unlike other political organizations, we do not believe these principles are outdated. Our government has become a problem because these principles are ignored not followed. We need to return to a government that protects all innocent life; a government that protects liberty, not suppresses it; and a government that allows the free pursuance of happiness, not regulation of it. In the spirit of the Declaration of Independence it is time to remove power from that 'faraway' government in Washington, D.C. and return it to the states and local communities." (Philosophical statement is from the U.S. Taxpayers Party Website.)

Some other parties which have been consistently active in recent national elections include:

The Green Party—"The Greens/Green Party USA is part of the worldwide movement that promotes ecological wisdom, social justice, grassroots democracy, and non-violence." (This statement is from the Green Party Website.)

The Libertarian Party—"The Libertarian way is a logically consistent approach to politics based on the moral principle of self-ownership. Each individual has the right to control his or her own body, action, speech, and property. Government's only role is to help individuals defend themselves from force and fraud." (This philosophical statement is from the Libertarian Website.)

Natural Law Party—"The Natural Law Party stands for prevention-oriented government, conflict-free politics, and proven solutions designed to bring national life into harmony with natural law." (This philosophical statement is from the Natural Law Party Website.)

The New Party—"The New Party believes that the social, economic, and political progress of the United States requires a democratic revolution in America—the return of power to the people. Our basic purpose—reflected both in our own governance and in our aspirations for the nation—is to make that revolution happen. At present, in America, the people do not rule. And they must, if we and our children are to lead lives of dignity, decency, and fulfillment." (This philosophical statement is from the New Party Website.)

Matching.

1.44	_____	incumbent	**a.** having the larger number in the house of Congress, assuring strong voting power in decisions of legislation.
1.45	_____	challenger	
1.46	_____	landslide defeat	**b.** losing by a sizable margin in an election.
1.47	_____	majorities	**c.** a person who currently holds an office.
			d. a person who doesn't hold an office but who is trying to unseat an incumbent.

Answer *true* **or** *false.*

1.48 _____ The Republican Party began as a series of anti-slavery political meetings held in the Midwest in 1854.

1.49 _____ John C. Fremont was the first Republican presidential candidate to win the office in 1856.

1.50 _____ Abraham Lincoln was the Republican president during the Civil War.

1.51 _____ The Republicans won fourteen of the eighteen presidential elections held between 1860 and 1928.

1.52 _____ The Republican Party appealed to groups such as farmers, industrialists, merchants, and economists.

1.53 _____ William Howard Taft led a divided Republican Party in 1912.

1.54 _____ The Bull Moose Party was formed by Theodore Roosevelt in 1912.

1.55 _____ The Democrats were in power from 1932 to 1952.

1.56 _____ The Republicans controlled the House of Representatives but not the Senate in 1948.

1.57 _____ Beginning with Dwight D. Eisenhower, the Republican Party would be in office from 1952 through 1972.

1.58 _____ The Democrats won the presidency in 1976, 1980, and 1996.

Fill in the blanks.

1.59 "The Libertarian way is a logically consistent approach to politics based on the moral principle of

self- _____ ."

1.60 Name five third parties listed: _____

_____

1.61 A person who currently holds an office is a(n) _____ .

1.62 The Prohibition Party was founded in 1869 solely for the purpose of preventing the manufacturer and sale of alcoholic beverages in the United States.

The Prohibition Party is an example of _____ .

1.63 The left-wing protest party that was formed in 1919 was the _____

_____ .

1.64 The Populist Party of the 1890s was an example of a party formed chiefly to help a

_____ .

✓ **CHECK** _____ _____
                    Teacher   Date

↻ **Review the material in this section in preparation for the Self Test.** The Self Test will check your mastery of this particular section. The items missed on this Self Test will indicate specific areas where restudy is needed for mastery.

SELF TEST 1

Matching (each answer, 2 points).

1.01	_____ loose construction	**a.**	limits the Federal government to powers the Constitution specifically delegated to it
1.02	_____ faction	**b.**	gathering for the purpose of creating a Constitution to lay down the laws for running the U.S.
1.03	_____ Alien and Sedition Acts	**c.**	arrangement or groundwork laid to get a program going
1.04	_____ strict construction	**d.**	president is given power to deport any alien he deems dangerous
1.05	_____ Constitutional Convention	**e.**	allowing the federal government all powers not denied it within the Constitution
1.06	_____ provision	**f.**	a group that may not be in agreement with the general direction of the larger population

Fill in the blanks (each answer, 3 points).

1.07 The _____ party is the oldest political party in the United States.

1.08 The federal power of the country is known as the _____ government.

1.09 In the 1860 presidential election the Democratic Party ran two candidates,

_____ and _____ .

1.010 The only Democrats to serve as president from 1860 to 1916 were

_____ and _____ .

1.011 Name five third parties listed: _____

_____

1.012 A person who currently holds an office is an _____ .

1.013 The Prohibition Party was founded in 1869 solely for the purpose of preventing the manufacturer and sale of alcoholic beverages in the United States. The Prohibition Party is an example of a party

that _____ .

1.014 The left-wing protest party that was formed in 1919 was the _____ .

1.015 The Populist Party of the 1890s was an example of a party formed chiefly to help a

_____ .

Match these items (each answer, 2 points).

1.016 _____ George Washington

1.017 _____ Alexander Hamilton

1.018 _____ Thomas Jefferson

1.019 _____ John Adams

a. secretary of the treasury

b. first president

c. second president

d. third president

Fill in the blanks (each answer, 3 points).

1.020 The Federalists believed in a(n) _____ of the Constitution.

1.021 The Federalists believed that the _____ should possess all powers not specifically denied to it.

1.022 The Anti-Federalists believed in a(n) _____ of the Constitution.

1.023 Today the two major political parties are the _____ and

the _____ .

1.024 The Democrats won all the elections from 1828–1860 except in 1840 and _____ .

1.025 Name three Democratic presidents.

_____

_____

_____

1.026 Name three Republican presidents.

_____

_____

_____

Matching (each answer, 2 points).

1.027 _____ coalition

1.028 _____ Bull Moose Party

1.029 _____ Dwight D. Eisenhower

1.030 _____ Jimmy Carter

1.031 _____ United We Stand Party

a. formed by Theodore Roosevelt in 1912

b. Republican president

c. temporary alliance of political parties

d. Democratic president

e. formed by Ross Perot in 1992

Answer *true* **or** *false*. (each answer, 2 points).

1.032 _____ The Republican Party began as a series of anti-slavery political meetings held in the Midwest in 1854.

1.033 _____ John C. Fremont was the first Republican presidential candidate to win the office in 1856.

1.034 _____ Abraham Lincoln was the Republican president during the Civil War.

1.035 _____ The Republicans won fourteen of the eighteen presidential elections held between 1860 through 1928.

1.036 _____ The Republican Party appealed to groups such as farmers, industrialists, merchants, and economists.

1.037 _____ William Howard Taft led a divided Republican Party in 1912.

1.038 _____ The Bull Moose Party was formed by Theodore Roosevelt in 1912.

1.039 _____ The Democrats were in power from 1932 to 1952.

1.040 _____ The Republicans controlled the House of Representatives, but not the Senate in 1948.

1.041 _____ Under Dwight D. Eisenhower, the Republican Party was in office from 1952 through 1972.

1.042 _____ The Democrats won the presidency in 1976, 1980, and 1996.

The Anti-Federalist would limit the Federal government strictly to: (check one) (2 points).

1.043 _____ managing of foreign affairs.

_____ coining of money.

_____ the powers the constitution delegated to it.

Mark the sentences that are *TRUE* (each answer, 2 points).

1.044 _____ The Republican Party began as a series of anti-slavery political meetings held in the midwest in 1854.

_____ Rural areas will tend to vote more for the liberal party.

_____ During the election of 1824, Andrew Jackson won the most electoral votes, but not the majority needed to be elected president.

_____ The Anti-Federalist would limit the Federal government strictly to the powers the constitution delegated to it.

_____ Third parties play a highly important role in the strengthening the two major parties.

_____ If a political party puts people above the needs of its party it is known as partisan politics.

Mark the statements that are *TRUE* (each answer, 2 points).

1.045 _____ The Democrats blamed the Republicans for the Stock Market Crash of 1929.

_____ The Democrats won the presidency in the 1990s but lost control of the Congress.

_____ The Democratic party won considerable political strength during the Civil War.

_____ The Anti-Federalists were one of the first two American political parties; they wanted a strong central government.

_____ The "Era of Good Feelings" was a period from 1816–1824 where there was only one political party: the Democrat-Republicans.

The Democrats fought almost bitterly at times over: (each answer, 2 points).

1.046 _____ banking policies.

_____ slavery issues.

_____ tariff rates.

_____ all of the above.

Matching (each answer, 2 points).

1.047 _____ economic unrest

1.048 _____ Whig party

1.049 _____ carried

1.050 _____ challenger

1.051 _____ incumbent

1.052 _____ landslide defeat

1.053 _____ scandal

1.054 _____ Stock Market Crash, 1929

a. a party formed mainly to fight the Democratic party and Andrew Jackson

b. in a national election, a candidate who was able to win the vote in a particular state

c. a public shame or disgrace brought about by illegal or unethical actions

d. an uneasiness due to the lack of stability in the financial market

e. saw the market lose so much power that many people lost their fortunes in a matter of days

f. losing by a sizable margin in an election

g. a person who currently holds an office

h. a person who does not hold an office but who is trying to unseat an incumbent

$\frac{134}{167}$ **SCORE** _____ ✓ **CHECK** _____ _____

Teacher Date

2. THE WORKINGS OF POLITICAL PARTIES

> "My fellow-citizens, no people on earth have more cause to be thankful than ours, and this is said reverently, in no spirit of boastfulness in our own strength, but with gratitude to the Giver of Good who has blessed us with the conditions which have enabled us to achieve so large a measure of well-being and of happiness."
>
> — *President Theodore Roosevelt, presidential inaugural address, 1905*

Section Objectives

Review these objectives. When you have completed this section, you should be able to:

4. Understand how a political party is formed; from selecting candidates to financing a campaign.

5. Understand the organization of a party, from national conventions to local organizations.

6. Demonstrate knowledge of the nomination process and the strengths and weaknesses of closed vs. open primaries.

Vocabulary

Study these words to enhance your learning success in this section.

adopt	To accept and agree upon.
campaign	A unified and organized effort with a goal in mind.
campaign manager	The director of a political agenda whose goal is to place a chosen candidate in office.
controversial	Relating to an issue that may not be agreed upon by many different sides, causing many debates.
local level	A smaller, non-widespread scale.
national level	A country-wide scale.
nominate	To formally suggest and recommend a candidate for election.
plank	An issue upon which the campaign may build such as civil rights, taxes, energy, or education.
platform	The declared policy of a political group.
precinct	An election region or section of a community.
strategy	A plan of action.

HOW DO YOU CREATE A POLITICAL PARTY?

LET'S IMAGINE FOR A MINUTE ...

A Christian political party whose agenda would be to spread the Gospel around the country to everyone? Or maybe a Morality Party could be formed, with the chief candidate promising that within a year of election, all pornography would be cleaned from the airwaves, internet, and bookstores. Would it be good to have political parties such as these? People have debated these questions for years and years, but one question registers in many political peoples' minds: How do you start an American political party, anyway?

In 1992 the public was able to view an almost day-by-day attempt of billionaire Ross Perot to create a third party which would rival the power of the Democrats and Republicans. While his party did not achieve the power it desired, many people were able to observe the creation of a party which is still in existence today. Newspaper and television accounts gave step-by-step proceedings of Perot's selection of **campaign managers** and strategies. The American party system has a very complex structure from the **national level** down to the **local level** and at first it would appear to be impossibly intimidating. Through the years, however, these parties have refined their structure similar to a smooth running engine. In this section we shall examine the functions of the political parties: the process of selecting candidates, designing the platform, conducting and financing the campaign, carrying out programs, and criticizing the party in office. We shall look at every level of party organization.

FUNCTIONS OF POLITICAL PARTIES

Political parties did not start "automatically." The Constitution of the United States made absolutely no provision for the selection and nomination of candidates, the method of conducting campaigns or the financing of campaigns for elections. It left the organization of political parties up to the people. As vital issues developed during Washington's administration, people began to take sides, just as people do today, over vital issues and problems that confront society. As these early groups discussed the issues that confronted them, organizations were formed and our first political parties developed.

Political parties have many functions. They are responsible for selecting the candidates they want to represent them in office. After the candidate for the party has been selected, the party program or platform is designed for the coming campaign. Each party must finance its **campaign** properly so fund-raising is one of the most important functions of the party. If it wins the election, the party is also responsible for carrying out the programs it designed before and during the campaign.

SOME PARTIES LAST THE DURATION OF ONLY ONE PRESIDENTIAL ELECTION.

Selecting the candidates. Few candidates or office seekers are **nominated** outside the party lines. It is important that parties do the job of selecting candidates because the number running for public office must be small if one person is to get enough of a majority to win. Party Republicans will therefore choose leaders who will reflect their ideas and party Democrats will do the same. After the candidates are chosen by their respective parties, the voters are given an opportunity to choose between them.

Designing the platform. The platform or program on which a party's candidate stands is put into writing and is **adopted** by the party at its national convention every fourth year. The parts of this platform are presented to the people in the form of **planks** or issues. Each plank represents a principle or point of view, such as civil rights, taxes, energy or education, for which the party is willing to fight. Because both major parties try to appeal to as many voters as possible, the issues are seldom clear-cut. Party **platforms** have often been compared to those of buses or streetcars, to get in, not to stand on. Most candidates will pledge that, if they are elected, they will help translate these ideas into law. Candidate Douglas, for instance, might say, "If you want lower taxes, vote for me. I will reduce your taxes." Once the candidate has been selected and the platform has been adopted, then the campaign is conducted.

Conducting the campaign. Few candidates for state or national offices could be elected without the support of their party. The party prints and distributes literature and contracts and pays for radio and television time including as much prime time as possible. The party does everything it can to sell its candidate to the voters. The party coins campaign slogans to help reflect the position of the party and its candidate. Billboards along all the major highways are plastered with names and pictures of the candidates. The party collects as much information as possible and distributes this information on behalf of its candidate. It is not uncommon to find bumper stickers and posters distributed everywhere. The party will often search for information that will work against the opposing candidate. They will broadcast this information in hope of influencing the voters on election day. The national committee assigns leaders to go to certain states to help campaign for their party's candidate, especially in states where the opposition may be stronger.

Political campaigns waged by rival organizations focus the spotlight of public attention on the candidates, their qualifications, and their stand on the issues. It may seem to be an avalanche of information heaped upon the public! The public is bombarded with party slogans, campaign promises, speeches, and sound bites every day during the heat of the campaign. Locally, party workers strive to get people out to vote in their **precincts** on election day, sometimes even offering free transportation and babysitting services. Every effort is made to get the voter to the polls to vote for the man or woman of their choice. If a candidate appears to be headed for a loss, he or she may concede the election to the other candidate, which means that they are acknowledging their defeat. After the election, the losers normally congratulate the winners and then start making plans for the next election.

Financing the campaign. It takes more money to win an election than many people may realize. For example, the 1996 Federal Election Commission reported that Texas Senator Phil Gramm spent over $9,600,000 on his campaign—and he didn't even win the Republican presidential nomination. Millions are spent by each front-runner in an effort to keep his name in the public consciousness. With the exception of extremely wealthy persons, most candidates cannot possibly finance their own campaigns on a district, state, or national level without the support of the party they represent.

The party acts as the central agency for collecting funds for all its candidates and often campaigns for all of these candidates as a unit. The party distributes funds among them. If a candidate does not have a good chance of winning, he may find that the party will not allot him as much money as it would to a candidate who has an excellent chance of winning. The party prefers to spend the money that has been contributed on candidates who will win and this increases the party's power.

The problem of how to regulate the raising and spending of campaign funds is vital. A law passed in 1966 allows each taxpayer to mark a box on his income-tax return requesting that one dollar of his tax (or two dollars for couples) go into a presidential campaign fund to be shared by the parties. This law was suspended in June 1967, and reinstated in 1972. Congress has also considered numerous proposals for permitting tax deductions for political contributions up to $100, for requiring television stations to offer reduced rates for television campaigning, and for putting new limits on campaign spending.

CAN YOU IMAGINE PAYING $35,000 FOR A PLATE OF FOOD?

Fund-raising comes in different forms for political parties. The parties have to depend largely on private donations for their campaign funding. They also hold plate dinners that range from $50 to $35,000 or more a plate. Other donations come from corporations.

The political parties keep a careful eye on the reactions of the public throughout the United States. With so much at stake, the party that is out of office doesn't want the nation to start favoring the party in power. The party in office is usually held responsible by the public for running the government and for the achievement of its

| Can you imagine paying $35,000 for a plate of food?

HISTORY & GEOGRAPHY 1203
LIFEPAC TEST

Name _____

Date _____

Score _____

7D

86

Fill in the blanks (each numbered activity, 2 points).

1. If a political party puts the party agenda above the needs of the people it is known as

    _____ .

2. The Federalists believed in a _____ of the Constitution.

3. Name six Republican presidents._____

    _____

4. Who was the last Democratic president before Bill Clinton?_____

5. In 1888 the _____ or secret ballot was introduced in the United States.

6. The federal power of the country is known as the _____ government.

7. The only Democrats to serve as president from 1860 to 1916 were

    _____ and

    _____ .

8. A person who currently holds an office is an _____ .

9. The Populist Party of the 1890s was an example of a party formed chiefly to help a

    _____ .

10. The Federalists believed that the _____ should possess all powers
    not specifically denied to it.

11. In most of the 150,000 election precincts around the United States, either one or both major

    parties have a precinct _____ or _____ .

12. The _____ committee sends political leaders to certain states to campaign for their party's candidate.

13. In the early days of our democracy, voting was done _____ .

14. In the party _____ method, the names of the parties appear at the tops of the columns, and the titles of the various offices are shown at the sides.

15. The members of the election board are selected by the _____ or the

    _____ .

16. In absentee voting, a person obtains a ballot from his county election officer either in person

    beforehand or by _____ .

17. The Australian ballot is another name for a _____ .

18. On the _____ ballot only the names of the candidates for the highest office appears on the ballot.

19. The _____ is a handicap because the voters cannot possibly learn enough about the candidates for all offices to vote intelligently.

Answer *true* **or** *false* (each answer, 2 points).

20. _____ George H. W. Bush was a Republican president.

21. _____ In most states you do not have to pay dues or carry a membership card to be part of a political party.

22. _____ John C. Fremont was the first Republican presidential candidate to win the office in 1856.

23. _____ The Republicans won fourteen of the eighteen presidential elections held between 1860 through 1928.

24. _____ William Howard Taft led a divided Democratic Party in 1912.

25. _____ The Democrats were in power from 1932 to 1952.

26. _____ George Washington was a Democratic-Republican president.

27. _____ Andrew Jackson was a Republican.

28. _____ A taxpayer can be involved in the financial part of the election process by marking a box on his/her tax return requesting that a certain amount of his tax go into the presidential election fund.

29. _____ The Australian ballot was introduced in the United States in 1888.

30. _____ Some states require that local elections must come during the in-between years when no national elections are held.

How can you become a member of a political party? (2 points)

31. _____ pay back dues since the last presidential election

_____ registering to vote with the party you wish to join

_____ you are a member of the party your parents were members of

How often is the party platform written? (2 points)

32. _____ every two years

_____ every four years

_____ every year

How can a Republican state chairman become a member of his party's national committee? (Choose all that apply) (each answer, 2 points).

33. _____ if most members in the Congress from his states are Republican

_____ if his state has a Republican governor

_____ by paying party dues

_____ his state cast electoral votes in the last election for the Republican candidate

_____ by applying for membership

Match the words with their definitions (each answer, 2 points).

34. _____ Stock Market Crash, 1929

35. _____ majority

36. _____ Whig party

37. _____ scandal

38. _____ carried

39. _____ landslide defeat

40. _____ economic unrest

41. _____ incumbent

42. _____ American Communist Party

a. party formed to fight the Democratic party and Andrew Jackson in the 1830s

b. in a national election, a candidate who was able to win the vote in a particular state

c. a public shame or disgrace brought about by illegal or unethical actions

d. an uneasiness due to the lack of stability in the financial market

e. financial panic which saw the market lose so much power that many lost their fortunes in days

f. having the larger number in a house of Congress, assuring strong voting power in legislation

g. losing by a sizable margin in an election

h. a person who currently holds an office

i. left-wing protest party that was formed in 1919

What is TRUE about the Anti-Federalists? (Choose one) (2 points)

43. _____ would limit the Federal government strictly to managing of foreign affairs

_____ would limit the Federal government strictly to coining money

_____ would limit the Federal government strictly to the powers the constitution delegated to it

_____ would limit the Federal government strictly to Acts of War

Which one is NOT the function of political parties? (2 points)

44. _____ selecting the candidate

_____ calling for a recount

_____ conducting the campaign

_____ designing the platform

Match the words with their definitions (each answer, 2 points).

45. _____ loyal opposition

46. _____ Franklin D. Roosevelt

47. _____ controversial

48. _____ Ronald Reagan

49. _____ faction

50. _____ Phil Gramm

a. elected president four times

b. An issue that may not be agreed upon by many different sides

c. praised for making the economy strong during the 1980s

d. spent over 9 million dollars in his presidential bid in 1996

e. takes a firm stand on the program of the administration and publicize its views

f. a group that may not be in agreement with the general direction of the larger population

Mark the statement that is _TRUE_ (2 points).

51. _____ The federal power of the country is known as the central government.

_____ The Republican party is the oldest political party in the United States.

_____ The Australian ballot is for the nobility only.

Check the statements that are _TRUE_ (each answer, 2 points).

52. _____ To vote a split ticket requires a knowledge of the qualifications of every candidate.

_____ In order to vote, you must be 18 years of age and must vote in your designated precinct.

_____ At the polling place you will need to show three forms of identification.

_____ One way to cut down on the number of elections would be to lengthen the term of office for elected officials.

_____ Your name and address will be verified at a registration table.

_____ All state officials are elected every two years.

_____ The president and vice president are elected once every four years.

program. If a Democratic president and Congress have been elected, they are considered responsible for laws passed and actions taken, even though many of these laws and actions may have been supported by the Republicans. Thus, in the past, the Democrats have received both praise and blame, depending on the point of view, for such programs as Social Security, civil rights or the Vietnam War. On the other hand, the Republicans of the President Eisenhower administration were credited with the National Defense Education Act and the building of the St. Lawrence Seaway. Down through the years, administrations have been under fire for various issues. For Ronald Reagan, it was a concern of who received firearms for battle in what was known as the "Iran-Contra Affair." For George H. W. Bush, it was a lack of consideration for the country's economy. For Bill Clinton, it was for personal morals. Conversely, the same men were praised for their good efforts while in office. Ronald Reagan received high accolades for strengthening the economy, as did Bill Clinton. George H. W. Bush was much praised in his no-nonsense approach to Iraq's threats in the Persian Gulf War.

The party out of office will look forward to gaining some seats in the Senate and House during state elections. For instance, even if the party gains a seat in Hawaii, a seat in Idaho and a seat in Texas, those may be the necessary votes that would help the party sway particular votes in Congress. The party out of office, desiring to get in, keeps a critical eye on the party in power to discover mistakes and to use those mistakes to their own advantage in the next campaign. However, this function is more than campaign **strategy**. A duty of the "loyal opposition" is to take a firm stand on the program of the administration and publicize its views. It must bring to the attention of the public any misuse of power, any serious blunders or errors of judgment and any violation of constitutional principles by the party in control of the government. Various means are used, such as press conferences by minority party leaders and rebuttals of presidential speeches. The give-and-take of the opposing parties might seem overbearing at times, but the positive note is that such competition not only gives the public information on those in office but also keeps all of the candidates aware that they are being scrutinized with as much vigor as they are scrutinizing others.

| Task Force 155 gathering during Operation Desert Storm in the Persian Gulf War

---

Matching.

2.1 _____ precinct

2.2 _____ plank

2.3 _____ campaign

2.4 _____ strategy

2.5 _____ local level

2.6 _____ platform

a. a plan of action

b. on a smaller, non-widespread scale

c. the declared policy of a political group

d. an election region or section of a community

e. an issue upon which the campaign may build each represents a principle or point of view

f. a unified and organized effort with a goal in mind

Fill in the blanks.

2.7 George H. W. Bush was praised for his efforts in the _____ War, but was

criticized for his poor efforts in strengthening the nation's _____ .

2.8 What are planks in relation to the party platform? _____

_____

2.9 How can the average taxpayer be involved in campaign financing? _____

_____

2.10 A duty of the "_____" is to take a firm stand on the program
of the administration and publicize its views.

2.11 The parties have to depend largely on _____ for their
campaign funding.

Choose one.

2.12 What is the function of political parties?

_____ selecting the candidate

_____ designing the platform

_____ conducting the campaign

_____ campaign financing

_____ all of the above

2.13 How often is the party platform written?

_____ every two years

_____ every four years

_____ every year

2.14 Which committee sends political leaders to certain states to campaign for their party's candidate?

_____ election committee

_____ national committee

_____ campaign committee

2.15 How much was spent by candidate Phil Gramm on his presidential bid?

_____ 1.6 million dollars

_____ 7.6 million dollars

_____ 8.6 million dollars

_____ 9.6 million dollars

"But in another sense, our new beginning is a continuation of that beginning created two centuries ago when, for the first time in history, government, the people said, was not our master, it is our servant; its only power, that which we the people allow it to have."

— President Ronald Reagan, 1985

Vocabulary

Study these words to enhance your learning success in this section.

appointee	One who is nominated or designated to a position.
committee	The group of leaders who make the major decisions in the political party's election strategy.
electoral votes	The votes given to each state to cast for a national candidate for president of the United States.
mass meeting	The convention that mobilizes the national agenda and announces the candidates for the national election.
patronage	Appointing individuals to political offices.
public relations	The effort to establish a favorable impression with the populace.
specific leaders	Chairman of the national committee and presidential candidate.
war chest	Money designated for the purpose of conducting a winning campaign.

ORGANIZATION OF A POLITICAL PARTY

Millions of dollars are spent each election season, as political parties open up their "**war chests**" and pour out funds for TV ads, bumper stickers, radio announcements, campaign headquarter rentals, and more. The political parties of America take this business serious; not only are careers made or broken in a single campaign but the very direction of the country could depend on the outcome. The Democrat and Republican parties are complicated organizations that have strong inner structures. Both parties are highly organized at the national, state, and local levels and follow a closely mapped out agenda. At each level the parties have three basic units: the **mass meeting**, the committee, and **specific leaders**. The relationship of each unit varies at the three levels of government. It also varies from one state or community to another.

National conventions and committees. In theory, the national convention of each party has the final authority in party matters. However, the national convention actually has very little power. The national convention of each party meets only once every four years, when it nominates the candidates for president and vice president of each party.

The national convention also goes through the motions of electing the national committee, which acts for the party between conventions. Each state party, in reality, chooses its representatives on the committee. The national committee of both major parties consists of one committeeman and one committeewoman from each state and from the District of Columbia, Guam, Puerto Rico, and the Virgin Islands. The Republican National Committee includes each chairman of certain state committees. A Republican state chairman becomes a member of his party's national committee if (1) his state cast its **electoral votes** for the Republican candidate in the preceding presidential election, (2) most members of the Congress from his state are Republicans or (3) his state has a Republican governor.

Both the Democratic and Republican national committees have their headquarters in Washington, D.C. They meet only one to three times a year. A main task of each party committee is to organize its next national convention. It chooses the city where the convention will meet and makes arrangements for a smoothly run convention. It prepares campaign literature; secures speakers; arranges tours for the candidates from city to city and state to state; contracts for billboards, radio, and television time; and assists the state and local committees to start their political machinery rolling. The national committee members organize into working committees to provide money, publicity, and speakers. Most work of the national party organization is done by the national committee chairman and his staff. The national chairman is the specific leader who takes on the role of making the campaign a success.

The chairman of the national committee is generally selected by the party candidate for president. He is usually an outstanding party figure who has organizing ability and a great deal of popular appeal and money-raising ability. During presidential election years, the chairman serves as national campaign manager and fund-raiser for his party. He decides where the campaign funds are to be spent and where the campaigning is to be heaviest. The chairman acts for the national **committee** in directing the public relations of the party. He assists the president in patronage matters by recommending **appointees** for federal jobs. Because appointees are cleared through his office, he grants favors where they do the most good, rewarding faithful party workers with jobs. Jobs are the fuel for the party machine.

The national chairman of the party out-of-power is also a busy man. His primary duty is to organize a program of positive education about the party for the public, to build up the party image, to direct publicity, and to keep the machinery from getting rusty. In other words, he keeps the party active on every level of the organization and takes political advantage of every mistake the majority party might make. The national chairman also organizes the national headquarters of his party. He is the chief decision maker within the national organization, but the headquarters staff, which consists of more than one hundred permanent members, does the detailed work for the party. It has campaign, **public relations**, and research divisions.

The major parties also have state committees. Both the Democratic and Republican parties have a state committee in each state. In most states the committee members are chosen in party primaries or at conventions. The state committees organize and manage campaigns for state offices and assist in local campaigns. They also raise money, make arrangements for primary elections, and organize the state conventions.

The chairman of the state committee is the official head of the state party. The committee formally elects him, but the governor, a United States senator from the state, or a group of powerful local officials actually hand-picks the chairman. In most states these officials are also powerful enough to lead the party and to control the state committee. In some states, however, the committee chairman is an effective leader and controls or even chooses key state party officers.

Local organizations can stay just as busy as the national parties. Both of the two major political parties have a county committee in most counties of the United States. Committee members are chosen by county conventions or in primaries. The county committee elects the county chairman. He maintains communication with the state party organization and, in most states, is a delegate to the state committee. County chairmen have a great **patronage** power, which they use to sway the votes of delegates at both state and national party conventions. Below the county committees are the city, ward, and precinct organizations. Leaders of these organizations have the closest contact with the voters. City and ward committeemen are selected in local conventions or primaries. In some states precinct committeemen or captains are also chosen in primaries. In others the county committee selects them.

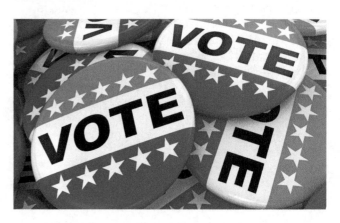

DO YOU KNOW YOUR PRECINCT?

The United States has approximately 150,000 election precincts. In most of them, either one or both major parties have a precinct captain or committeeman. This official prepares the party poll book, which lists the names of the voters in his precinct and to which party, if any, they belong. He and his assistants try to make sure that all members of their party are registered to vote.

There has been a history of abuse in American politics on the local level. In decades past, precinct captains or committeemen have done unethical acts in order to reach their objectives. They have sought votes for their party by assisting voters and would-be voters in many ways. For example, they have helped immigrants become citizens, bailed out prisoners under arrest, found jobs for unemployed persons, and sometimes even given out charity. However, in many cities, the local party leaders and political bosses have lost the great influence they once had, while "watchdog" groups see to an election's honesty.

Government welfare programs and rapid economic growth have made many voters less dependent on the help of the precinct leader. Ever-present media attention scares a lot of election wrongdoing away. Still, voters must be always aware that there should be care taken at election time to see that the proper authorities are present to make voting honest.

Matching.

2.16 _____ committee

2.17 _____ specific leader

2.18 _____ appointee

2.19 _____ patronage

2.20 _____ war chest

2.21 _____ electoral vote

a. one who is nominated or designated to a position

b. appointing individuals to political offices

c. money designated for the purpose of conducting a winning campaign

d. the vote each state is given to cast for a national candidate for president of the United States

e. the chairman of the national committee and the presidential candidate

f. the group of leaders who make the major decisions in the political party's election strategy

Fill in the blanks.

2.22 The Chairman of the National Committee is usually chosen by

_____ .

2.23 The headquarters for both major parties are located in _____ .

2.24 The power to appoint, called _____ , held by the county party chairmen can be used to influence the votes of delegates at state and national conventions.

2.25 How are committee members chosen in most states? _____

_____

2.26 In most of the 150,000 election precincts around the United States, either one or both major

parties have a precinct _____ or _____ .

2.27 "Watchdog" groups see to an election's _____ .

Check all that apply.

2.28   The basic unit(s) of each party at each level are

_____   mass meeting.

_____   committee.

_____   public relations.

2.29   How can a Republican state chairman become a member of his party's national committee?

_____   If most members in the Congress from his states are Republican.

_____   If his state has a Republican governor.

_____   By paying party dues.

_____   His state cast electoral votes in the last election for the Republican candidate.

_____   By applying for membership.

2.30   Which are duties of the national chairman?

_____   Campaign manager and fund-raiser.

_____   Campaign fund spending and fund management.

_____   Public relationships.

_____   Assisting the president in awarding loyal party workers.

_____   All of the above.

Answer *true* **or** *false*.

2.31   _____   The national Convention meets every 4 years to nominate candidates for president and vice president.

"In the midst of these pleasing ideas we should be unfaithful to ourselves if we should ever lose sight of the danger to our liberties if anything partial or extraneous should infect the purity of our free, fair, virtuous, and independent elections."

— *John Adams, 1797*

Vocabulary

Study these words to enhance your learning success in this section.

announcement . . . . The individual fills out documentation and pays a filing fee to announce that he seeks a political office.

caucus . . . . A gathering of party leaders to talk over possible candidates.

closed primary . . . . The voter declares his party allegiance and votes for the ballot of his own party.

county convention . . . . Delegates nominate most county officers and chose delegates to the state convention.

declaration of candidacy . . . . Person wishes to be a candidate for the party, so he makes an announcement of intention.

direct primary . . . . The members vote, by secret ballot, to choose their candidate for the general election.

open primary . . . . Qualified voters vote for the candidates without revealing their party membership.

party-raiding . . . . Members of one party move into the primary of the other party to choose candidates.

plurality . . . . The most votes cast, but not necessarily a majority.

state convention . . . . Delegates nominate candidates for offices and Congress, and delegates to the national convention.

NOMINATIONS AND ELECTIONS

THERE IS SERIOUSNESS BEHIND THE FUN! You may have seen a Democratic or Republican convention on network television and been taken aback by the party atmosphere. What fanfare and excitement! It seems as if most of the events are centered around one big celebration, but behind all the whistle, banners, and streamers, there are serious goals being reached. These political conventions have an agenda that hopefully will lead to a successful run into the White House. Candidates are being nominated, which leads up to an election. Nomination is the first step in the election selection process, and often it can be more important than the election itself. Dictators have been quick to recognize and take advantage of this fact. Their policy is: "Give us the right to name the candidates and you may vote for whomever you please." In American politics, the nomination process is a very careful agreement of many thousands of people who try to select the person who most nearly represents their goals and political desires. Lots of strategy occurs during nominations - do we present this person as our strongest candidate? Does he have what it takes to convince the population that he is best? How well will he serve if he wins? How bad will it hurt us if he loses?

Nominations are not limited to a free society, but it is important to remember that in a suppressed society the nomination and elections are almost a mockery. You might be surprised to know that Mussolini, Hitler, and Stalin all held elections. With great fanfare they pointed out that almost all of the voters cast their ballots. At first it seemed that indeed the percentages appeared to put the democracies to shame, but the democracies were quick to point out that the captive peoples of suppressed societies had no real freedom of choice or consent. They not only were required to vote, but also they were forced to vote for the candidates hand-picked by the dictator. American politics offers a highly competitive yet open-society approach to selecting candidates.

In this section, we shall examine the processes of nominating candidates for office, voting in elections, and making voting more effective. One of the most important roles of the citizen is to exercise his right to vote. The freedom of choice and consent helps to make *the* government a stronger democracy.

NOMINATING CANDIDATES FOR OFFICE

Except for the candidates for the presidency and vice presidency, the nomination of public officers has been left almost entirely to the states. We elect over 500 members of Congress, about 10,000 state officers-governors, legislators, and over 500,000 local officials. Since both major parties name candidates for many of these positions, the total is well over a million nominations. Five different nomination methods have been used up to the present day. These methods are (1) caucus, (2) convention, (3) **direct primary**, (4) petition, and (5) announcement.

The caucus. The earliest device for nominating candidates for state offices and for seats in Congress was the legislative caucus. People would gather together to discuss the pros and cons of each possible candidate. The term caucus comes from the Algonquin Indian language and means "to talk," and a caucus is a gathering of party leaders to talk over possible candidates.

In the beginning, members of the state legislatures met in caucus to draw up the slate of candidates for the various state and congressional offices. In local affairs, however, the nineteenth century caucus had become one of the regular means by which candidates were secretly named by local political leaders. The people took no part in the nominating process—it was a privately arranged affair.

In our nation's first three presidential elections no system of nomination was used and there was no caucus desired. The members of the electoral college simply agreed twice on George Washington and once on John Adams. With the coming of political parties in 1800, though, the candidates for president and vice president were chosen by the caucus. A group in Congress representing one of the two main parties—Federalists or Democratic Republicans— would meet in a caucus and put up their party candidates for president and vice president.

The caucus method lost favor after 1828, after the followers of Andrew Jackson made a strong argument that it was being seriously abused. Therefore, with the extension of suffrage, the caucus method of nomination began to disappear from the national scene. The **caucus** is far from gone, however. It is still used in many local elections today in the United States.

CONVENTION TIME: DELEGATES NOMINATE AND "FINE-TUNE"

The convention. The party convention is a meeting of delegates. These delegates may be elected by the people in a district or may be chosen by the party leaders themselves. Two types of conventions were used after 1830. The **county convention** came into existence first and it nominated most county officers, elected the county chairman and later chose delegates to the **state convention**. State conventions soon began to meet and to nominate all candidates for state offices and members of Congress. The state convention also nominated the delegates to the national convention of the party.

In general, party leaders prefer the convention system because it gives them opportunity to take care of the other party business besides nominating candidates. At these gatherings the party can "fine-tune" its organization, finding where it is weak and working to correct the weakness. It can judge the candidates from the standpoint of popularity in different sections of the state and can arouse party enthusiasm among the leaders. This enthusiasm can be carried home to the local level. For these reasons the convention method was the most common method of nominating candidates after 1835. It remained popular until shortly after 1900 when the direct primary replaced it in many states, but it is still used on the national level. In some states both a convention and a direct primary are held. Candidates in Massachusetts, for example, can enter the primary election as endorsed by the convention. Some, however, enter without such endorsement.

The direct primary. Political bosses gradually came to dominate the conventions. Fraud, bribery, and corruption were all common in the conventions. For this reason states abandoned the convention method of nomination. Nearly all the states now use the direct primary or a combination of convention and primary.

The direct primary is a party election. The members of both the Republican or Democratic parties vote, by secret ballot, to choose the candidate who is to represent their party in the general election. Any person who desires a political office may have his name put on the primary ballot of his party in one of the following three ways: (1) a simple **declaration of candidacy**; (2) a declaration plus payment of a fee; (3) the presentation of a nominating petition signed by a given number, or a certain percent, of the voters in his party. California, for example, requires every petition of candidacy to be filed by a certain number of "sponsors" who must swear that they know the candidate personally and consider him qualified for the office he is seeking.

OPEN PRIMARY VS. CLOSED PRIMARY: WHAT'S YOUR PARTY LOYALTY?

Two types of primaries are used in the United States. In the **open primary**, all qualified voters may vote for the candidates of the party they desire without revealing their party membership. For example, Mr. Jones gets a Republican ballot and a Democratic ballot, both the same size and color. He marks one ballot and puts it in the ballot box. The other is folded and discarded. Voters of all parties as well as independents thus enjoy complete freedom of party choice.

The weakness of the open primary is the fact that it lends itself to "**party-raiding**." Members of one party can thus move into the primary of the other party to choose candidates whom they will more likely defeat in the final election. Some of the open primary states are Wisconsin, Michigan, Idaho, Minnesota, Montana, and North Dakota.

In the **closed primary**, the voter must declare his party allegiance and ask for the ballot of his own party, which he then marks. Independents are excluded.

The closed primary has the advantage of building up the party strength and unity. It helps to make both the party and the candidates mutually responsible for its program. Most of the states have the closed primary. What is the practice in your state? The state of Washington has an interesting system known as the blanket ballot system. It has also been referred to as the wide open primary. Under this plan, the voter is given one ballot. The ballot has the names of the candidates for each office in each party. The voter makes his choice regardless of the party label of the candidate for whom he votes. This system encourages party switching, with emphasis on the best man rather than party loyalty.

Run-off primary. In most states the candidate who receives a **plurality**, the most votes cast, but not a majority, is the candidate of that party in the general election. However, most southern states have provided for a second primary or run-off election to decide which candidate gets a majority. In two other states the winning candidate must receive at least 35 percent of the votes of his party. If he fails to obtain this percentage, the nomination is made by a convention called for that purpose.

Nomination by petition. It is not necessary for a candidate to be supported by a political party or to be nominated at the party primary. Although they provide for the primary, most states allow prospective independent candidates to be nominated by petition and to have their names placed on the ballot in the final election. This nomination requires more signatures than is required of those who wish their name placed on the primary ballot. It is generally required that the petition for nomination be filed after the primary election, and most states prohibit candidates who were defeated in the primary from filing as independent candidates after the primary election.

Nomination by self-announcement. In most towns and villages the candidates for office are put on the ballot by the simple method of self-announcement. A person decides that he would like to be a town councilman; therefore, he makes a public **announcement** to this effect. He files papers with the proper officers and pays a filing fee, and his name is placed on the ballot. Many of the nonpartisan officers, such as members of the board of education, are nominated in this manner. It is used in small areas, for public service and for nonpaying positions.

Matching.

2.32 _____ direct primary

2.33 _____ declaration of candidacy

2.34 _____ convention

a. a meeting of delegates for the purpose of preparing for an election campaign

b. person wishes to be a candidate for the party, he will make this announcement of intention

c. a party election. The members vote, by secret ballot, to choose the candidate who is to represent their party in the general election

Answer *true* **or** *false*.

2.35 _____ Mussolini, Hitler, and Stalin all held elections.

2.36 _____ In some states, both a convention and a direct primary are held.

Fill in the blanks.

2.37 The word *caucus* comes from the Algonquin Indian language and means _____ .

2.38 By using the caucus the people took no part in the _____ process.

2.39 During the first three presidential elections, the _____ chose the president and the vice president.

2.40 In 1800 the candidates for president and vice president were chosen by _____ .

2.41 Though the caucus has disappeared from the national scene, it is still used on the

_____ level.

2.42 The party convention is a meeting of _____ .

2.43 The delegates may be chosen by the _____ in a district or chosen by the

_____ .

2.44 The two types of conventions that came into being after 1830 were the _____

and _____ conventions.

2.45 The county convention nominated:

_____   _____   _____

2.46 The state conventions nominated all candidates for:

_____   _____   _____

2.47 Why do party leaders prefer the convention system?

_____ .

2.48 What were three negative characteristics of political conventions?

_____   _____   _____

2.49 A person can get his name put on the primary ballot of his party by

_____ .

2.50   What are the two types of primaries?

_____

_____

2.51   What is an open primary? _____ .

2.52   What is a closed primary? _____ .

2.53   What are three states still have the open primary?

_____

_____

_____

2.54   What is a wide open primary? _____

_____

2.55   Two methods of nominating a candidate are by _____ and

_____ .

2.56   An independent candidate may file a petition of nomination after the _____ election.

2.57   A candidate who makes a public announcement must then file papers with the proper

_____ and pays a(n) _____ , and his name is then placed on the ballot.

2.58   Most states prohibit candidates who were defeated in the primary from filing as

_____ candidates after the primary election.

2.59   The five methods of nominations used today are:

_____

_____

_____

_____

_____

2.60   The nomination of public officers has been left almost entirely to the _____ .

✓ **CHECK** _____ _____
                                    Teacher   Date

↺ **Review the material in this section in preparation for the Self Test.** The Self Test will check your mastery of this particular section as well as your knowledge of the previous section.

SELF TEST 2

Answer *true* **or** *false* (each answer, 2 points).

2.01 _____ A presidential candidate does not need private financing. He can actually run a campaign using only his own personal money.

2.02 _____ Planks are parts of the party platform in the form of issues that are presented to the people. Civil rights, taxes, and energy are a few examples of the issues.

2.03 _____ A taxpayer can be involved in the financial part of the election process by marking a box on his/her tax return requesting that a certain amount of his tax go into the presidential retirement fund.

2.04 _____ Both the Democratic and Republican parties have a state committee in each state.

Fill in the blanks (each answer, 3 points).

2.05 Bill Clinton was a _____ president.

2.06 In most of the 150,000 election precincts around the United States, either one or both major

parties have a precinct _____ or _____ .

2.07 The parties have to depend largely on _____ for their campaign funding.

2.08 How can someone get his name put on the primary ballot of his party?

_____

2.09 An issue that may not be agreed upon by many different sides is called a

_____ issue.

2.010 The power to appoint or distribute people to governmental or political positions is called

_____ .

Choose one (each question, 2 points).

2.011 What is NOT the function of political parties?

_____ selecting the candidate

_____ conducting a census

_____ conducting the campaign

_____ campaign financing

_____ designing the platform

2.012   Who was praised for his efforts in the Persian Gulf War, but was criticized for his poor efforts in strengthening the nation's economy?

_____   Bill Clinton

_____   George H. W. Bush

_____   Ronald Reagan

2.013   What committee sends political leaders to certain states to campaign for their party's candidate?

_____   election committee

_____   national committee

_____   campaign committee

Match the words with their definitions (each answer, 2 points).

2.014   _____   "watchdog" group

2.015   _____   Reagan

2.016   _____   faction

2.017   _____   open primary

a.   president during the 1980s.

b.   sees to an election's honesty.

c.   voters may vote for the candidates of the party they desire.

d.   a group that may not be in agreement with the general direction of the larger population.

Check the statements that are *TRUE* (each answer, 2 points).

2.018   _____   The federal power of the country is known as the central government.

_____   Ronald Reagan was praised for making the economy strong during the 1980s.

_____   The Republican party is the oldest political party in the United States.

_____   A watchdog group is where the people raise public concern for domestic pets.

_____   Phil Gramm spent over 9 million dollars in his presidential bid in 1996.

3. VOTING

Not required for school study

> "And my first act as president is a prayer. I ask you to bow your heads: Heavenly Father, we bow our heads and thank You for Your love. Accept our thanks for the peace that yields this day and the shared faith that makes its continuance likely. Make us strong to do Your work, willing to heed and hear Your will, and write on our hearts these words: *'Use power to help people.'* For we are given power not to advance our own purposes, nor to make a great show in the world, nor a name. There is but one just use of power, and it is to serve people. Help us to remember it, Lord. Amen."
>
> — *President George H. W. Bush, 1989*

Section Objectives

Review these objectives. When you have completed this section, you should be able to:

7. Explore the possibilities and ideas for making voting more effective and efficient.
8. Understand the process and variations of voting worldwide.

Vocabulary

Study these words to enhance your learning success in this section.

appointment . . . . A designation to serve, based upon ability and other qualifications.

general election . . . . This follows the primary election; voters determine which of the nominated candidates shall hold office.

independents . . . . Voters with no party affiliation.

polling official . . . . A designated authority at each voting precinct who sees to the fairness of the election.

primary . . . . An early election in which delegates select and nominate candidates for office.

referendum . . . . The submitting of a proposed public measure for voting by the general public.

short ballot . . . . A ticket for voting that shows only the names of the candidates for the highest offices.

split ticket . . . . Voting for the best candidates for each office regardless of party.

straight ticket . . . . A vote for all candidates of one party for all offices.

voting booth . . . . A device used in elections; its privacy curtain or shield ensures the citizen of secrecy while voting.

voting machine . . . . A mechanism used in elections; with a system of buttons and levers, the voter has no need of writing utensils.

MAKING VOTING MORE EFFECTIVE

The method of voting has changed from "oral voting" of ages past to the use of the secret ballot in American election precincts today. The use of **voting booths**, the **voting machine**, and **polling officials** have all become a part of our voting system. Even though many nations use the American system of elections as a model, voting still needs to be made more effective. Less than half of the eligible voters vote in a national election. Many questions arise as to the effectiveness of the voting system in the United States. Why do people not go to the polls as much as they should or vote as intelligently as they might? Some possible remedies to the problem are the effective use of the short ballot and the separating of local, state, and national elections. Let's present some questions that could help make voting more effective:

Could we limit the "long ballot?" If you were to study the ballots from different states in a general election, you would find that they differ considerably in length. In a recent election in one state, the ballot was almost nine feet long! The people were asked to vote, not only for national, state, and local officers, but on many initiative and **referendum** measures as well. With such a long ballot the voters cannot possible learn enough about candidates for all offices to act intelligently. As a result, candidates lacking in ability are sometimes put into office. The long ballot is a handicap to good government because it puts a heavy "homework" load on the voter to find out about all the issues and candidates.

Is the "straight ticket" a responsible way to vote? Straight ticket voting is encouraged by the existence of the long ballot with its bewildering array of offices and candidates. In voting a straight ticket the voter merely marks his X at the top of the ballot beside the name of the party of his choice. This procedure means that he votes for all candidates of that party for all offices. Voting machines even have levers for a straight party vote. An extremely long ballot makes the temptation strong to vote the straight ticket as the easy way out. In doing so, however, the voter is saying in effect "Every candidate of my party is better than every

OFFICIAL BALLOT LABEL
JOINT ELECTIONS
HARRIS COUNTY, TEXAS
NOVEMBER 4, 1997
INSTRUCTIONS FOR VOTING A PUNCH CARD BALLOT

HOW TO MARK YOUR BALLOT WHEN VOTING FOR CANDIDATES AND PROPOSITIONS
1. Vote for the candidate of your choice in each race by making a punch hole in the Space provided adjacent to the name of that candidate.
2. To vote "For" or "Against" a proposition on the ballot, punch a hole in the space provided adjacent to the statement that indicates the way you wish to vote.

REPLACING A SPOILED BALLOT
If you make a wrong punch, tear, or deface your ballot, return it to the election official and obtain another. YOU MAY NOT RECEIVE MORE THAN THREE, BALLOTS IN SUCCESSION

DEPOSITING THE BALLOT
Check your ballot after voting to make sure that the holes are actually punched through. Deposit your ballot in the ballot box. Do not fold your ballot.

VARIABLE RACES FOR PAGE 6
CITY OF HUSTON, TEXAS
CARRERAS VARIABLES EN LA PAGINA NUM, 6
CIUDAD DE HOUSTON, YEXAS

Council Member, District A	*Merroro del Consejo, Distnto A*	Council Member, District E	*Merroro del Consejo, Distnto E*
Berenda Flynn Flores	139 ◊	Erik Rivera	139 ◊
Dave E. Jones	140 ◊	**Council Member, District F**	*Merroro del Consejo, Distnto F*
David Wilson	141 ◊	James B. Neal	139 ◊
Chris Branson	142 ◊	Charles Hammer	140 ◊
Dawn Evans	143 ◊	Ray F. Driscoll	141 ◊
Liz Lara-Carreno	144 ◊	Brandon Rasch	142 ◊
Allen Barrilleaux	145 ◊	**Council Member, District G**	*Merroro del Consejo, Distnto G*
Ken Urmy	146 ◊	Karen Kay Kelley	139 ◊
Council Member, District B	*Merroro del Consejo, Distnto B*	Elissa Pendragon	140 ◊
George W. Singelton	139 ◊	**Council Member, District H**	*Merroro del Consejo, Distnto H*
Alan Baratta	140 ◊	Felix Fraga	139 ◊
Council Member, District C	*Merroro del Consejo, Distnto C*	Carmen Orta	140 ◊
Peter Aldred	139 ◊	Justin Care	141 ◊
Council Member, District D	*Merroro del Consejo, Distnto D*	Marcia Olivarez	142 ◊
Ray Martha J. Wong	139 ◊	**Council Member, District I**	*Merroro del Consejo, Distnto I*
Gil Jones	140 ◊	James Partsch-Galvan	139 ◊
		Al Christopherson	140 ◊

candidate of the opposing party." Party leaders love this kind of loyalty, but the quality of democracy suffers in the process.

Why not utilize the "split ticket" more often? The alternative method is to vote a split ticket. Voting a split ticket means voting for the best candidates for each office regardless of party. **Independents** split their tickets regularly. This method requires a knowledge of the qualifications of every candidate running for office, something quite unlikely in the case of a long ballot.

By dealing with a way to let the voters be more responsible and yet not overworked, we can encourage more voter action and higher intelligence in making decisions in the voting booth.

THE SHORT BALLOT: HIGHER OFFICES ONLY!

The short-ballot movement could help alleviate the problem. The remedy for the problem of the long ballot, according to some thinkers, is the **short ballot**. Only the names of the candidates for the highest offices appear on this ballot. The other offices are then filled by **appointment**, preferably under the civil-service system. For example, in the state elections, only the governor, lieutenant governor, and members of the legislature would be elected under the short-ballot system. All other state offices would be filled by appointment on the basis of ability and qualification. The result would be a more responsible and efficient government. The few elected officials could be held accountable for their actions and they would be encouraged to appoint the best possible team members to get essential work done. The National Short Ballot Organization, with Woodrow Wilson as its president, started in 1909. This group has since united with other organizations working for reform of our election system.

The use of the short ballot has been slow in spreading, but it is gradually being used in more and more city, county, and state elections. The national government has been the best example in America of the short ballot. Of all the Federal officials, we elect only the president, vice president, and members of Congress.

Another idea is to limit the frequency of elections. Because so many offices are filled by the vote of the people, elections are frequent. The people vote for a president and vice president every four years and for the whole House of Representatives and for one third of the Senate every two years. In some states certain officers are elected every four years, and in others every two years. In some county and local political subdivision, officers are elected annually. Add to these the **primaries**, which in most states precede these elections, and you have an idea of how often people are asked to vote.

Sometimes elections appear to be held too frequently. The people of one of our larger cities went to the polls four times between January and the **general election** in November, making a total of five elections in ten months. Frequent elections not only cost money, but also they tend to make it difficult getting a majority of the people to vote. One way of cutting down the frequency of elections would be to lengthen the terms of our elected officials.

Another way would be to cut out any election when all the persons running are unopposed.

Separate national and local elections for more attention to local matters. Another criticism of elections is that national, state, and local elections come on the same day in most cases, which means that national issues often overshadow important local matters. A sweeping election victory by one popular presidential candidate often carries along with him party candidates from senators down to city councilmen. Highly qualified candidates of the opposing party may thus be defeated at the state and local levels by weaker candidates who ride into office on the coattails of the president. To avoid this problem some states have required that local elections must come during the "in-between" years when no national elections are held. Other states have set elections for local and state officers at a different time of year; but again, the difficulty is too many elections.

Matching.

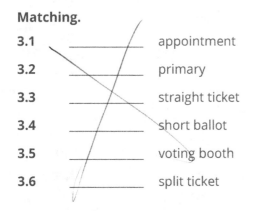

3.1	_____	appointment
3.2	_____	primary
3.3	_____	straight ticket
3.4	_____	short ballot
3.5	_____	voting booth
3.6	_____	split ticket

a. voting by marking an "X" at the top of the ballot beside the name of the party of choice

b. an early election in which delegates select and nominate candidates for office

c. voting for the best candidates for each office regardless of party

d. a ticket for voting that shows only the names of the candidates for the highest offices

e. a device used in elections; its privacy curtain or shield ensures the citizen of secrecy while voting

f. a designation to serve, based upon ability and other qualifications

Fill in the blanks.

3.7   The long ballot is a handicap because _____ .

3.8   The long ballot encouraged _____ voting.

3.9   The alternative to voting a straight ticket is to vote a _____ .

3.10   To vote a split ticket requires a knowledge of the qualifications of every _____ .

3.11   On the _____ ballot, only the names of the candidates for the highest office appears on the ballot.

3.12   The president and vice president are elected once every _____ years.

3.13   One way to cut down on the number of elections is to not have an election when all the persons running are _____ , which happens frequently.

Answer *true* **or** *false*.

3.14   _____   In state elections, only the governor, lieutenant governor, and members of the state legislature would be elected under the short-ballot system.

3.15   _____   With the long ballot system all less important state offices would be filled on the basis of patronage.

3.16   _____   We use the short ballot to elect the president, vice president, and members of Congress.

3.17   _____   We elect one-third of the Congress every two years.

3.18   _____   All state officials are elected every two years.

3.19   _____   One way to cut down on the number of elections would be to lengthen the term of office for elected officials.

3.20   _____   A criticism of elections is that national, state, and local elections come on the same day.

3.21   _____   Some states require that local elections must come during the in-between years when no national elections are held.

> "[Independence Day] ... will be the most memorable epoch in the history of America. I am apt to believe that it will be celebrated by succeeding generations as the great anniversary festival. It ought to be commemorated as the day of deliverance, by solemn acts of devotion to God Almighty. It ought to be solemnized with pomp and parade, with shows, games, sports, guns, bells, bonfires, and illuminations, from one end of this continent to the other, from this time forward for evermore."
>
> — *John Adams*

Vocabulary

Study these words to enhance your learning success in this section.

absentee voting	Process for those who cannot be present at their polling place because of health or obligation.
Australian ballot	A secret ballot, originated in Australia.
contested election	If a losing candidate feels that fraud has occurred he may call the commission to recount the votes.
election board	Selected by district election board, a group that sees to the fairness and efficiency of an election.
inspector	One who is responsible for the proper conduct of the election.
office-bloc arrangement	Titles of offices appear across the ballot; the candidates of parties for each office are below the titles.
oral voting	Older form of voting where voters would call out the name of the candidate.
party column method	Names of the parties appear at tops of the columns; titles of various offices are shown at sides.
poll watcher	A citizen who is paid by the parties to keep a watchful eye on the voters and the officials.
polling place	Specific voting area; each voter is assigned a particular place within the district where he lives.
secret ballot	Ballot that is kept private and distributed only at the polling places and only by the election officials.

VOTING IN ELECTIONS

Voting is a citizen's right in America. Terry shows up at evening college classes, munching a doughnut and wearing an American flag sticker. "What's with you and the sticker and doughnut?" asks George. Terry swallows. "I just voted in my precinct at the fire station!" George turns pale. "Oh, man!" he exclaims, "I almost forgot! My polling place is at the library. I think I have about twenty minutes!" Terry waves to him as George leaps into his car and shouts, "I'll tell the professor you'll be a bit late for class!" George and Terry don't pass up the opportunity to involve themselves in a very special part of their U.S. citizenship. While many adults are guilty of apathy at the polling place, both of these young men are joining millions of other people across the country in taking their voting rights seriously.

ARE YOU REGISTERED TO VOTE?

Voting is a privilege, not a requirement as it is in some countries. When the founding fathers of our country met in what is now called Independence Hall in Philadelphia, they were concerned with individual freedoms. Through all of the debates, compromises, and political maneuvering, the body of delegates fought for the best way to grant American citizens certain liberties. One of the liberties which was agreed upon in those many meetings in Philadelphia was the right to vote. That voting right spread from its initial privilege to white men only, to cross gender, race, and even age lines. It is an opportunity that should not be taken lightly. Such a simple thing as voting involves many areas, from the polling places and election officers to the types of ballots used in elections. You may know the major political parties, but do you know about the **secret ballot**, **absentee voting**, **contested election**s, the handicap of the long ballot, the straight ticket versus the split ticket, the short ballot movement frequency of elections, and separating national and local elections?

Polling places give access to the voters of the area. Every county, district or city is divided into precincts, with a fairly equal number of voters in each. The aim is to have one polling (voting) place for every few hundred voters, and the average is four hundred per precinct. The voting place for each precinct is usually a public building, such as a church, school, police station, fire station or library building. In some states private homes are used as voting places; however, this procedure is often expensive. Because the county pays from $10 to $50 a day for the use of a private home, the election officials too often have rented the homes of party workers as political patronage.

Election officers maintain order and fairness at the polling place. At every polling place are **inspectors** and judges who are responsible for the proper conduct of the election. Generally three to five election officials chosen by an **election board** are at each polling place. With the exception of a few states where one party controls the state, these officers must come from both parties. In addition to the election officials, **poll "watchers"** are at the **polling places**; they are appointed and paid by the parties to keep a watchful eye on the voters and the officials. Each county or election district has an election board whose members are selected by the county supervisors or the district election board. in some states these officials are appointed by the county clerk or the county court.

VOTING: THE POLLING PLACES HELP WALK YOU THROUGH THE PROCEDURE.

The secret ballot is the accepted voting procedure in America. Jeff is voting in his very first presidential election. He heads to his polling place and arrives at 8:30 in the morning. His particular polling place is at a local elementary school where he is surprised to see quite a number of people already filing in to vote. He passes a table with coffee and smiling people asking him if he needs any assistance. He asks them where he signs in and is directed to a table at the middle of the gymnasium floor. He shows his voting card and his driver's license. The kind lady sitting at the table points him to a voting booth, where Jeff enters, draws a curtain and fills out a ballot in secret. In a matter of minutes he's on his way, but not after he has received a small sticker on his lapel which proclaims him as a voting citizen. As trivial as it may seem, Jeff is proud to wear the sticker and let everyone know he cares enough to vote.

As you know, voters in a national election will be casting their ballots for president and vice president once every four years. However, if you have not been eligible to vote in a state election, you may be surprised at the number of office candidates hoping for your vote. From governor to judges, you are given the right to elect servants to state offices. In some states, the legislature or the governor will appoint judges to office, but there are still many states who leave this decision up to the citizens.

In the early days of our democracy, **oral voting** was used in a number of states. The voters went to the polling place and shouted to the judges the names of the candidates for whom they were voting. The candidates were present, and they knew who voted for them and who voted against them. An employer also knew how his employees voted, and vice versa.

A little later the printed ballot came into use. Each party printed its own special-colored ballots with the names of its candidates. These ballots were distributed before the election and the voter simply brought the colored ballot of his party to the polls and cast his vote openly. By this method, the political bosses knew how everyone voted, and they could punish those who failed to vote the "right" way by denying them any services or jobs.

Not until 1888 was the so-called Australian ballot introduced into the United States. It was used in Louisville, Kentucky, in the city elections. Several months later it was adopted by Massachusetts and today it is used throughout the country.

The **Australian ballot** has four distinctive features: (1) it is a secret ballot, (2) it includes the names of all candidates from all parties, (3) it is prepared by the state or county and is printed at public expense and (4) it is distributed only at the polling places and only by the election officials. The ballot is arranged in one of two ways. One is the **party column method** where the names of the parties appear at the tops of the columns, and the titles of the various offices are shown at the sides. The other is the **office-bloc arrangement**, which puts the titles of the offices across the ballot, then the candidates of both parties for each office are placed below the titles.

Voting procedure. Let us pretend that you have reached the proper voting age in your state and have fulfilled the requirements for voting. Just how will you proceed to vote? Assuming that you have registered in time, and that you are a qualified voter, you will probably receive from the county clerk or other election official a card telling you where you are to vote. The announcement usually will be posted in several places in your precinct about a week before the election.

On election day, you will go to your voting place. You can recognize the polling place because it will display the United States flag. Upon entering, you will be asked to give your name and address. Some states require that you present your voter identification card and sign the voting book. One of the election officials will check the registry to see if your name is listed and if you are qualified to vote in that precinct. If everything is found in order, another election official will give you a ballot. You then go to a booth where you mark your ballot in secret and fold it. Having completed this procedure, you hand the folded ballot to the election officer, who deposits it in the ballot box. Thus, you complete your responsibility as a voting citizen of your town, county, state, and nation.

After the polls close—they are open for eight to twelve hours—the officials begin the task of counting the ballots. This task often takes hours, and the election officials are usually up until the early hours of the morning after the election. In some states voting machines have taken the place of paper ballots. The names of all candidates, each with a separate lever, appear across the face of the machine. The voter walks in and closes the curtain behind him. This automatically opens the machine. Then he simply pulls the levers which indicate the names of his choices. When he opens the curtain that has concealed him, the machine records his vote.

Voting machines have these advantages: they make fraud impossible, they assure absolute secrecy, and they do away with the need for numerous officials to count the votes. Votes are tabulated automatically as they are cast. Machines are increasing in popularity and may eventually be used nationwide. Most of the big cities already use them. It is estimated that well over half of the voting is now done by machine.

Vote-by-mail. Nearly all of the states allow those who are absent on business, or those who are ill or physically disabled, to vote. Under the **absentee voting** system, the ballots are received beforehand. The voter marks this ballot and then swears before a notary public that he is a duly registered and qualified voter. He then sends his ballot to the county clerk. More than half of the states allow people to vote through the mail. The voter is usually required to submit a request form for a ballot which places a signature on file for validating the ballot. The ballot is mailed out prior to the election. The voter can fill in the ballot, place it in the envelope that is provided, sign and date the envelope, and then mail it prior to the election.

Contested elections. Sometimes an election is so close that the outcome is in doubt until the last

ballot is in. Close elections have often occurred in our history, including gubernatorial elections, senatorial races, and even presidential elections. In such cases, the losing candidate may accept the results or he may believe that a recount of the votes will change the results. If he is convinced that evidence of a fraud exists, he can contest the election. In the former case he simply demands a recount, and the election commission is required to make it. If the charge of fraud is made, the case comes under the jurisdiction of the courts. Because contested or disputed elections are always a possibility, most states require that the ballot boxes be sealed and kept in a safe place for several months after the election.

Matching.

3.22 _____ polling place

3.23 _____ inspector

3.24 _____ oral voting

3.25 _____ absentee voting

3.26 _____ office bloc arrangement

3.27 _____ party column method

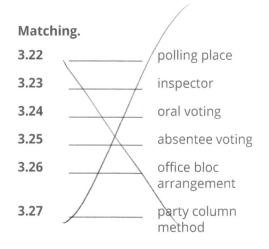

a. one who is responsible for the proper conduct of the election

b. an older, less private form of voting where the voters would call out their vote

c. names of the parties appear at the tops of the columns; titles of various offices are shown at the sides

d. titles of the offices appear across the ballot, candidates of parties for each office are below the titles

e. specific voting area; each voter is assigned a particular place within the district where he lives

f. process made for those who cannot be present at their polling place because of health or obligation

Fill in the blanks.

3.28   Each county, district, or city is divided into _____ .

3.29   The average number of voters per precinct is _____ .

3.30   Four types of public buildings used for polling places are:

_____   _____

_____   _____

3.31   There are generally between _____ to _____ election officers at each polling place.

3.32   The members of the election board are selected by the _____ or the

_____ .

3.33   In the early days of our democracy, voting was done _____ .

3.34   In 1888, the _____ or secret ballot was introduced in the United States.

3.35   The Australian ballot was first used in _____ .

3.36   List four distinctive features of the Australian ballot.

_____   _____

_____   _____

3.37   A contested election means that the losing candidate is demanding a _____ .

3.38   Explain the process necessary for casting your vote.

_____

_____

_____

3.39   Nearly all states allow those who are absent on _____ , or those

who are _____ or _____ to vote.

3.40   In vote-by-mail, a person obtains a ballot from his county election officer either in person

beforehand or by _____ .

3.41   In vote-by-mail, a person marks the ballot and then swears before a _____

_____ that he is a registered and qualified voter. He then sends his ballot to the

county _____ .

Answer *true* **or** *false*.

3.42 _____ Inspectors and judges are responsible for the proper conduct of the election.

Choose one.

3.43 Election officers are chosen by the

_____ people.

_____ election board.

_____ national convention.

_____ caucus.

3.44 What is the advantage for the use of voting machines?

_____ fraud is nearly impossible

_____ assure absolute secrecy

_____ do away with the need for numerous officials to count ballots

_____ all of the above

✓ **CHECK** _____ _____
                              Teacher   Date

Before you take this last Self Test, you may want to do one or more of these self checks.

1. _____ Read the objectives. Determine if you can do them.
2. _____ Restudy the material related to any objectives that you cannot do.
3. _____ Use the **SQ3R** study procedure to review the material:
   a. **S**can the sections.
   b. **Q**uestion yourself again (review the questions you wrote initially).
   c. **R**ead to answer your questions.
   d. **R**ecite the answers to yourself.
   e. **R**eview areas you did not understand.
4. _____ Review all vocabulary, activities, and Self Tests, writing a correct answer for every wrong answer.

SELF TEST 3

Fill in the blanks (each answer, 3 points).

3.01   In the early days of our democracy, voting was done _____ .

3.02   In an Australian ballot, the names of all candidates appear on a _____ ballot.

3.03   In the party _____ method, the names of the parties appear at the tops of the columns and the titles of the various offices are shown at the sides.

3.04   In the office _____ arrangement, the titles of the offices appear across the ballot, then the candidates of both parties for each office are placed below the titles.

3.05   Inspectors and judges are responsible for the proper _____ of the election.

3.06   The average number of voters per precinct is _____ .

3.07   The members of the election board are selected by the _____ or the

_____ .

3.08   Nearly all states allow those who are absent on _____ to vote.

3.09   In vote-by-mail, a person obtains a ballot from his county election officer either in person

beforehand or by _____ .

3.010   In vote-by-mail, a person marks the ballot and then swears before a _____

_____ that he is a registered and qualified voter. He then sends his ballot to the

county _____ .

3.011   The Australian ballot is another name for a _____ .

3.012   The alternative to voting a straight ticket is to vote a _____ .

3.013   To vote a split ticket requires a knowledge of the qualifications of every _____ .

3.014   On the _____ ballot only the names of the candidates for the highest office appears on the ballot.

3.015   The president and vice president are elected once every _____ years.

3.016   One way to cut down on the number of elections is to not have an election when all the persons

running are _____ , which happens frequently.

3.017   The _____ is a handicap because the voters cannot possibly learn enough about the candidates for all offices to vote intelligently.

Answer *true* **or** *false* (each answer, 2 points).

3.018 _____ There are generally between 3 and 5 election officers at each polling place.

3.019 _____ A primary is an early election in which delegates select and nominate candidates for office.

3.020 _____ In state elections, only the governor, lieutenant governor, and members of the state legislature would be elected under the short-ballot system.

3.021 _____ We elect one-third of the Congress every two years.

3.022 _____ All state officials are elected every two years.

3.023 _____ One way to cut down on the number of elections would be to lengthen the term of office for elected officials.

3.024 _____ Some states require that local elections must come during the in-between years when no national elections are held.

Which one is *FALSE* concerning the use of the voting machine? (2 points)

3.025 _____ fraud is nearly impossible

_____ it was invented in 1898

_____ it does away with the need for numerous officials to count ballots

_____ it assures absolute secrecy

Match the words with their definitions (each answer, 2 points).

3.026 _____ referendum

3.027 _____ short ballot

3.028 _____ election officers

3.029 _____ a criticism of elections

3.030 _____ the Australian ballot

a. was introduced in the United States in 1888

b. used to elect the president, vice president, and members of Congress

c. chosen by the election board

d. national, state, and local elections come on the same day

e. the submitting of a proposed public measure for voting by the general public

Check the statements that are *TRUE* (each answer, 2 points).

3.031 _____ A school is an acceptable building used for a polling place.

_____ A fire station is an acceptable building used for a polling place.

_____ A church is an acceptable building used for a polling place.

_____ A local hamburger restaurant is an acceptable building used for a polling place.

_____ A library is an acceptable building used for a polling place.

15

A contested election means that the losing candidate calls for a: (check one) (2 points).

3.032 _____ primary.

_____ press conference.

_____ recount.

_____ caucus.

Check the statements that are _TRUE_ concerning your voting rights and responsibilities (each answer, 2 points).

3.033 _____ You must be 18 years of age.

_____ You must vote in your designated precinct.

_____ At the polling place you will need to show three forms of identification.

_____ There will be a ballot box to receive your voting ballot, if a ballot is used.

_____ Your name and address will be verified at a registration table.

_____ There is a small fee for voting but you will be reimbursed through your tax refund.

_____ If you have broken any laws you cannot vote.

$\frac{76}{95}$ **SCORE** _____ ✓ **CHECK** _____ _____
                                              Teacher   Date

↺ **Before taking the LIFEPAC Test, you may want to do one or more of these self checks.**

1. _____ Read the objectives. Determine if you can do them.
2. _____ Restudy the material related to any objectives that you cannot do.
3. _____ Use the **SQ3R** study procedure to review the material.
4. _____ Review activities, Self Tests, and LIFEPAC vocabulary words.
5. _____ Restudy areas of weakness indicated by the last Self Test.